PRENTICE-HALL
HISTORY OF MUSIC SERIES
H. WILEY HITCHCOCK, editor

FOLK AND TRADITIONAL
MUSIC OF THE
WESTERN CONTINENTS

second edition

FOLK AND TRADITIONAL MUSIC OF THE WESTERN CONTINENTS

BRUNO NETTL

University of Illinois

with chapters on Latin America by
Gérard Béhague (University of Illinois)

PRENTICE-HALL, INC., ENGLEWOOD CLIFFS, NEW JERSEY

Library of Congress Cataloging in Publication Data

NETTL, BRUNO
    Folk and traditional music of the western continents.

    (Prentice-Hall history of music series)
    Includes bibliographies and discographies.
        1. Folk music—History and criticism.   2. Music,
    Primitive.   I. Behague, Gerard.   II. Title.
    ML3545.N285 1973   781.7'09182'1   72-10010
    ISBN   0-13-322941-6
    ISBN   0-13-322933-5 (pbk)

ML
3545
N285

68662

FOR GRACE

Printed in the United States of America

10 9 8 7 6 5 4 3 2 1

© 1973, 1965 by Prentice-Hall, Inc.
Englewood Cliffs, New Jersey

PRENTICE-HALL INTERNATIONAL, INC., *London*
PRENTICE-HALL OF AUSTRALIA, PTY. LTD., *Sydney*
PRENTICE-HALL OF CANADA, LTD., *Toronto*
PRENTICE-HALL OF INDIA PRIVATE LIMITED, *New Delhi*
PRENTICE-HALL OF JAPAN, INC., *Tokyo*

FOREWORD

Students and informed amateurs of the history of music have long needed a series of books that are comprehensive, authoritative, and engagingly written. They have needed books written by specialists—but specialists interested in communicating vividly. The Prentice-Hall History of Music Series aims at filling these needs.

Six books in the series present a panoramic view of the history of Western music, divided among the major historical periods—Medieval, Renaissance, Baroque, Classic, Romantic, and Contemporary. The musical cultures of the United States, Latin America, and Russia, viewed historically as independent developments within the larger western tradition, are discussed in three other books. In yet another pair, the rich yet neglected folk and traditional music of both hemispheres is treated. Taken together, the eleven volumes of the series are a distinctive and, we hope, distinguished contribution to the history of the music of the world's peoples. Each volume, moreover, may be read singly as a substantial account of the music of its period or area.

The authors of the series are scholars of national and international repute—musicologists, critics, and teachers of acknowledged stature in their respective fields of specialization. In their contributions to the Prentice-Hall History of Music Series their goal has been to present works of solid scholarship that are eminently readable, with significant insights into music as a part of the general intellectual and cultural life of man.

H. WILEY HITCHCOCK, *Editor*

PREFACE

Dividing the world into two halves for the purpose of investigating and discussing its traditional and folk or its so-called ethnic music is perhaps a dangerous proposition. But if such a division must be made, it seems logical to group together Europe, sub-Saharan Africa, and the Americas. During the last several centuries, these areas have come greatly under the influence of Western civilization and its music—and they have influenced Western high culture also—while the rest of the world appears to have been more under the aegis of the oriental high cultures. Moreover, in an American publication it seems appropriate to treat together those areas of the world which, broadly speaking, are responsible for the musical culture of the Americas today: Europe, Negro Africa, and aboriginal America. Finally, the areas covered here can be thought to have produced about half of the world's music and musical styles, if such concepts can be quantified at all. On the other hand, there is not much unity but there is a tremendous variety of musical styles, values, functions, and instruments in the part of the world that is the subject of this volume.

Our approach is essentially geographic. After two chapters dealing with the general characteristics of traditional music and its cultural context, and with some of the methods used to study folk music, we devote four chapters to Europe, one to sub-Saharan Africa, and three to the Americas. It has been impossible, of course, to survey comprehensively the music of each area, nation, and tribe, and we must content ourselves with examples of the kinds of musical styles that are found, and with sampling the types of songs that are sung, the various uses to which music is put, and the plethora of instruments past and present. The musical examples are intended to illustrate points made in the text rather than to serve as a representative anthology of musical forms; but most of the things discussed are musically illustrated, and a few of the most important and unusual instruments are depicted.

This revised edition differs from the original in a number of respects. Wherever possible, errors have been corrected. Several chapters have been substantially expanded, largely in the direction of providing more discussion of the role of music in culture and of recent developments in the traditional musics as they continue their existence in modern urban culture. Most important is the inclusion of an entirely new chapter on folk music in Latin America by my colleague, Dr. Gérard Béhague, who has also revised and added to the section of music of Afro-American peoples in South America and the Caribbean, in Chapter 10.

I should like to express my thanks to the various publishers, collectors, and authors who have given permission to quote musical and textual material; individual credit is given with each quotation. I am indebted to William P. Malm for advice and criticism and for arranging to have the exquisite line drawings of instruments by the prominent Japanese artist Masakazu Kuwata. I am also grateful to H. Wiley Hitchcock for advice and guidance and to my wife for technical assistance.

B.N.

CONTENTS

Contents

ONE

FOLK AND TRIBAL MUSICS
IN THEIR CULTURAL SETTING

INTRODUCTION

We are concerned here with a body of music called ethnic, folk, or traditional, as it is found in Europe, most of Africa, and the Americas. This music consists essentially of two groups of styles and repertories: (1) folk music, which is found in those cultures and areas in which there is also a longtime development of urban, professional, cultivated musical tradition, something that is often called "art" or "classical" music, and (2) tribal music, the music of nonliterate cultures, i.e., those without a tradition of literate, sophisticated musical culture living alongside the musical folk culture. The latter kind of music is frequently called "primitive," but the term is to be used with caution. The world's tribal musical cultures are not in essence different from the cultivated ones, except that they have less in the way of music theory and of professionalization of

1

musicians; and they have no musical notation. Quantitatively, their musics are simpler than the art musics of the world. (But even this statement is only generally true; for example, the rhythmic structures of African music are often much more complex than those of nineteenth century European classical music.) Nevertheless, the musical creations of tribal cultures are genuine works of art; they can be analyzed, judged, and appreciated in much the same terms as can the great masterpieces and all other compositions of Western music, if one views them in the context of their own cultural background.

Although we really have no way of telling just what happened in the musical history of all the world's cultures, we may perhaps assume that an earlier stage of the musical development of all cultures, including the modern ones, was something like the musical culture of contemporary tribal and folk societies, in the sense that it involved mainly people who were not professional musicians, and that it consisted of music that all of the people could understand and in which many or most could participate. Then, among some peoples, there must have taken place the development of a separate musical life for an educationally sophisticated and economically or politically powerful segment of the population, while the rest of the people held on to the older musical tradition. In Western civilization, we tend to be dominated by this more sophisticated musical culture, which includes our concert music and also the vast body of popular music. We are much less aware of the folk traditions that, before the invention of recording and radio, were dominant, especially in the rural parts of Europe and the Americas, and that still live in relatively isolated pockets of society. But we are beginning to realize the great influence that folk music has had on urban musical culture, and we are also beginning to understand the ways in which the musical folk culture has changed under the influence of the urban mass media, but still remains somewhat intact.

We are concerned, then, with two kinds of music, the folk and the so-called primitive, which really—when they are first heard by the novice —have very little in common. European and American folk music is, after all, part of our own cultural tradition as members of Western culture. The traditional music of the American Indians and Africans is generally quite outside our experience. Moreover, each nation, each tribe, has its own music, and one kind of folk music may sound quite unlike another; Indian and African music are quite dissimilar, indeed, as different as two kinds of music can be. Our only justification for including such a large group of music in a single volume is the fact that in each culture in the Western half of the world this is the music that is used by a large number of people.

Contemporary academic musicians tend to concentrate on the

degree to which a piece of music is unique and on the complexity of its structure and texture; and they may not care particularly whether it is understood by many listeners, by a few professionals, or even by the composer himself. In tribal and folk musics, the values are usually turned around. Uniqueness may not be important, and the innovator may be discriminated against; but a new song must be acceptable to others in order to live. This distinction is important, even if the case for it has sometimes been overstated.

Early students of folk music believed that in a tribal or folk community all individuals knew all of the songs in the repertory and could perform them more or less equally well. It is true that in order for a song or other music to be viable in such a culture, it must be understood and accepted by a large segment of the population. But we know that in African societies there have for a long time been musicians recognized as such; we know that American Indian shamans or medicine men knew more songs than other members of their tribes; and we are aware that in European folk cultures individuals who knew many songs and could sing well were singled out for recognition. Moreover, in all of these cultures, there was a tendency for certain songs or pieces to be reserved for specific groups, such as men, women, children, members of religious cults, political subdivisions, etc. Thus it is impossible to conclude that there is a difference *in essence* between the musical cultures of primitive tribes and those of the modern Western city. The simplest tribal group and the most advanced group of avant-garde musicians (which throughout the world has perhaps only a few thousand adherents) are at different ends of one continuum, and most of the world's musics fall at various points between them. And a great deal of the world's music is at borderlines between such conventional categories as tribal, primitive, folk, popular, and classical.

If there are specific features common to all of the musics discussed in this volume, they are (1) ready acceptability to large segments of the society in which they exist, and (2) the fact that they live in and are preserved by oral tradition.

ORAL TRADITION

To say that a culture has oral tradition means simply that its music (like its stories, proverbs, riddles, methods of arts and crafts, and, indeed, all its folklore) is passed on by word of mouth. Songs are learned by hearing; instrument making and playing are learned by watching. In a literate musical culture, music is usually written down, and a piece conceived by a composer need never be performed at all during his lifetime; it can be discovered centuries later by a scholar and resurrected. But in a folk or a nonliterate culture, or even in a sophisticated culture without musical notation, a song must be sung, remembered, and taught by one generation to the next. If this does not happen, it dies and is lost forever. Surely, then, a piece of folk music must in some way be representative of the musical taste and the aesthetic judgment of all those who know it and use it, rather than being simply the product of an individual, perhaps isolated, creator.

As we have just indicated, a folk song must be accepted or it will be forgotten and die. There is another alternative: if it is not accepted by its audience, it may be changed to fit the needs and desires of the people who perform and hear it. And since there is not, in the case of most folk or tribal music, a written standard version which people can consult, changes made over the years tend to become integral to the song.

Of course this kind of change occurs for several reasons and at various levels. Imagine, for instance, that a Kentucky or an Alpine mountaineer makes up a folk song—both melody and words. He may compose the melody by putting together snatches of other songs he knows, or simply by humming aimlessly until he hits upon something that strikes his fancy, or by systematically changing a melody he already knows. (We know very little about the way in which composing is done in folk and nonliterate cultures, just as we really know next to nothing about the mental processes involved in composing sophisticated music.) This man then teaches his song to his three sons. Son number one is a musical fellow who has a television set and occasionally goes to the city (where he hears more complicated music) and over the years, he whittles away at the song, changing notes here and there, adding ornaments, and evening out the meter, until he has made very substantial changes, which he no doubt considers improvements. Son number two likes to sing, but has a poor musical memory. He forgets how the song begins but remembers the second half of the tune. In his rendition, the song, which originally had, say, four different musical phrases (ABCD), consists only of a repetition of the last two and now has the form CDCD. (This is what evidently happened in the case of an old English and American song, "The Pretty Mohea," which is often sung to a tune with the form AABA. The last two lines, repeated, seem to have become the tune of a popular hillbilly song, "On Top of Old Smoky.") Son number three moves to Mexico, and while he likes to sing his father's song, he becomes so saturated with Mexican popular and folk music that his version of the song begins to sound like a Mexican folk song with the kind of rhythmic and ornamental structure characteristic of that country's tradition. You can imagine what might happen at a family reunion: the three sons sing their three versions, and while a person who knew the old man and his song the way it was first sung would surely realize that the sons have sung three versions of the same song, a newcomer to the group might hardly guess that the sons' songs actually were descendants of the same original. Add a few generations, and one song has become a large number of variants. The original form is forgotten and can no longer be reconstructed from the later versions.

HOW DOES TRADITIONAL MUSIC ORIGINATE?

We have looked at the way in which folk music comes to us. Most of it is quite old, but it has changed. To be sure, new songs are made up in most cultures at all times. In some cultures, many new songs are composed every year or every generation; in others, only a few new ones may appear in a century. But a great deal of the material, in all cases, is old, and thus we frequently hear about the great antiquity of folk and primitive music. But we must keep in mind the fact that this music, no matter how far back its roots, has probably undergone a great deal of change—because people wanted to improve it, because they forgot parts of it, or perhaps because they felt it necessary to make it sound like other music that they were hearing. Folk and primitive music, then, have for us the fascinating quality of being both old and contemporary, of being representative of a people's ancient traditions as well as an indicator of current tastes. And they are simultaneously the product of individual composers and of the creativity of masses of people. This historical development—far more than the artistic merit of the individual composition, which may be considerable in the opinion of some, but which may also seem insignificant in comparison to Bach fugues and Brahms symphonies—is the main justification for a detailed consideration of traditional music on the part of modern urban students and musicians.

We have implied that folk music is composed by individuals, but that subsequent to the original act of composition, many persons may make changes, thus in effect re-creating a song. This process, called "communal re-creation," is one of the things that distinguish folk music from other kinds. But the way in which folk music is created has not always been recognized. Among the earlier definitions of folk music, that which stresses the anonymity of the creator is one of the most persistent. According to this definition, a song whose composer is unknown is a folk song. Of course there is a fallacy here; should our ignorance of the identity of a composer make such a difference in our classification of musics? Still, there is some truth in this view, for the composers in European folk music and in most nonliterate cultures are indeed not known to scholars. Moreover, they are not usually known to the members of their own culture; in most of the cultures with which we are concerned here it makes little difference just who makes up a song. There are exceptions, of course; in some Plains Indian tribes people remember very specifically who "made" a particular song, or who "dreamed" it (some tribes believe that songs come to people in dreams).

It was believed by some nineteenth-century scholars that folk songs were made up by people improvising in groups. Actually this is rare, if indeed it occurs at all. Controlled improvisation under the leadership of a music master does seem to occur here and there—in the gamelan orchestras of Java and Bali, for instance, and among the Chopi of Southeast Africa. We have reports of American black slaves in the nineteenth century making up songs by calling to each other and gradually arriving at a song-like formula. But this kind of "communal creation" is rare. Nevertheless, those who formulated the theory that folk songs are the product of the communal mind were not unwise, for they must have realized the importance of the contributions of generations of singers, players, and listeners in determining the final form of the song (but is it ever really final?). Of course, folk songs are normally composed by individuals, and in the case of Western European folk music these may be professional composers, popular song writers, churchmen, and sometimes even the great masters of music. There are many instances of tunes from the classics—Schubert's "Linden Tree" and Papageno's aria from Mozart's *Magic Flute* come to mind—which have been taken over by the folk tradition.

When speaking of the importance of change, in folk and tribal music, that is due to communal re-creation, let us not fail to realize that the amount of change that a song undergoes is also determined by the culture's view of change. Some of the world's cultures regard change as a positive value—the modern United States is certainly a good example— while others regard an adherence to tradition as immensely important; the culture of India is one of many possible examples. On the whole, folk and tribal cultures have tended to avoid rapid change, at least until confronted with modern technology. But there is variation even within a group of related and similarly complex societies. For example, the Pueblo Indians of the southwestern United States resisted change much more than did the Indians of the North American Plains, and this difference in attitude affected many aspects of their history, including the recent history of their music. Thus, while we must assume that we never find complete stability and that some change always results from oral tradition and communal re-creation, rapid and dramatic change occurs in some cultures, while slow and often barely perceptible change occurs in others.

FOLK MUSIC AS NATIONAL EXPRESSION

The idea that folk music is closely associated with a people, a nation, or a culture has long been widely accepted. In some languages, the words for "folk music" and "national music" are the same. This popular notion is quite opposed to that which deems music a "universal language." Neither is really correct or objective. Of course, it is possible to identify music as music, whether it is in a style known to us or not. Music is a universal phenomenon, but each culture has its own, and learning to understand another culture's music is in many ways like learning a foreign language. No culture can claim a body of music as its own without admitting that it shares many characteristics and probably many compositions with other neighboring cultures. But we must also assume that some of the essential and distinctive qualities of a culture somehow find their way into its music. Balancing the idea of traditional music as a national or regional phenomenon against the concept of folk music as a supranational kind of music is one of the fascinations of this field.

At the root of the concept of uniting nation and musical style is the idea that a nation's folk music must somehow reflect the inner characteristics of that nation's culture, the essential aspects of its emotional life—its very self. This feeling has at times given rise, among the general population as well as among folk song scholars, to a politically nationalistic view of folk music. Unfortunately, folk music has at times been made the tool of aggressive and racist policies. This was to an extent the case in Nazi Germany, where the high quality of German music was extolled and the "poorer stuff" of Slavic folk song was denigrated, and in the Soviet Union during the 1950s, when traditional folk tunes of all peoples, including the non-Slavic minorities in Soviet Asia, were fitted with words praising Lenin and Stalin, collective farms, and the dictatorship of the proletariat. Although we may question the authenticity of music treated or arranged in this way, and while we may wonder whether it is really representative of or accepted by a nation's culture, it behooves us to study this use of folk music in order to understand its importance in the political and cultural processes.

There is some validity to the notion that the folk music of a nation or a tribe has a special relationship to its culture. We have spoken of the need for general acceptance of a song if it is to be remembered. There are other points. For example, it seems likely that the general character-istics of a language—its stress patterns, its patterns of intonation, and of course the structure of its poetry—are reflected in the music of its people. Moreover, if we plotted the characteristics of the folk music of each people—the characteristics of its scales, its melodic movement, its rhythm, and so on—and if we fed this information, nation by nation, into a com-puter and examined the results statistically, we would probably find that no two peoples have identical styles of music. And while various musical characteristics may be present in the music of many peoples, each people has its own particular proportion and combination of musical traits, and these interact in a unique way.

Studies of this sort have actually been carried out by a group of scholars headed by Alan Lomax.[1] Using many characteristics of music, they plotted the typical stylistic "profile" of many musical cultures, find-ing correlations between certain kinds of music and certain culture types, but also finding each unique. According to Lomax, the favorite song style of a culture reflects its style of social relationships. Thus he be-lieves that the difference between Middle Eastern music (which is prevail-ingly soloistic and has long, drawn-out, ornamented melodies) and African music (which is frequently performed by ensembles or choruses, requires close cooperation by the musicians, and contains a lot of polyph-ony) is due to differences between these cultures in their attitudes towards cooperation, sex, and the stratification of social classes. Whether this theory will in the end prove correct is not yet known, but it does make us aware of the fact that each culture has its distinctive music, and that this distinctiveness is probably in some way related to the basic values and attitudes of the culture.

Despite the distinctiveness of each people's music, the musical relationships between neighboring peoples may be very close. It has been shown many times that melodies and songs travel from people to people. A tune may appear as a ballad in Germany and (in slightly differ-ent form) as a Christmas carol in Poland, as a dance song in Slovakia, and so on. It is possible, of course, that the same tune was made up separately in each of these countries, but this is not likely. The more complex an idea or a cultural artifact is, the smaller the possibility that it was in-vented more than once by different people. And a song, even a very simple one, is, after all, a complicated creation. Very likely a melody found in several countries was simply taught by people on one side of the border to friends on the other side, or taught in many communities by a wandering minstrel. The tune could be easily learned, but the words were strange, could not be readily translated, thus were replaced by a

---

[1] Alan Lomax et al., *Folksong Style and Culture* (Washington: American Association for the Advancement of Science, 1968).

poem in the language of the second country. But since the tune did not fit perfectly into the repertory of the second country, since it did not have the characteristics of that country's preferred musical style, it was gradually changed to make it conform. If the styles of the two countries involved were very different, the song would probably not take root at all in the second country but would be dropped. It so happens that the various folk music styles of Europe are rather similar, and probably for this reason there are many tunes that have spread from people to people until they covered the entire continent. In contrast, when Spaniards and Englishmen settled North America, they did not absorb into their repertories many, or perhaps any, tunes of the American Indians, probably because, among other reasons, they were too strange for absorption into their style.

We see that songs can be passed from culture to culture. The same is true, to an extent, of musical characteristics or, as we frequently call them, stylistic traits. A type of scale, a kind of rhythm, a way of singing can be passed from one people to another without a simultaneous passing of songs. If one country has a particular kind of technique—for example, antiphony, the alternation between two groups, each singing a phrase at a time—that technique can be taken up by the people in a second country, who may then impose it on their own songs. There is some evidence that this actually happened in North America. Antiphonal technique is highly developed in some African cultures, and when Africans came to America as slaves, some began living with certain Southeastern Indians, both as slaves and as refugees from slavery. The Indians, who already practiced some singing in which a leader and a chorus alternated, seem to have started using the specifically African variant of this technique in their own songs. It is obvious that in spite of the national or tribal identity of a folk music style, there is much sharing of songs and of ways of performing music among the peoples of the world.

Discussion of the uniqueness of each people's musical style brings us to a consideration of authenticity. This concept is rooted in the idea that each culture has a primordial musical style of its own, and that songs and traits learned at a later date in its history are not properly part of its music. An authentic song is thought to be one truly belonging to the people who sing it, one that really reflects their spirit and personality. To be sure, each culture has its unique musical style, but within this there may be subsumed a number of varieties, some of them resulting from the introduction of new techniques of composition and of new inventions, such as instruments, or from contacts with other cultures. All of the kinds of music that reside within a culture are worthy of study and are important for an understanding of that culture. We are entitled and, indeed, obligated to find out and interpret the differences in age among certain songs, the difference in complexity among various strata of the repertory of a culture, and the attitudes that members of a culture take towards various kinds of music that they perform. But that is quite different from deciding that a particular kind of music is the "authentic" music of that culture, and that other kinds of music, particularly those that have come about under the pressure of outside influences, are somehow inferior, debased, or contaminated, and not worthy of attention. We may even be justified in saying that the majority of the musics in use in the world today are in some way hybridized, as a result of contact among widely divergent cultures. Surely this is true of most of the "popular" musics in use; Western popular music has elements of African musical styles, Middle Eastern popular music is a mixture of traditional and Western. The same is true of older and less modernized tribal or folk musics. A too narrow identification of one kind of music with each culture or nation is, in the long run, related to the gross and widespread misconception that simple cultures, folk and tribal, are capable of learning only one kind of music. The facts seem to provide another picture: the culture type, economic development, and range of long-term outside influences of a people help to determine the limits of its musical development and its favorite style, but within these limits there is ample room for variety and change.

HISTORICAL PERSPECTIVE

A characteristic of folk and tribal music that is frequently stressed is its great age, although often it is not certain whether the age of individual songs or of musical styles is meant. But to assume that each people is, for all time, tied to one kind of music is to assume that no change has ever occurred in its tradition. This view we cannot accept, for we can observe change in the world's folk music traditions going on constantly. And while change may have been accelerated in recent times by the rapid Westernization of many non-Western cultures and by the growth of mass media, we must assume that change also occurred in the more distant past. After all, migrations of peoples have always taken place, cultural diffusion and acculturation have occurred at all times, and there is no reason to believe that peoples who have learned from each other to use the wheel, to construct instruments, and to smelt iron should have refrained from exchanging songs.

It is rarely possible to reconstruct the music history of a culture with oral tradition alone, but we can find out something about the growth, change, and geographic movements of musical styles, instruments, and even specific songs from their geographic distribution through-out the world, from archeological investigation of instruments, and from observation of the types of change that have occurred recently. But the fact that a culture has, today, a limited repertory does not mean that it may not, in prehistoric times, have possessed musical styles that were later forgotten or that merged with new materials learned from outside influences.

About the history of folk and tribal musics, then, we can make only the most general sorts of statement. We must assume that there has been a history, that change, rapid or slow, took place. In general, but probably not always, simple musical styles were followed by more complex ones. Several kinds of change were involved: changes in the repertory, brought about by the introduction of new compositions; changes in the uses of music and of attitudes towards music; and changes in individual compositions, e.g., the addition of new musical phrases, or of ornamentation, or of harmony to an extant song, or perhaps the changing of a song from one mode to another, as from major to minor. And finally, we must assume that in general (but certainly with exceptions), those cultures which are exposed most to outside influences also had a more rapidly changing music history than do the more isolated ones, and that societies whose culture changes rapidly also exhibit more rapid musical change than do those with greater cultural stability.

MUSIC IN CULTURE

The foregoing paragraphs may give the impression that we reject the concept of authenticity outright. To be sure, there seems to be little to justify some of its implications. We are approaching the study of folk music with the assumption that we are studying the musical expression of many people. And we cannot neglect any aspect of this expression simply because it is not ancient, or because it was brought from the outside, or because it does not seem to reflect the personality of the culture. On the other hand, we are not concerned here with music that is disseminated primarily by the mass media of radio, television, and records, although this music today has an enormous role in the world, and although some of it is closely related in style to the orally transmitted musics that are our subject. Similarly, we shall not deal with arrangements of folk songs as performed by professional urban musicians, nor shall we deal with rock, jazz, and country and Western music, except to mention their ultimate derivation, in part, from folk styles. This exclusion may seem arbitrary, since there is an unbroken historical line connecting rural folk music and urban popular music, but the entire field of world music is historically interrelated and arbitrary lines must be drawn for practical reasons. Thus the concept of authenticity has its practical uses: we are discussing, in this volume, that part of the music of the world's Western continents which was and is entirely or largely maintained in oral tradition.

But we are also interested in the music of particular groups of people. Those classified as nonliterate or tribal cultures can be defined with no great difficulty. Until recent times, for instance, there was no doubt that all American Indians were in this category. In the nineteenth century, there were individual Indians who learned to read, and some became learned; later, some became anthropologists who studied their own cultures. But the Indian languages were not written down except under the stimulus of white missionary scholars, and in each Indian tribe, more or less all the people shared one kind of music.

In the folk cultures of Europe and America it is more difficult to separate the folk music from the sophisticated, cultivated, or fine art of music, or from popular music. The distinction is gradual and unclear. The musical life of cities and courts, directed by trained professional musicians with the use of written music, is certainly different from that of the villages in which music is passed on by oral tradition and in which most of the people participate actively without much specialization. But some folk music also exists in the cities, and some influence from the cities has always trickled down to the villages and at times inundated them. Everyone has a bit of folk heritage; on the other hand, the folk songs of most areas in Europe and America have for centuries undergone some influence from the sophisticated music of the cities. The popular music of the cities seems to occupy a sort of middle ground. We can draw no sharp line.

Much has been said about the differences between folk and art music as far as their use or functions in the culture are concerned. We frequently hear the statement that folk and primitive music are "functional," while art music is not, or less so. This would imply that folk and primitive music always accompany other activities in life, and that art music is always "art for art's sake." There is some truth in this distinction, but the overall picture is a very complex one.

If we scrutinize the role of music in Western civilization, we find that music is not at all solely a giver of pleasure and a device for aesthetic edification. On the contrary, it is frequently designed to accompany activities of all sorts. We need to mention only church music, dance music, marching music, and the background music of drama, film, and television. On the other hand, the ideal kind of music, the music generally considered as best and greatest by those most concerned with music, is the music designed primarily for hearing in recital or concert. Thus we would be right in stressing the role of music in Western civilization as being one not involving other activities, but only because this is the idealized role of music, not because most music necessarily conforms to this image. And, to be sure, we generally respond by describing music as beautiful rather than judging its suitability for its particular function.

The converse picture is, on the whole, found in folk and tribal cultures. We are frequently told that all folk music accompanies other activities, that it never fills a role of entertainment, that it does not provide simple enjoyment. Of course this is not the case; there are many examples, in European folklore and in African and American Indian cultures, of music's being used as entertainment. Individual singers may entertain groups or themselves with music. In some African cultures, music is performed by professional or semi-professional musicians to entertain. But generally speaking—and here there are great differences among the world's cultures—the traditional music is focused towards functionality. Songs are typically referred to as "good" or "powerful," indicating that it is not the aesthetic quality of the song but the manner in which it fulfills its task (persuading the spirits, accompanying a dance, or giving an account of history) that is essential. Is it possible to indicate for any culture the main function of its music? No doubt, in any culture, music has many uses. But seen in the overall perspective of a culture, and compared to other activities, music may in each society have one special role. In some tribal cultures, music has essentially an enculturative function, that is, it serves to introduce members of the tribe to various aspects of their own culture. Elsewhere, its main function may be specifically religious in the strict sense, that is, it may be used as a language in which the supernatural or divine is addressed. Elsewhere again, music is the tribal "stamp of approval" for an activity; the activity must be accompanied by the appropriate music in order for it to be carried out correctly. Or music may be an important force for tribal unity and cohesion. In modern Western culture, all of these functions are present, but the fact that our most valued musical creations are intended for concerts and for entertainment (in the broad sense of that word) indicates that in our lives music has a different role from that which it has in most tribal and folk societies.

THE GENESIS OF FOLK MUSIC

The way in which Western folk music (or, for that matter, the folk music of Asian civilizations) came about is a fascinating one. The question whether "the folk creates" or whether it only utilizes material created by a higher social stratum has frequently been asked. We have already stated that all music is composed by individuals. The old belief that folk music rises, like a mist, from the collective consciousness of the village or band is hardly worth an argument. But the source of the materials used in folk music is still a bone of contention. Tribal cultures, of course, must have acquired their songs and the musical components of these songs from their own creativity or possibly from occasional outside contacts, although it is sometimes argued that even the remote primitives have had contact with the high cultures of the world, and that they have derived their musical accomplishments by absorbing the music of the high culture, diluted though it may be by passing through tribes and nations. Thus it may be argued that the Indians of South America, some of whose music is exceedingly simple, must in primordial times have derived their style from that of China; and there are remote similarities to substantiate this theory. This, however, is quite different from the everyday contact that has existed between folk and art music in some European countries. In Europe, it is sometimes thought, both the songs and the style of music in each nation are derived from the same nation's art music. This idea, based on a theory known by the German term *gesunkenes Kulturgut* (debased culture), assumes that the folk communities are inherently incapable of creating music or literature or art, and that instead they assimilate what trickles down to them from the sophisticated society of the cities. A time lag is assumed as well, so that the kind of style found in German art music in one century, for instance, is likely to turn up in its folk music centuries later. No doubt there has been a great deal of influence bearing from the cities on the folk culture. We know of folk songs that had their origin in the city, and we know of sophisticated dances that decades later became folk dances. But we cannot accept the notion that all folk music is simply debased city culture. The evidence of folk song influencing the sophisticated composer—from Schubert and Liszt to Bartók and Enesco—is too great. Rather, let us accept a theory of mutual give-and-take to describe the relationship between folk and art music.

Let us now summarize, on the basis of the considerations given in this chapter, the criteria we shall use for determining the materials to be discussed in the rest of this volume. Defining tribal music is not too difficult, but defining folk music is not an easy task. Several criteria can be used, but each, applied alone, is unsatisfactory. The main one is the transmission by oral tradition. Folk music, in its native setting, is not written down. As a result its compositions develop variants, and the original form of a folk song is rarely known. Folk music may originate anywhere, but it is most frequently created by untrained, nonprofessional musicians, and performed by singers and players with little or no theoretical background. Folk song is frequently old, and the style of folk music may be archaic. But folk and nonliterate cultures do have a music history; they allow their music to change, their compositions to be altered, and their repertory to be turned over. Folk music is frequently associated with other activities in life, but it also serves as entertainment. And most important, since folk music is the musical expression of a whole people or tribe, or a significant portion of a culture, it must be performed and accepted in order to remain alive.

BIBLIOGRAPHY AND DISCOGRAPHY

Introductions to the general nature of traditional music and its functions in society and as an aspect of human behavior are not numerous. Among the best are some of the articles in Funk and Wagnalls' *Standard Dictionary of Folklore, Mythology and Legend,* edited by Maria Leach (New York, 1949–50): "Song" (by George Herzog), "Dance" (by Gertrude P. Kurath), and "Oral Tradition" (by Charles Seeger). An overview of traditional musics, nation by nation, appears in *Grove's Dictionary of Music and Musicians,* 5th ed. (New York: St. Martin's Press, 1954), under the heading "Folk Music." A survey of non-Western music, especially in its historical perspective, appears in the first volume of *The New Oxford History of Music* (London: Oxford University Press, 1957). Alan P. Merrian, *The Anthropology of Music* (Evanston: Northwestern University Press, 1964), provides much material on the role of music in various nonliterate cultures.

Several scholarly periodicals specialize in non-Western and folk music; among them, we should note *Ethnomusicology* (Journal of the Society for Ethnomusicology); *Journal and Yearbook of the International Folk Music Council; Asian Music; Jahrbuch für musikalische Volksund Völkerkunde; Selected Reports* of the UCLA Institute of Ethnomusicology; and *African Music.* Bruno Nettl, *Reference Materials in Ethnomusicology* (Detroit: Information Service, 1961) is a bibliographical guide to the whole field.

Some articles of interest that explore specific aspects of traditional music everywhere and that are relevant to points made in this chapter are Alan Lomax, "Folk Song Style," *American Anthropologist,* LXI (1959), 927–954; Maud Karpeles, "Some Reflections on Authenticity in Folk Music," *Journal of the International Folk Music Council,* III (1951), 10–16; and K. P. Wachsmann, "The Transplantation of Folk Music from one Social Environment to Another," *J-IFMC,* VI (1954), 41–45.

A number of records and record sets give examples of the music of many of the world's cultures. These are listed here, although they could also have been listed following Chapter 2 and in some cases later chapters: *Music of the World's Peoples,* ed. Henry Cowell (4 albums), Folkways

FE 4504–4507; *Primitive Music of the World,* ed. Henry Cowell, Folkways FE 4581 (a smaller selection overlapping with the former); *Columbia World Library of Folk and Primitive Music,* compiled by Alan Lomax (over 20 records, partly reissues of older recordings, partly new material collected by Lomax and others); *The Demonstration Collection of E. M. von Hornbostel and the Berlin Phonogrammarchiv,* Folkways FE 4175 (reissue of an early collection that attempted to show the great variety of the world's musical styles); *Man's Early Musical Instruments,* Folkways P 525; *An Anthology of the World's Music,* Anthology records; and the UNESCO Collection, comprising sets of African and Asian music.

TWO

STUDYING THE STYLE

OF FOLK MUSIC

Music of any sort, but folk and tribal music especially, should be examined in two ways: (1) for itself, that is, its style and structure, and (2) in its cultural context, its function, and its relationship to other aspects of life. Eventually, of course, a blending of the two approaches should be achieved. The second has been briefly covered in Chapter One. We have tried to show how folk music and the music of nonliterate cultures, despite their diversity, differ as a group from other kinds of music in their origin, transmission, and cultural role. We should now like to devote a few pages to the question of musical style. In order to talk about music we need to develop a vocabulary, and talking about or describing folk music and the music of non-Western cultures requires special adaptations of the technical vocabulary normally used for describing the music of Western civilization. Also, in order to distinguish the various styles of folk music throughout the world from each other, we should have some idea of what is common to all or most of them. Here, then, we wish to talk about the music itself, not about the use that is made of it, nor about the words of the song, nor about the instrument used to play it.

We are interested in finding out how a piece of music is put together, what makes it tick. We also want to know what aspects of music characterize a repertory of a community or a country or a tribe, and we want to know what it is that distinguishes the musical sound of one culture from that of another. Answering these questions, i.e., describing musical styles, is something that ultimately requires great sophistication. Some published descriptions of music seem to defy understanding even by trained musicians. On the other hand, a layman with no background at all can, by listening and repeated listening, learn a great deal about how a piece of music is put together. In the case of folk and tribal music, which tends to be quantitatively simpler than the sophisticated music of the trained composer, analysis by listening rather than by examining a score is normally not too difficult. The reader of these pages is advised to listen to records of folk music as much as possible.

It is important to realize that a music is something like a language. It must be understood to be appreciated. The listener must know that certain kinds of sounds are signals, for example, of points of tension, of relaxation, of beginnings or endings of musical thoughts. A music, or perhaps we may say a musical repertory, is a system with an internal logic, structure, and typical modes of expression. And this is true whether the music is written by professional trained composers, as in Western classical music; whether it is composed by sophisticated professionals who do not use musical notations, such as the composers of Indian classical music; whether it is by the formally untrained composer of folk and tribal cultures who may not be able to explain what he is doing; whether it is an improvisor of Middle Eastern music who, as it were, composes on the spur of the moment; etc. In no music is material made up simply at random. The absence of an articulated music theory does not imply the absence of rules which a composer must follow; on the contrary, the composer in a folk or tribal culture is likely to be surrounded with musical limitations, to which he feels it necessary to adhere. (This is partially related to the need of having one's compositions accepted by performer and listener in order for the music to remain alive.)

Since in folk and tribal cultures "rules" of composition are not stated by music theorists and composers, we must derive them from the music itself, and the statements in the following chapters regarding the characteristics of various musics may be regarded as partial or introductory statements of the rules and logic of their musical systems. These brief statements are of necessity superficial, for if we delve with sufficient depth into any musical repertory, we discover that it is a system of communication with a complicated "grammar," "syntax," and "vocabulary" of musical materials and devices.

SOUND AND SINGING STYLE

The first thing that strikes a listener when he hears an unfamiliar musical style is the overall sound, which has many components but among whose chief traits are tone color and texture. Musical cultures differ in their sound ideals. The way in which the human voice is used, particularly, is characteristic of a culture and tends to be maintained throughout the variety of forms, scales, rhythmic patterns, and genres in its repertory. The way in which American Indians sing is quite different from that of Africans; Spanish folk singers sound different from English ones. One needs to hear only two seconds of Arabic singing to identify it as Middle Eastern. The characteristics of singing in a culture may reflect characteristics of speech and language, but there are sufficient exceptions to make us suspicious of any simple explanation that automatically relates these two methods of communicating.

Describing the characteristics of a singing style in words is difficult. We speak of such things as degrees of vocal tension, use of vibrato or tremolo, presence or absence of sharp accentuation of tones, loudness, ornamentation such as trills and grace notes, nasality, and so on. It is interesting to find that in many cultures, the sounds of instruments have characteristics similar to those of the singing style. Thus the violin playing of India sounds very much like Indian singing, and very different indeed from European violin playing.

The overall sound of music characterizes a musical culture in other ways as well. Sub-Saharan Africa, for example, may be characterized by a multiplicity of simultaneous sounds, and we find polyphony, that is, part-singing or ensemble music. But in addition we also find attempts by single musicians to produce several simultaneous sounds even when the means to do so are limited, and we find that there are always attempts to make these simultaneous sounds contrast with each other, as in the use of unrelated instruments in an ensemble or in the simultaneous use of widely divergent rhythms. In contrast, the music of South and West Asia is usually soloistic, and when several instruments play together, they tend to approximate each other in their tone colors.

It is important to realize that while the musical style of a culture may change rapidly, its singing style and overall sound patterns change very slowly; thus this is one of the traits of music that is most characteristic of a culture and that is closely tied to the value structure of other aspects of life.

Realizing the relative stability of singing style and sound ideals in a culture, we may be tempted to tie them to heredity and race. We may assume that the way in which the voice is used by Indians or Africans is related to the peculiarities of their race, their appearance, the color of their skin. But there is no evidence to support this view. Africans and Indians can learn to sing in the styles of other cultures, and indeed, Europeans and Americans, with sufficient effort, can learn to sing in Indian, African, and Chinese styles. The integrity of national or tribal singing styles has other roots. Every people has musical traits which are of great importance for maintaining its cultural identity, whether the musicians are able to verbalize about this or not; and singing styles and sound ideals in music are evidently among these traits. On the other hand, all aspects of music are definitely parts of culture, and the cultural and racial boundaries of the world do not coincide precisely, if at all.

FORM

Having noted the general character of the sound of a music, perhaps the best way to begin analyzing it, whether one hears it or sees it written out, is to find the large subdivisions and the broad tendencies of formal design. Is it made up of several large sections which contrast markedly? Are the sections of equal length? Does the tempo change considerably or suddenly in the course of the piece? Are any of the sections repeated? Is the whole piece repeated several times? If so, are the repetitions more or less exact, or are they variations of the first rendition? Do the sections correspond to sections or lines of the same length in the verbal text? These are the kinds of questions an intelligent listener must ask.

Simultaneously, we should watch for the arrangement of the performance, and this is especially important in studying music from a recording. We want to know whether the piece is performed by a single performer or a group, and whether there is alternation. Do several performers sing or play in unison, or does each have his own part?

Having identified the several sections of a piece, we must try to establish the relationships among them. One way to do this is to give each of them a letter, and to repeat the letter when the section is repeated. When one section is a variation of a previous one, we give it a superscript number: thus A^1 is a variation of A. When a section is new but seems

somewhat reminiscent of a previous one, we can indicate this by a superscript letter so that B^a is a section reminiscent of A. For example, the song
in Example 2-1 could be analyzed with the following letters: AA^1BA^1.

EXAMPLE 2-1. German folk song, "O du lieber Augustin," learned by the
author from oral tradition.

Sometimes the interrelationship is more complex, as in Example
2-2, where a section reappears at different pitch levels. It could be described by letters $AA^1{}_5A^2{}_5A$, A_5 being a transposition, a perfect fifth
higher, of A.

Forms such as AABB, ABBA, and ABCA appear frequently in
European folk music. All these forms have in common the use of four
musical lines, perhaps of equal length. But the internal differences are
significant. Example 2-1 presents a theme, then a contrasting line, and
returns to the theme. Example 2-2 is based on a single theme which, perhaps for the purpose of providing variety, is presented at different pitch
levels. But they both share a quality of being rounded off, which most
typically forms the basis of strophic songs, in which a melody is repeated
several times with different words.

EXAMPLE 2-2. Hungarian folk song, from Zoltán Kodály, *Folk Music of
Hungary* (London: Barrie and Rockliff, 1960), pp. 61–62.

Tempo giusto

In the music of some non-Western cultures, songs don't have clearly marked endings or forms that are precisely predetermined. The following Navaho song (Example 2-3) is made up of an occasionally regular, but sometimes irregular, alternation of three sections (marked A, B, and C in the transcription). The sequence of the sections is AABBCBAB-BCBAABABBCB, etc.

EXAMPLE 2-3. Navaho Indian song, from Bruno Nettl, *North American Indian Musical Styles* (Philadelphia: Memoir 45 of the American Folklore Society, 1954), p. 47.

In the discussion of musical styles of tribal and folk cultures, we must keep in mind the limitations that are imposed by the lack of a musical technology (i.e., notation and music theory) and the absence of intensive training of the musician by professionals. These limitations amount to relatively simple forms as well as the use of strong unifying factors which act as mnemonic devices. A drone (as in the lowest pipe of the bagpipes), the use of the same musical material in each voice of a part-song, the reappearance of a musical motif at different pitch levels throughout a song, a repeated rhythmic pattern, a simple tonal structure with clearly marked tonic and reciting tones—all of these are devices that are arrived at unconsciously but are eagerly accepted by the folk community because they help the folk singer and his audience to organize the musical material in their minds and clarify its structure, thus making oral tradition a more feasible process.

POLYPHONY

Most of the music we deal with in this volume is monophonic, which means that only a single tone is heard at a time, and there is no accompaniment except that of drums, rattles, or other percussive sound. But there is a good deal of European, American, and Latin American folk music, and a great deal of African music, that has more than one tone sounding at a time or more than one melody at a time or has perhaps accompaniment with chords. Several terms have been used to describe such music; perhaps the most satisfactory one is "polyphony," which we will use here to include all music that is not monophonic, whether it consists of a singer's own simple accompaniment with his guitar or of a chorus or of a group of different instruments playing a complex interrelationship as in chamber music.

In a style of polyphonic music that is strange to one's ears, it may be difficult to describe just what is going on. There is not much point, when describing folk music from Russia or from South Africa, in trying to apply labels used for Western art music, such as "organum," "fugue," "conductus," and the like, to music that developed quite outside Western European musical culture.

A better way to begin describing a polyphonic piece is to decide whether the various parts being sung or played at the same time are of equal importance, or whether one stands out as the leading or solo part. Then one can try to describe the melodic relationship among the parts. For example, do they use material based on the same tune or theme, or do they use more or less independent tunes? If the latter is the case, one should decide whether the relationship among the different voices or instruments produces imitation or canon, the most common manifestation of which is the round (the same tune performed at different time intervals); or parallelism (the same tune performed at the same time at different pitch levels); or heterophony (something like variations of the same tune played or sung simultaneously). At this point, also, one would like to know how much of the music is composed, and what aspects of it, if any, are improvised. It would also be important to know which aspects of the music had to be performed the way they are, and in which the performer had a choice and the right to make changes on the spur of the moment.

A further point to be considered is the way in which the musicians and listeners in another culture perceive polyphony. Do they concentrate on the effects of the simultaneities, such as chords, and on their progression, or do they listen to the progression of the individual melodies as they proceed side by side? We can hardly make judgments about this on the basis of simple listening, and extensive field research is necessary in order for us to be sure of our ground. But we must at least be aware of the fact that different cultures may perceive the same music differently, and that our own perception may or may not be relevant.

RHYTHM AND TEMPO

We can learn a good deal about the rhythmic character of a culture's music, or of a single piece of its music, also simply by listening. We want to know, for example, whether the music is organized in measures that recur more or less regularly throughout, and where exceptions occur. If we can perceive a repeated unit of beats and accents, we may conclude that the music is "metric." We can check this by tapping our foot regularly and seeing whether the tapping fits the music. We also want to know whether a drum or rattle accompaniment, if any, coincides with the rhythmic units of the melody. Then, quite aside from the meter, we may also describe rhythm in terms of the lengths of the notes found in a piece. This is something that cannot be found out quite so easily by listening, but can be described with the use of written notation.

We want to know, for example, whether most of the notes are of one length, whether two note-lengths predominate (as, for instance, quarters and eighths, in Example 2-4), or whether perhaps there are notes of all sorts of lengths, from half notes to sixty-fourths.

The tempo of a piece is also important here. We want to know whether it is fast or slow. Here our intuitive judgment cannot always be trusted. A piece that a Western listener considers fast (perhaps because of the speed of the drum accompaniment) may be considered slow by a person from the culture that produced it. One way to find an objective measure of tempo is to divide the number of notes in a melody by the number of minutes the piece takes; this would express the tempo in terms of average number of notes per minute. Another way is to ascertain the speed of the "pulse" or "beat," if there is one; it may be the most frequently used note-length in the melody, or the length of stroke of the percussion accompaniment.

There are many other factors that make up the rhythmic character of music. The degree of accentuation of stressed notes, already mentioned above as an aspect of singing style, is a characteristic feature of rhythmic style. The very presence or absence of meter, the degree to which performers deviate from it, the use of different meters simultaneously, the amount of contrast between the longest and shortest notes, and typical rhythmic motifs, such as dotted rhythms (♪♩♪♩) or more complex patterns that recur, are examples of things to look and listen for.

EXAMPLE 2-4. Shoshone Indiane Peyote song, from David P. McAllester, *Peyote Music* (New York: Viking Fund Publications in *Anthropology,* no. 13, 1949), song no. 73. Reprinted by permission of David P. McAllester and Wenner-Genn Foundation for Anthropological Research.

MELODY AND SCALE

We come now to the aspect of music that has been of greatest interest to students of folk and nonliterate cultures—melody. This aspect is probably the most difficult to study or describe. A simple approach to an understanding of melody involves consideration of the melodic contour. We wish to know whether the melody of a piece generally rises, falls, remains at the same level, proceeds in a curve, or moves in large leaps, and so on. Listening to the overall movement of the tune is thus important. We are also interested in the ambit, or range, of a tune—that is, the distance, in pitch, between the highest and lowest tones. This can be found with little difficulty by listening. Then we come to consideration of the scale.

The uninitiated listener to non-Western music, and to the folk music of Eastern Europe and even perhaps some Western European folk music, is often struck by the curious, possibly unpleasant sound of it. It may sound out of tune to him, and he will have trouble reproducing the tones and intervals if he tries to sing it. Also, he will be unable to reproduce the tones correctly on a piano. The reason for this is that the tone systems and scales of much non-Western music do not conform to these scales used in the music of Western civilization. Under no circumstances should this statement be taken to imply that the Western system of music is somehow a world standard, that it is more natural or more rational than other systems. While certain musical systems may appear to correspond more closely to natural laws (e.g., acoustical, biological, or psychological), we must assume that all musics are man-made to an equal extent, and that all of them are in some way based on the rules of nature. In this respect, all of them are equally worthy of independent study, and the fact that some diverge from the average more than others is not to be the basis of value judgments. Thus the "peculiarity" of certain scales or tone systems to our ears is due to the "particularity" of the tone system with which we have grown up.

A scale may be defined as the pitches used in any particular piece of music such as song. A tone system, on the other hand, is all the pitches used in a whole body of songs or pieces in the same style. One way to describe a scale is to count the number of different pitches or tones that appear in it. From this kind of description are derived such terms as "pentatonic," which denotes a scale consisting of five tones; "tetratonic," a scale of four notes; "tritonic" (three tones); "hexatonic" (six); and "heptatonic" (seven). The mere number of tones, however, doesn't really determine the character of a scale to any great extent; the reason for the curious sound of some non-Western music is not to be sought in the number of tones used.

The distance in pitch between the tones is probably a more important indicator of tonal character than their number. Thus we may find one pentatonic song that uses the scale, A-B-D-E-G and another one that uses the tones, A-Bb-B-C-D. Each uses five tones, but one uses large intervals, the other very small ones. The number of interval arrangements that can be found in folk music is almost infinite, but the listener should decide whether the intervals he hears are, on the whole, large, small, or medium, and get an idea of the character of the scale that he is hearing.

In some cultures there are intervals smaller than the half tone, that is, smaller than anything that can be produced on the piano. More commonly we find intervals intermediate in size between those used in the Western tempered system. Thus the "neutral third," an interval found in various cultures, is halfway between a major and a minor third. Of course, in Western civilization we use several different pitch standards. The intervals on the piano are somewhat different from those produced on the violin. But we have a range within which an interval is considered "in tune." Although "A" is normally supposed to be 440 vibrations per second, a pitch of 435 or 445 would still, by most persons, be considered "A." Presumably a similar range of acceptability exists in the musical system—expressed, or unconsciously taken for granted—of each culture. And probably one may deviate from pitch more in some musical styles than in others and still operate within the acceptable norm.

Another important feature of musical scales is the hierarchy in importance and function of the individual tones. Most frequently there is one tone which is the basis of the scale; it is apt to appear at the end of a piece and is called the tonic. Another tone, perhaps higher and used with great frequency, may be called "dominant." Other tones may appear with average frequency, and still others may be rare. Individual tones may also have particular functions, such as appearing typically just before or after certain other tones, thus providing the listener with signals indicating points of the musical structure.

In short, the scale of a composition can and should be a capsule diagram of its melodic materials and rules.

In many ways, the music of non-Western and some folk cultures sounds strange, confusing, and downright unacceptable to the uninitiated listener. There is a tendency in earlier musical writings, and in present-day remarks of the uninformed, to assume that such music has no structure and no laws, that it is chaotically improvised. The frequent tendency to label it "chant" indicates an assumption that the music is simply a vehicle for ceremonial words, and that it has little interest of its own. Nothing could be farther from the truth. The intricacy of much of this music—its consistent and logical structure—makes much of it a marvel of artistry. Its simplicity is dictated by the fact that it must be memorized, and by the lack of notation available to the composer. Careful listening can, however, clear up much of the apparent confusion. Intervals that sound out of tune will not, once they are heard recurrently in several songs of one tribe, sound so harsh. Of course, all non-Western and folk music is not alike, so that learning one musical language, such as that of the Plains Indians, does not by any means assure knowledge of another, such as West African. But as in learning languages, so in learning musical styles, each succeeding "foreign" style is easier to assimilate than the previous one.

DESCRIPTION OF A CULTURE'S MUSIC

The sections just completed—dealing with sound, form, polyphony, rhythm, and melody—have concentrated on understanding the musical style of an individual piece of music. We find it perhaps even more necessary to describe the style of a whole body of music—all Sun Dance songs of one Plains Indian tribe, or all music of the Basongye tribe, or even the whole body of music in the Plains, or of one European folk culture such as the Rumanian. Of course, we cannot assume that all music in a culture will sound like the one example included on a single record, or even that all songs of a given tribe exhibit the same characteristics. Nevertheless, we frequently hear statements such as "the Ibo have this kind of music" or "Spanish folk music sounds like that." Fortunately for the serious scholar in our field, there is a good deal of stylistic unity in the folk music of each culture. Such unity is probably greatest in the world's simplest cultures and gives way to increasing diversity as the cultures get more complex.

The description of the musical style of a whole culture is bound to be essentially a statistical statement. There are few traits of music that don't occur at least to a small degree in many cultures, but the extent to which they occur varies and is important. When we say, for example, that most of the scales of the Arapaho Indians are tetratonic, that is, they have four tones, we must add that there are also many songs with five or six tones, some with three, and a few with seven. When we say that English folk songs are essentially modal, which implies seven tones to the scale, we must realize that all sorts of other scales also appear. We also face a problem in distinguishing among several kinds of a culture's music: the oldest and perhaps most authentic music, the recent imports and the results of outside influences, and the atypical creations which don't really belong. (Or can we make this distinction?)

In the other chapters of this survey, we will be describing musical styles along with their cultural background. We must admit at the outset that we don't really know enough about the folk music of Europe, Africa, and the Americas to give a reliable or definite description. Many songs have been collected, many recordings are available; but the job of analyzing the songs and of describing the styles in scholarly terms has actually just begun. The statements that will be made in this volume will sometimes have to be impressionistic, based on knowledge of only a small segment of a people's music. We can only indicate examples of the kinds of things that occur. We cannot give a complete picture, but we hope that the partial picture presented will stimulate the reader to strike out on his own in order to learn more.

RESEARCH IN TRADITIONAL MUSIC:
ETHNOMUSICOLOGY

Perhaps a few words about the way in which research in folk and non-Western music is done will help the reader to understand some of the procedures and statements in the following chapters. The field that provides research in this area is now known as ethnomusicology. Before about 1950 it was commonly called comparative musicology, and it is a sort of borderline area between musicology (the study of all aspects of music in a scholarly fashion) and anthropology (the study of man, his culture, and especially the cultures outside the investigator's own background). Research in ethnomusicology consists essentially of two activities, field work and desk or laboratory work. In past decades it was customary to keep these activities quite distinct. Those who went into the "field"—to villages, reservations, or colonies, to make recordings—were not necessarily trained in the techniques of analysis and description that form the main part of the "desk work." Conversely, the armchair ethnomusicologists rarely went into the "field." In recent times it has been assumed that the best work would result if the same person did both the field research and the later analytical work. It is now taken for granted that almost every ethnomusicologist is, at various times, both a field and a "desk" worker.

The distinction between the field worker who is interested only in recording music and the one who is interested in music as a factor of culture and as a form of behavior is also disappearing. It is true that these two different approaches to ethnomusicology are and continue to be recognized, but recently ethnomusicologists have come to realize that one cannot record and study the music of any people effectively without understanding the cultural context in which the music lives. At the same time, they realize that discussing the uses that a culture makes of music, its attitudes towards music, and the way in which music reflects the values of the society is likely to be meaningless without an understanding of the music itself. Thus it is true that ethnomusicology has two sides, or two approaches, the musicological and the anthropological, but they are both essential, at least to some degree, for each individual scholar and student; they are complementary.

There are many different types of field projects that an ethnomusicologist may undertake. He may go to study the music of an entire people, such as the Yoruba of Nigeria or the people of Afghanistan, but aside from providing an introductory survey, such a project would be useless in the context of the amount of knowledge available today because it would be superficial. More fruitful is the study of a particular type of music or the musical culture of an individual community, of a particular group (such as a minority) in a community, or even of an individual musician. The approach of the field worker varies with the project and the emphasis. He may simply record music and take down, from the statements of his informants, the necessary information on its cultural background. Or he may observe musical events as they occur. He may learn aspects of the musical system by learning how to perform the music himself; this can be done particularly effectively in those cultures which have established formal musical training. He may devise techniques, such as musical aptitude tests based on the people's own music, questionnaires or various approaches involving statistics. In general, we may divide field research into several categories: (1) eliciting material (music and information about it) from informants in special recording or interviewing sessions; (2) observing culture as it operates, from the field worker's view as an outsider; (3) participating in the culture as a student and performer; and (4) gaining insights from special tests which oblige the informants to think about their culture in ways to which they are not accustomed.

Obviously, the complexity and difficulties of ethnomusicological field work are considerable and not to be underestimated by the novice who tries his hand at it. The person who goes off to record the music of an African tribe or a Balkan village must know, in advance, a good deal about the culture of the people he will visit. Once there, he must use certain techniques to be sure that he gains access to the individuals who know songs, and that he makes representative samplings of the music. He should not, for example, try to record only one kind of song. Thus a collector of folk songs in the Virginia mountains should not try to record only old English ballads. If he does so, not only will he miss much other valuable material, but he may also alienate the singers, since they will probably consider other songs equally valuable, and he may not even succeed in hearing as many old English ballads as he would if he had taken a more broad-minded approach. He must get to know people in the community very well. A three-day field trip is usually not very successful; ideal field work requires months and years of stay, with follow-up visits to see how songs and also how attitudes toward music have changed.

Whatever the field worker's specific approach, he should take a broad view of his task. Turning on the tape recorder or learning how to play an instrument is only a small part of his job. He should find out what his informants think about the songs they sing; what they consider a good song or a bad one, and why; how they learn songs; how they compose; who the good musicians are and what makes them good musicians; what kinds of songs the culture has (according to the tribe's own classification; what kinds of terms they use, if any, to talk about music; what kinds of music outside their own they have had contact with; what activities each song is designed to accompany, if any; what the status of the musician in the society is; and so on. The field worker may have to use special eliciting techniques. David McAllester, for example, widely known for his collecting of Navaho music, says that he persuades the Indians to sing for him by singing folk songs or even Indian songs to them.[1] It may be useful to find an informant who will assume the role of teacher to the field worker. It is necessary to record the same song as it is sung by different people in a community, or by the same person at different times, in order to find out what aspects of a song remain stable and which ones are subject to change by improvisation; also how much a song changes in a given period of time. But no matter how much an ethnomusicologist prepares himself before a field trip and how much he learns from books and records, the first week in the field will convince him that somehow everything is different from his expectations, and that there is no substitute for seeing the situation at first hand.

TRANSCRIPTION AND ANALYSIS

Arriving back at his office with a collection, the ethnomusicologist must set about analyzing and describing the music. He may do this simply by listening with techniques something like those described in the first pages of this chapter. More likely he will want to set at least some of the music down on paper in notation. This process is called transcription.

Since our ordinary system of notation was devised essentially for the music of Western civilization, and since its purpose is to help a performer carry out the composer's intentions rather than to describe the musical actions of the performer, it is not surprising that the system is rather imperfect for the descriptive use to which it must be put in ethnomusicological transcription. The fact that the rhythms and scales of non-Western and folk music do not always fit into the Western system makes it all the more difficult to reproduce such music in conventional notation. Yet, although various special systems have been devised, most scholars have returned to the conventional one despite its shortcomings.

[1] David P. McAllester, *Enemy Way Music* (Cambridge, Mass.: Peabody Museum of American Archaeology and Ethnology, Harvard University, 1954).

It is one, after all, that can be easily mastered and that is already understood by individuals who are acquainted with music. It can be used in folk song collections that serve the double purpose of being scholarly descriptions of music and providing music to be performed. Some transcribers have added special symbols where the, conventional system of notation is wanting. For example, intervals smaller than half-steps are frequently indicated by placing a "plus" (higher) or a "minus" (lower) above a note.

Careful listening to even a simple folk tune indicates that a considerable number of musical events take place in every second of singing. The question is whether we should try to capture each of these or whether we should restrict our notation to the main lines. The ethnomusicologist, careful and thorough, would like to capture all. If he has a talented ear and enormous patience, he will come up with a very intricate notation. This procedure was followed by Béla Bartók, not only a great composer but also one of the most important scholars of folk music, who collected vast numbers of Hungarian, Slovak, Yugoslav, and Rumanian folk songs. Example 2-5 shows one of his transcriptions of Yugoslav folk music. Below the melody in all its detail is a less complicated version of the song that gives only the main notes.

EXAMPLE 2-5. Serbo-Croatian folk song, with complex and simplified transcriptions by Béla Bartók and Albert B. Lord, *Serbo-Croatian Folk Songs* (New York: Columbia University Press, 1951), p. 154.

Of course, the important thing in transcribing is to be objective, to write down what actually occurs and not what the transcriber, with his ear used to a particular musical idiom (usually the Western one), may think he hears. And make no mistake about this: what one hears is conditioned not only by what sound is actually produced, but also by what sound one's ear is attuned to and expects. Consequently, transcribing is a process that requires hearing and rehearing a piece; a minute of music may take two hours to transcribe.

In order to save time and increase accuracy and objectivity, several attempts have been made to devise machinery that would measure pitch and transcribe music. These range from a monochord—simply one stretched string with a graduated table to show vibration rates—invented by Jaap Kunst, to elaborate electronic devices based on the oscilloscope and on computers. The most recent devices are usually called melographs. There are three important forms, one invented by Charles Seeger and used at the University of California at Los Angeles, another developed in Israel, and a third invented by a group of Norwegian scholars headed by Olav Gurvin.[2] These machines produce detailed graphs, as shown in Example 2-6 (in which the top section indicates amplitude or rhythm, which is derived from volume; the series of dots in the middle indicates the time, the space between two dots equalling one second; and the bottom section indicates pitch movement or melody). Such graphs must be retranslated into a more musically meaningful form—like conventional notation with all its deficiencies. Even so electronic transcription holds great promise for future research in music that lives in oral tradition.

[2] Charles Seeger, "Prescriptive and Descriptive Music Writing," *Musical Quarterly*, LXIV (1958), 184–95; Karl Dahlback, *New Methods in Vocal Folk Music Research* (Oslo: Oslo University Press, 1958).

EXAMPLE 2-6. Graph of an automatic transcription of part of a Norwegian folk song; from Karl Dahlback, *New Methods in Vocal Folk Music Research* (Oslo: Oslo University Press, 1958), p. 127.

Transcription of the musical sound into some kind of notation system is only one of the techniques used by ethnomusicologists to prepare their material for analytic conclusions. Processing musical data with computers, counting various kinds of intervals and note values, tracing the development of a musical motif from the beginning to the end of a performance, comparing various versions of one song, classifying a repertory in groupings that are internally related, comparing the structure of a melody with that of its accompanying verbal text—all of these are examples of the kinds of things that are frequently done together with, or in some cases, instead of, transcription.

All of these techniques are, however, only stepping stones for the ethnomusicologist to get at the central questions of his field: What is the nature of music throughout the world? What does music accomplish in culture generally? Why do different cultures produce different musics? And in each individual culture? What are the conditions under which music changes? By what processes does it change?

BIBLIOGRAPHY

Methods of analysis and approaches to describing musical styles in their various phases are set forth in Curt Sachs, *The Wellsprings of Music* (The Hague: M. Nijhoff, 1962); Alan Lomax, *Folk Song Style and Culture* (Washington: AAAS, 1971); several articles by Mieczyslaw Kolinski, especially his "Classification of Tonal Structures," *Studies in Ethnomusicology* I (1961), 38–76, and B. Nettl, *Theory and Method in Ethnomusicology* (New York: Free Press, 1964). Many publications deal with methods of analyzing individual aspects of music. Among them are Sirvart Poladian, "Melody Contour in Traditional Music," *J-IFMC*, III (1951), 30–35; Mieczyslaw Kolinski, "Consonance and Dissonance," *Ethnomusicology*, VI (1962), 66–74; Kolinski, "Determinants of Tonal Construction in Tribal Music," *Musical Quarterly*, XLIII (1957), 50–56; and Curt Sachs, *Rhythm and Tempo* (New York: Norton, 1953), chapters 1 and 2.

General works about the field of ethnomusicology, its history and theories, are Jaap Kunst, *Ethnomusicology*, 3rd ed. (The Hague: M. Nijhoff, 1959) and Bruno Nettl, *Theory and Method in Ethnomusicology*, Mantle Hood, "Music, the Unknown" in *Musicology* (Englewood Cliffs, N.J.: Prentice-Hall, 1963), and Hood, *The Ethnomusicologist* (New York: McGraw-Hill, 1971). Other discussions of research methods appear in Alan P. Merriam, "Ethnomusicology, Discussion and Definition of the Field," *Ethnomusicology* IV (1960), 107–14; and his "Ethnomusicology Revisited," *Ethnomusicology* XIII (1969), 213–29. A special issue of *Ethnomusicology* (vol.

VII, no. 3, Sept. 1963) is devoted to questions of identification and methodology of the field.

A directory of ethnomusicological archives in the United States and many other nations is currently being published by the Society for Ethnomusicology. For an earlier view of such archives, see George Herzog, *Research in Primitive and Folk Music in the United States, A Survey* (Washington: ACLS, 1936). The standard work on musical instruments is Curt Sachs, *The History of Musical Instruments* (New York: Norton, 1940); important dictionaries of musical instruments are Curt Sachs, *Real-Lexicon der Musikinstrumente* (New York: Dover, 1964) and Sibyl Marcuse, *Musical Instruments: a Comprehensive Dictionary* (Garden City: Doubleday, 1964). The basic book on dance, despite its considerable age, is Curt Sachs, *A World History of the Dance* (New York: Norton, 1937). An excellent survey of recent research in non-Western dance is Gertrude P. Kurath, "Panorama of Dance Ethnology," *Current Anthropology*, I (1960), 233–54. *Ethnomusicology* VII (1964), 223–77, contains a detailed symposium on transcription and analysis on the basis of a single Bushman song.

THREE

THE GENERAL CHARACTER
OF EUROPEAN FOLK MUSIC

"What is Europe? Is it an aggregate of separate cultures or an integral unit? And what is European folk song? A single body of music or simply a group of separate styles as large in number as the continent's nations and languages?" These questions are asked by Walter Wiora,[1] a leading authority on folk music, and they are good questions with which to begin a discussion of European folk music. Of course, a qualified "yes" can be said to each of these questions. In some ways, European folk music is indeed a single corpus of musical style. The various European folk musics have much in common, but each country—in some cases each region, each district, and each community—has its own music and its own style. In this chapter we would like to devote ourselves to exploring the unity of European folk music. In Chapters Four, Five, and

[1] Walter Wiora, *Europäischer Volksgesang* (Cologne: Arno Volk Verlag, 1950), p. 5.

Six we will try to discuss the special characteristics of regions and countries.

We have pointed out that it is very hard to state concretely just how much difference there is between one kind or style of music and another. One way of telling that a musical style is similar to another one, the second of which you already recognize, is that the first of the styles also appeals to you. If this is true, and a person who is acquainted with British folk music finds Russian folk song more appealing than the music of Polynesia, then Russian and English folk song are indeed more similar to each other than are the English and the Polynesian. This has to do, of course, with the fact that folk music styles, like languages, exhibit greater or lesser degrees of relationship. Just as it is usually easier to learn a language that is closely related in structure and vocabulary to one's own, it is easier to understand and appreciate a folk music style similar to one that is already familiar. (This hypothesis does not, however, explain the fascination that an utterly strange music may immediately hold for a previously unexposed listener; but obviously there are many things that determine what kind of music will speak to an individual. Familiarity, however, is one of the strongest criteria.)

If we use this only very moderately reliable measuring device, we must admit that most of the European styles are rather similar to each other. And, on the whole, those that are geographically close to each other are also the most closely related in terms of musical style. There are a number of characteristics which we find to be present throughout Europe—with the usual pockets of exception, of course—and throughout that part of the world inhabited by descendants of Europeans.

We really know very little about the history of European folk song. We have little evidence as to the age of individual songs, although some idea can be gained from the notations of folk songs made by composers ever since the Renaissance. But in such cases we don't know whether a song was really part of the folk tradition, or whether it was an art or popular song that later moved into the realm of folklore. We also know little about the age of the various styles of folk music in Europe. Still, we are sure that for centuries there has been a close relationship between the art music of the continent and its folk music. How could it be otherwise? Villages and cities could not live without some mutual contact. In the early Middle Ages, wandering minstrels carried their tunes from court to village and from country to country. The villagers of the Middle Ages attended church and heard Gregorian chant. The composer at the court of a minor duke in seventeenth-century Germany drew his performers from the village musicians living on his lord's estate. We have ample evidence for assuming a constant relationship between the folk musician and his sophisticated counterpart.

All of this contact was accelerated by the invention and rapid dissemination of printing after the fifteenth century, especially in Western Europe. We tend to think of the folk and the art music traditions as living essentially separate lives, but this is surely erroneous not only in a consideration of European culture but also in the case of those Asian civilizations that have similar stratification. The folk musics of China, India, the Islamic world, and elsewhere all bear important similarities to the art musics of their countries. And in Europe, where printing provided a particularly good and rapid method of dissemination, especially of the words but to an important extent also the music of song, the relationship has been especially close.

Of course the effect of art music on folk music is dependent on the existence of a well-developed fine-art tradition in music. Such a tradition evidently did not exist to a large degree before the Middle Ages, and it did not come to Eastern Europe until even later. There are those who believe that the styles of European folk music evolved to a state similar to their present one before the time (perhaps a thousand years ago) when sophisticated composers first began to influence folklore; that the folk styles are an invaluable remnant of precultivated times, even of prehistoric eras. This belief can be neither substantiated nor negated. But we are probably safer in believing that the styles of European folk music developed sometime in the Middle Ages, and that this happened to some extent under the influence of the art music that was also developing at the time. This, after all, might account for the rather considerable degree of homogeneity in European folk music.

THE STROPHIC FORM

The most characteristic trait of European folk songs is their "strophic" structure. We tend to accept such a structure in which a tune with several lines is repeated several times, each time with different words, as normal. But this kind of arrangement is not so common elsewhere in the world, and it ties the European nations together as a musical unit. The length of a song with stanzas (called strophic song in technical terminology) can vary greatly, from a short bit such as that in Example 3-1 to a relatively elaborate piece such as that in Example 3-2.

It is important to realize, however, that strophic songs are found also in other parts of the world. They appear in some North American Indian cultures, in the Middle East, in Asia and Africa. Their basic principle is that a tune, or a portion of a tune, can be sung more than once, with different words; and this principle is accepted at various

EXAMPLE 3-1. Slovak folk song with short stanza, learned by the author from oral tradition.

EXAMPLE 3-2. Irish folk song, "Patty McGinty's Goat," collected in New-foundland by MacEdward Leach, transcribed by Bruno Nettl.

levels in a multitude of musical styles. Indeed, in some of the world's simplest styles, the repetition of a single musical motif, with slightly or completely different words, is common. But the more or less exact repetition of a fairly detailed musical organism with several different sets of words as the basic and by far predominant type of organization is unique to Europe; and, interestingly, it is important in all types of European music—folk, art, and popular music; East and West, North and South.

The special character of the strophic song is derived from a peculiar trait of European poetry—folk poetry as well as that of the sophisticated poets. This is the tendency to arrange poems into units of two, three, four, five, six, or more lines. Such units, called stanzas or strophes, have a form that is repeated; the interrelationship of the lines is repeated, but the words—or at least most of them—are not. The lines may be interrelated by the number of syllables or of poetic feet per line, or, more commonly, by a rime scheme. But in any event, some sort of structure is given to the stanza quite aside from the meaning of the words. The words themselves, of course, progress through the poem, telling a story or expressing the poet's feelings about practically any subject. But the structure of the stanza is repeated. We don't know, of course, whether such a strophic structure in the poetry came first, or whether it was invented to fit the music of a song; this may be a case of the "chicken-and-egg" dilemma. But logically, it is a simple transition from a repeated poetic structure to a repeated melody, with the words and their content changing from stanza to stanza.

For example, the following stanza of the famous English ballad, "Barbara Allen," shows us some of the traits of the poetic unit typical in European folklore:

> *Oh yes I'm sick, I'm very sick*
> *And death is in me dwelling;*
> *No better, no better I ever shall be*
> *If I can't have Barb'ry Allen.*

Even if we saw the complete poem without music and without the printer's divisions into stanzas, we could easily figure out that it is arranged into stanzas, because: (1) lines 2 and 4 rime (also lines 6 and 8, lines 10 and 12, etc.), and (2) every fourth line ends with the words "Barb'ry Allen." In other songs and in other languages, there are different characteristics of the stanza, different ways of identifying the stanza as a unit. But the same kind of musical structure, strophic, with its repetition of a few musical lines, is found throughout Europe (if not in all songs) and is simply an accompaniment to and analogue of the poetic structure.

The close relationship between the words and music of a song is carried even further in European folk song. The lines of music and text usually coincide, and the points at which the music comes to a temporary rest are also those at which a sentence, phrase, or thought in the words is completed. There is, moreover, a close relationship between the smaller segments of musical and linguistic structure, for example, between stress and accent, and between the length of tone and of syllable, although the nature of this relationship varies from nation to nation because of the differences in structure among the various languages. In art song, this relationship has often been refined, and the rough edges resulting from oral tradition are smoothed out.

CHARACTERISTICS OF EUROPEAN SCALES

We have mentioned its basic strophic structures as a reason for our belief that European folk music is essentially a stylistic unit. Let us also briefly discuss the unity of the continent with regard to individual elements of music—scales, meter, intervals, and manner of singing.

The scales of European folk song exhibit great variety. Most typically, there are songs with only two or three different tones (these are most frequently children's ditties or game songs), there are songs with five tones (pentatonic scales), and others with six or seven tones. But the kinds of intervals, the distances in pitch, among the tones are not quite so diverse. The tendency is for European folk songs to use intervals that fit into the diatonic system, a system of tones that we can hear by playing the white keys of the piano. The diatonic system consists of major and minor seconds and of intervals produced by adding seconds. Throughout Europe, it seems that the most common intervals in folk music are the major seconds and the minor thirds. Unfortunately, we do not yet have statistics to prove this definitively, but a thorough inspection of a few representative song collections would be convincing. Other intervals are also found, of course, and occasionally there are intervals that do not fit into the diatonic system and which could not even be reproduced approximately on the piano. Also, in folk singing the intervals are not sung with the degree of precision found on the piano, and deviation from a standard norm seems to be somewhat greater in folk than in concert music. Nevertheless, adherence to the diatonic intervals seems to be one of the great general characteristics of European folk music.

Of course, other cultures also use scales which fit into the diatonic system. In some Asian civilizations, music theory that is almost parallel to that of Europe (so far as the arrangement of pitches in a scale is concerned) has been developed, and intervals approximately the size of major seconds are probably found in the vast majority of world musics. Nevertheless, the almost perfect adherence of European folk song to this diatonic system is one of the chief characteristics of the continent.

Going into a bit more detail, we find that a great many of the songs that use seven tones can be explained, as far as their tonal material is concerned, in terms of the modes (Dorian, Phrygian, Lydian, Aeolian, Mixolydian, Locrian, and Ionian) that are used to classify Gregorian chant (in slightly different form) as well as other medieval and Renaissance music. This fact has led some scholars to believe that the styles of European folk music actually originated in the chants of the church. While we must concede the possibility of a great deal of influence of church music on folk song, it seems useful to consider these modes as only a system for classifying the latter. As such, it can be used to classify only those songs which actually have seven tones. For instance, Example 3-3 could be considered a Mixolydian tune transposed up a fourth.

EXAMPLE 3-3. Russian folk song in the Mixolydian mode, from Elsa Mahler, *Altrussische Volkslieder aus dem Pečoryland* (Basel: Bärenreiter-Verlag, 1951), p. 43.

We might be tempted to classify tunes that have only five tones according to the same system of modes, pretending that two tones of the mode are simply absent. The trouble is that we could not prove which tones are lacking. A song with the scale A-C-D-E-G that ends on A could be considered either Aeolian or minor, if the tones that are lacking were B and F. But if they were B-flat and F the tune would have to be called Phrygian. And if the missing tones were B-flat and F-sharp the scale would not fit any of the above-mentioned modes at all. (See Example 3-4 for the various modes that can be fashioned out of a nucleus of five tones in the diatonic system.) Thus we can hardly accept the blanket statement, made so frequently, that folk music is "modal" in the sense of the Gregorian modes. But a great many European folk songs do fit into the modal system.

EXAMPLE 3-4. Diatonic modes based on a single group of five tones.

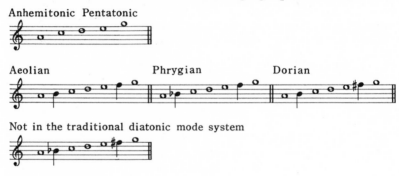

Anhemitonic Pentatonic

Aeolian   Phrygian   Dorian

Not in the traditional diatonic mode system

Pentatonic songs make up a large proportion of the European body of folk song; their scales are usually composed of major seconds and minor thirds, as in Example 3-5.

Pentatonic songs cannot, however—even with the special kind of pentatonic scale illustrated here—be considered as primarily a European phenomenon. This type of scale is one that Europe shares with a large part of the world, particularly with Northern Asia, with the American Indians, and with Negro Africa.

The same is true of the songs with two or three tones, illustrated in Example 3-6.

This very limited kind of scale is found in repertories throughout the world. There are some tribal cultures, particularly in the Americas and in Northern Asia, whose music hardly goes beyond it. This is true, for example, in the music of the Vedda of Ceylon (a people whose traditional music is now extinct, but whose songs were recorded, in rather small number, around 1900), and the songs of the last member of the Yahi

EXAMPLE 3-5. English folk song with a pentatonic scale, from Jan P. Schinhan, ed., *The Music of the Ballads* (Durham, N.C.: Duke University Press, 1957. *The Frank C. Brown Collection of North Carolina Folklore,* vol. 4), p. 184.

Scale:

EXAMPLE 3-6. Tritonic children's ditty, found in various nations with different sets of words.

Indians, the famous Ishi. In these cultures, however, an occasional fourth or fifth tone appears as well. We may feel that these cultures did not have the intellect to invent more complex scales, or to comprehend them when they heard them from other tribes. But this judgment is almost certainly false. In each culture, certain limitations are placed on musical development, and in these, the limitations were placed on the number of tones in the scale. The songs of Ishi exhibit considerable sophistication in other respects.

Cultures with more complex scale systems nevertheless tend to have some songs with only two or three tones, and this is also true of European folk cultures. In most cases (in Europe and elsewhere) these are children's songs, game songs, lullabies, and old ritual melodies. The melodies of epic poetry also frequently have few tones. The widespread geographic distribution of these scales, coupled with the simplicity of the songs which they usually accompany, has led some folklorists to believe that in Europe they constitute a remnant of an ancient musical culture. These scholars believe that all music must at one time have been as simple as this, and that such songs were driven into a corner of the repertory, just as those cultures which use only such songs were driven into the geographical corners of the world as newer, more complex music was invented. But this is only one of several possible explanations. The simple children's ditties of Europe may have nothing to do with the limited scales of the Yahi Indians, whose history may have included, in earlier times, more complex scales which gradually become more and more restricted in order to make possible the greater development of other aspects. It would be a mistake to take for granted the assumption that music everywhere moves consistently from simple to more complex forms. Thus the simplest songs of Europe may be the most archaic, but they are probably not representative of a stage in world music in which all music was based on two-tone and three-tone scales. If ever there was such a stage, it must have occurred many millenia ago, for we know that human culture, in many varieties, has been present in sophisticated forms for that long.

In summary, then, the seven-tone scales, with their modal arrangements, are a hallmark of European folk music, but they are not really limited to Western culture. The pentatonic scales are important in most if not all European traditions, but they are equally important in a large variety of non-Western cultures, in some of which they constitute the dominant scale type. The restricted two- and three-tone scales are found throughout the world, but except in a few isolated cultures, they constitute a small minority of the repertory.

METER AND SINGING STYLE

Most European folk music adheres to the concept of meter. This means that there is some regularity of recurrence in the accent pattern of the music, though such regularity does not by any means imply the predominance of common or triple meters without deviation. A good deal of European folk music can indeed be classed as isometric; that is, a single metric pattern, such as 4/4, 3/4, 6/8 (or even 5/8, 7/8, etc.), dominates the song. When several meters are used, these tend to appear in recurring sequences; thus a song, particularly one in Eastern Europe, may have a meter consisting of the regular alternation of 3/8, 4/8, and 5/8 measures (see Example 5-3). Music in which no metric pattern can be detected is not common in European folklore. Deviations from a metric pattern—for example, the elongation of tones at points of rest, near the endings of lines or of phrases—are common, as for instance that in

Example 3-7; but these deviations tend to reinforce the metric character of the music rather than to negate it. Thus another trait, found also, to be sure, elsewhere in the world, ties European folk music into a homogeneous unit.

EXAMPLE 3-7. English folk song, "Lady Isabel and the Elf Knight," from Cecil Sharp, *English Folk Songs from the Southern Appalachians* (London, New York: Oxford University Press, 1952), vol. 1, p. 7.

The metric character of European folk music is closely related to the metric organization of much of the poetry. Those peoples in which metric poetry is well developed are also those whose music most typically adheres to a simple meter. Those peoples in Europe (and they are mainly in Eastern Europe) whose poetry is organized in terms of syllable count rather than metric-foot count are also those which have a certain amount of nonmetric music, and which have more complex and more varying metric patterns in their folk music.

The manner of singing—use of the voice, movements and facial expressions, types of tone color—is another important feature. We have few guidelines according to which we can describe this phenomenon. Alan Lomax[2] is one of the few scholars who have paid attention to this important aspect of music. Lomax believes that it is possible to divide the world into relatively few areas each of which has a particular manner of singing that exists independent of the geographic distribution of other aspects of musical style such as melody, rhythm, and form. Europe, he finds, is rather complicated, for it possesses a number of singing styles that do not have contiguous distribution.

What we are interested in assessing, in a discussion of singing style, are those things that go into the singing of almost every tone, the things that make the sound of a singer and of his entire culture distinc-

[2] Alan Lomax, "Folk Song Style," *American Anthropologist*, LXI (1959), 927–54. See also his *Folk Song Style and Culture* (Washington: American Association for the Advancement of Science, 1968).

tive and recognizable immediately. Among the parameters of singing style already mentioned in Chapter Two are these: (1) degree of tension, or its opposite, called by Lomax "vocal width"; (2) amount of ornamentation; (3) raspiness; (4) accentuation, that is, degree to which individual tones are attacked with strength, and degree to which stressed tones are distinguished in loudness and sharpness from the unstressed ones; (5) nasality; (6) pitch level, i.e., the level of singing within the singer's natural vocal range; (7) vocal blend, i.e., the degree to which singers in a group blend their voices; (8) ornamentation; and others. Before Lomax, the Hungarian composer and folk song scholar Béla Bartók divided Hungarian and other European folk singing into two basic singing styles, "parlando-rubato" and "tempo giusto." The first of these is a singing style in which emphasis is on the words, there is not much strict adherence to tempo and meter, and there is a substantial amount of ornamentation. "Tempo giusto" implies greater stress on musical meter and tempo, and less on the words. Bartók found that both of these singing styles were found in Hungarian folk music, and both appear to be present in many European countries, although their definition must generally be adjusted somewhat differently for each culture. According to Lomax, however, there is in each culture one dominant singing style, and it can be identified rather easily in any small sampling of singing. His view is that the main singing style of each culture is determined by the character of that culture, and in particular by the types of relationships among people that are typical of that culture.

The three singing styles that Lomax assigns to European folk music are termed by him "Old European," "Modern European," and "Eurasian." The "Eurasian" style, which is found primarily throughout most of the high cultures of Asia, is represented in Europe in parts of the British Isles and France, in South Italy, and in the Mohammedan parts of the Balkans. The singing is high-pitched, strident, and harsh, and the singers' facial expressions are rigidly controlled or sad. The style lends itself well to long, ornamented tones and passages, and the character of the music is sweetly sad and melancholy. Lomax equates singing styles with certain types of social structure and, according to him, the Eurasian area is one in which the position of women is below that of men; they may be put on a pedestal, but they do not have equality.

The "Old European" style, according to Lomax, is found in the Hebrides, Northern England, Scandinavia, the Pyrenees, Czechoslovakia, Western Yugoslavia, Northern Italy, Germany, parts of the Balkans, the Ukraine, and the Caucasus. Here the singing is done with the throat relaxed, and the facial expressions of the singers are lively and animated. The tunes are simple and unornamented, and group singing is common. Cooperation among the singers in a chorus seems to have allowed polyphony to develop, and, says Lomax, possibly some of the polyphonic types of folk music antedated the development of polyphony in European cultivated music. In these areas, in any event, harmony was easily accepted. The idea of cooperation in music seems to have something to do with social cooperation, for the position of women in the "Old European" areas, according to Lomax, has been one of equality with men.

The "Modern European" style is, according to Lomax, a later layer which seems to have been superimposed on some of the other styles, perhaps because of the influence of the cities. It is found in most of England and France, in Hungary, Central Italy, and colonial America. This is the area of ballads and lyrical love songs. Singing, in contrast to the Old European style, is normally done by soloists or in unblended unison. The vocal quality is harsh and strained. Interest is more in the words than in the music.

Lomax's observations are certainly stimulating. He believes that the way in which people sing is more likely to remain constant than is the musical content of their songs. And he believes that a small sample of singing from a particular area or country will indicate the total singing style of that area. He seems to feel, accordingly, that each culture can sing in only one way (which is a theory that has been proved incorrect in various cultures, as for instance among the North American Indians). Lomax's observations lead us to conclude that Europe is not a unit as far as singing style is concerned, but that two or three styles of singing and voice production are found, and that each of these is supranational in character and cuts across the boundaries of politics, culture, and language. Also he shows that the two main European singing styles are not found to a great extent on other continents (except among descendants of Europeans).

WANDERING MELODIES

Quite aside from the characteristics of the elements of music, the content of the tunes found in Europe indicates that Europe is a historical unit. In the nineteenth century, some scholars began to be intrigued by what they came to call "wandering melodies," that is, by tunes whose variants were found in the folk traditions of widely separated countries. The existence of these melodies, or melody types, is also proof of the close relationship of art, church, and folk music. Melody types found in European folk music are also frequently found in hymns and art songs, particularly of the periods before 1700. They are probably not simply quotations of folk songs, in the sense of "quoting" something strange or exotic, as in nineteenth- and twentieth-century art music, but part and parcel of the basic material of art music.

Example 3-8 illustrates the phenomenon of "wandering melodies," or of widely distributed melody types. More extensive examples of related tunes found in larger numbers of countries, and including art

EXAMPLE 3-8. Tunes from Spain, Rumania, and England similar in structure and possibly genetically related, from Walter Wiora, *Europäischer Volksgesang* (Köln: Arno Volk Verlag, ca. 1950), pp. 50–51.

music, can be found in various publications, particularly in Walter
Wiora's *Europäischer Volksgesang*.[3] In a good many cases, it is quite
likely that the similar tunes found in several nations are indeed wandering melodies or, rather, variants of a single wandering melody. Whether
or not the three tunes in Example 3-8 are genetically related we cannot
say. Curiously, the variants of a tune found in separated countries are
usually accompanied by widely varying verbal texts. An English ballad
tune that has related forms in other countries will hardly be found outside England with a translation of the same ballad story. This very fact
may lead us to suspect that the existence of similar tunes in different
countries is not always, and perhaps not even frequently, simply the
result of a tune's migration. In any event, we cannot *prove* in most cases
that the tune has actually migrated. It is likely that traveling singers of
the early Middle Ages (their existence is documented) taught to the
peoples of many lands the original forms of many songs which developed
into groups of melodies related in the manner of Example 3-8.

    Another way of explaining the phenomenon of "wandering melo-
dies" is that the musical characteristics of European folk song have been
so homogeneous and have developed so much in the same direction
throughout the continent that similar tunes were composed independently in several countries. Given a certain restricted set of musical
characteristics—for the sake of argument, let's assume melodies composed
of five tones with seconds and thirds predominating, regular metric
structure, the tendency for the final sections of songs and of phrases to be
lower in pitch and more drawn-out rhythmically than the rest, and a
range of about an octave—it might be possible and even necessary for
similar tunes to spring up independently in several places at various
times. Thus the fact that there are some obvious similarities among the
tunes in the foregoing examples does not prove that all of them are de-
scended, through the use of communal re-creation, from a single parent

[3] Wiora, *Europäischer Volksgesang*, p. 5f.

tune. Whichever explanation is the correct one (and we may never know in many specific cases), the existence of similar tunes throughout the continent again shows us that Europe is an entity as far as its folk music is concerned.

SOME SONG TYPES FOUND IN EUROPE

Europe is a unit not only in the purely musical aspects of folk song. The cultural background and context as well as the words of the songs also indicate the essential integrity of the continent. There are certain types of songs that are found throughout Europe, though they are not present everywhere in the same proportion of quantity and importance.

One important song type is narrative song. Two main styles of songs that tell a story have been developed in Europe: epics and ballads. Narrative songs, particularly epics (distinguished from ballads by their length and heroic quality), are found outside Europe, in areas as divergent as the Great Basin of North American Indian culture, Persia, Borneo, and Japan; but only in Europe do they constitute one of the most important, indeed, perhaps, the preeminent, folk song type.

The ballad was developed in Europe in the Middle Ages—first, presumably, by song composers of city and court—and evidently passed into oral tradition and the repertories of folk cultures thereafter. The musical characteristics of the ballad are not different from those of most other kinds of folk song. Usually there are three to six musical lines and a number of stanzas. As far as the words are concerned, the ballad tells a story involving one main event. In contrast to the ballads, the epic songs are long, complex, and involve several events tied together by a common theme. Typically, the epic, as exemplified perhaps by the heroic songs of the Southern Slavs, does not have a strophic arrangement but tends rather to use a line which, with variations, is repeated many times. But there are sub-types of these genres and it is at times difficult to distinguish between them. (See Chapter Four for more detail about ballads, Chapter Six for epics.)

Love songs are important in many European countries (they are relatively rare in the folklore of other continents). They are more common in Western Europe than in the East, and characteristically they express love for another person in a melancholy or tragic setting. The music of love songs does not, on the whole, differ in style from that of other folk songs.

A number of ceremonial song types are common throughout Europe. Of course, the use of folk songs in an ecclesiastical setting is found. There are areas in which genuine folk hymns are sung; in Germany, a body of spiritual folk song became a partial basis of the Lutheran hymn, and the singing of "Kyrieleis" (a corruption of "Kyrie Eleison") in the rural communities was reported in medieval sources. But more typical are songs involving ceremonies that may have been practiced long before the advent of Christianity in Europe. Thus there are songs which revolve around important events or turning points in a person's life: puberty, birth, marriage, and death. In some countries these proliferated, as in France, where special songs for various events in a child's life (first words, first walking, etc.) were developed. The French have songs to urge a child to eat, to teach him to count, and so on. These are songs accompanying the so-called rites of passage which are important in practically every culture.

Also, there are songs involving the turning points in the year, such as the advent of spring, the summer and winter solstices, and the equinox. These have frequently been associated also with agriculture, and some have been attached, since the introduction of Christianity, to Christian festivals. Thus some pre-Christian winter solstice songs have become Christmas songs, as may have been the case of the popular German "O Tannenbaum." Pagan spring songs have sometimes become Easter or Whitsuntide songs. Again, these calendric song types are common in several nations of Europe.

Songs involving agriculture are also common, more so in Eastern than in Western Europe. Perhaps these songs should be generally regarded as work songs, since some of them actually aid in the rhythm of work, while others, such as the short tunes used by the Lapps to call reindeer, are functional in labor but not in a rhythmic sense. Another type of agricultural song, simply describing the work, is not sung during work but perhaps at social gatherings in the evening. Again, work songs are found also on other continents, but they are more common in Europe than in most other areas. As before, we cannot say that their style differs appreciably from the styles of European folk songs at large, although a few types of work songs do have special musical styles. Thus the Tribbiera of Corsica (Example 3-9), a type of work song sung while driving oxen around a small enclosure in which threshing is done, always has a form consisting of two sections with words, followed by a long, melismatic call.

Another characteristic type in European folk music is the humorous song. Musically this type does not differ especially from other songs, and of course humorous words can be associated with all sorts of song functions—ballads, work songs, children's songs, and so forth. One special type of humorous song found in many countries is the cumulative song.

EXAMPLE 3-9. Corsican "Tribbiera," from Wolfgang Laade, "The Corsican Tribbiera, a kind of work song," *Ethnomusicology* 6 (1962), 185.

It is not always uproariously funny or even mildly amusing, although some elements of humor are usually found and perhaps even the process of cumulation can be considered as having a humorous effect. A cumulative song is one in which each stanza, while presenting something new, also incorporates elements from the previous stanzas. Among the best known of these songs are "The Twelve Days of Christmas" and, of course, "Alouette."

Dance music is of course one of the main types of folk and ethnic music throughout the world. In Europe it is one of the important genres, and accompanies two main types of dance. According to Herzog,[4] the older dances are involved with rituals and ceremonies (round dances are especially characteristic here); these tend to be accompanied by relatively simple music. Dances that came into the European folk repertory at later times—and this includes most of those danced by couples, and many of the other kinds of social dances—have more complex music which shows, as does the dance itself, the influence of sophisticated musical cultures. However, while we can in good conscience make such broad generalizations about folk dance and dance music, we must also stress the tremendous variety of dances which exists in Europe. The dance seems to be one area of culture in which European trends are similar or closely related to those in other continents. Possibly this means that the older layers of European culture, those which antedate the introduction of Christianity and stem from a time when the European folk cultures would have been classed as primitive or nonliterate, have remained present in the dance more than in some other aspects of culture.

At any rate, mimetic dances (those which choreographically repre-

---

[4] George Herzog, "Song," Funk and Wagnalls' *Standard Dictionary of Folklore, Mythology, and Legend* (New York: 1949–50), II, 1035.

sent actions, events, feelings, persons, or animals) are found throughout European folk culture and in other continents as well. The same is true of dances with weapons (sword dances, for instance, performed in Scotland, Central Europe, and India), dances having sexual symbolism, and acrobatic dances, to name just a few. Gertrude Kurath[5] has made a survey of European folk dances and has managed to divide the vast array into several types, according to the form and style of dancing. For example, she distinguishes among circle, longway (line), and quadrille (square) dances, according to the formation used by the dancers. The point is, again, that each of these forms is found all over Europe, and that similar dances are performed in areas and countries with sharply contrasting cultures. Thus, Kurath cites the Maypole as used in dances of Spain, England, Germany, and Hungary; the "Hey," a technique in which two lines of dancers wind in and out of a circle, is found in England, Germany, Czechoslovakia, and Spain. Thus, in spite of national and regional peculiarities, we see again the basic unity of European folklore.

INSTRUMENTS AND INSTRUMENTAL MUSIC

Although singing accounts for a preponderance of music making, formal and informal, in the European folk music tradition, musical instruments are important, and instrumental music is of very great interest. While we can state with confidence that the participation of the population in singing is quite general, that is, most people in a folk culture can sing some songs and recognize many more, instruments are to a much larger extent the property of specialists. As we have pointed out, truly professional musicians, who have theoretical training and who make their living entirely through music, are not common in folk cultures. When they are found, they are usually instrumentalists. Instruments are typically played by only a small number of persons in a folk community, and these are usually professionals at least in the sense that they are recognized for their skill and called upon to perform on special occasions.

According to Curt Sachs[6] and others, the primitive instrumental styles of the world did not come about through simple imitation, on instruments, of vocal melodies. To be sure, vocal music must have come into existence before instrumental. But instrumental music presumably

---

[5] Gertrude P. Kurath, "Dance," Funk and Wagnalls' *Standard Dictionary of Folklore, Mythology, and Legend* (New York: 1949–50), I, 276–96.

[6] Curt Sachs, *The Wellsprings of Music* (The Hague: Martinus Nijhoff, 1962), p. 110f.

came about through the elevation of noise-making gadgets to really musical artifacts, through the coincidences of acoustic phenomena accidentally discovered, and through visual criteria used by craftsmen. For example, the maker of a flute may, in positioning the finger holes, be guided by the visual effect of the design more than by the pitches and intervals which a particular arrangement of these holes will produce. If this assumption is correct, it should not be surprising that the instrumental music of European folk cultures often seems quite unrelated to the songs found in the same area and sung by the same people. Also, there seems to be more stylistic variety in the instrumental music of Europe than in its vocal music, perhaps because of the limitations of human voice and ear as compared with the relative freedom allowed the instrumentalist, who needs to know only the right motions to make, but not necessarily how the music will sound before he plays it. Random improvisation and toying with an instrument may have a considerable effect on developing the styles of instrumental folk music.

Regarding the instruments themselves, we can make very few generalizations. They vary enormously in type, design, and origin, to say nothing of the musical materials which they produce. In so far as their origin is concerned, we can divide them roughly into four classes. (1) Among the simplest instruments are those which European folk cultures share with many of the simplest tribal cultures throughout the world, including rattles, flutes (with and without finger holes) usually made of wood, the bullroarer, leaf, grass and bone whistles, and long wooden trumpets such as the Swiss *Alphorn.* These (like the songs with the most restricted scales) tend to be associated with children's games, signalling practices, and remnants of pre-Christian ritual. Many of them actually function as toys, much as do their counterparts in simpler cultures. They are evidently archaic and became distributed throughout the world many centuries ago, but the fact that they are used as toys and for pre-Christian ritual does not necessarily mean that these rituals were, in earlier times, accompanied only by the simplest of musics. (2) A second group consists of instruments that were brought to Europe from non-European cultures in more recent times. They are much more complex, and evidently many of them were changed substantially after they were brought to Europe. Among them are bagpipes, simple fiddles such as the Yugoslav one-stringed gusle, the folk oboes and double-oboes of the Balkans, the banjo, and the xylophone. In general, the sources of these instruments were the Middle East and Africa. (3) Another group consists of instruments developed in the European folk cultures themselves, usually made from simple materials. A characteristic example is the Dolle, a type of fiddle used in Northwestern Germany, made from a wooden shoe. A more sophisticated one is the bowed lyre (sometimes also called the bowed harp), once widespread in Northern Europe and the British Isles, but now mainly confined to Finland. (4) A final, and perhaps the most important, group includes the instruments that were taken from urban musical culture and from the traditions of classical and popular music, introduced into folk cultures, then sometimes changed substantially. Prominent among these are the violin, bass viol, clarinet, and guitar. Some instruments used in art music during the Middle Ages and other early periods of European music history continued to be used in folk music into the twentieth century. Examples are the violins with sympathetic strings, related to the viola d'amore and still used in Scandinavia, and the hurdy-gurdy, related to the medieval organistrum and still played in France.

In Chapters Four through Six we shall explore European folk music in somewhat more detail. Unfortunately, even if comprehensive information were available we could not give the whole story on these pages. We cannot even give samples of the music of each nation. All we can do is to give some examples of what is typical, what is common, and what is particularly noteworthy, and then hope that the reader will continue delving into the specialized literature and, above all, proceed with listening in order to broaden his understanding of this fascinating area of European culture.

BIBLIOGRAPHY

The only general and comprehensive book on European folk music is in German, and it approaches its field from a very special viewpoint, attempting to show various historical layers evident in present-day traditions. Nevertheless, it is worth reading: Werner Danckert, *Das europäische Volkslied* (Bonn: Bouvier, 1970). Several collections of folk music in Europe that make it possible to compare the various styles are Leonhard Deutsch, *A Treasury of the World's Finest Folk Song* (New York: Howell, Siskin, 1942); Maud Karpeles, *Folk Song of Europe* (London: Novello, 1956); *Europäische Lieder in den Ursprachen* (Berlin: Merseburger, 1956), a collection published under the auspices of UNESCO; and Walter Wiora, *European Folk Song; Common Forms in Characteristic Modification* (Cologne: Arno Volk, 1966), a collection that illustrates the unity of European folk song by presenting variants of the same tunes or tune types from many countries.

Important general bibliographies of European folk music are Karel Vetterl, *A Select Bibliography of European Folk Music* (Prague: Czechoslovak Academy of Sciences, 1966) and *Annual Bibliography of European Ethnomusicology* (Bratislava: Slovak National Museum, 1966–   ). Ruth

Tooze, *Literature and Music as Resources for Social Studies* (Englewood Cliffs, N.J.: Prentice-Hall, 1955) provides material for the public school teacher. Walter Wiora, *Europäischer Volksgesang und abendländische Tonkunst* (Kassel: Hinnenthal, 1957) surveys the role of folk music in the history of European art music. *Handbuch der europäischen Volksmusikinstrumente,* a multi-volume encyclopedia of European folk instruments, is in preparation.

Introductions to the field of European balladry are Gordon H. Gerould, *The Ballad of Tradition* (Oxford: Clarendon Press, 1932) and William J. Entwistle, *European Balladry* (Oxford: Clarendon Press, 1939). The many variants of a single ballad text in several European nations are studied in Iivar Kemppinen, *The Ballad of Lady Isabel and the False Knight* (Helsinki: Published by the author, 1954). A short discussion of European epics is Felix Hoerburger's "Correspondence Between Eastern and Western Folk Epics," *J-IFMC,* IV (1952), 23–26. The entire epic tradition is discussed, but with emphasis on the Yugoslav forms, in Albert B. Lord, *The Singer of Tales* (Cambridge: Harvard University Press, 1960). Finally, a classic on folk song as a living artifact is Phillips Barry, "The Transmission of Folk Song," *Journal of American Folklore,* XXVII (1914), 67–76.

FOUR

THE GERMANIC PEOPLES

The Germanic peoples—that is, those peoples which speak Germanic languages—can be divided into three groups on the basis of their folklore: (1) the English, including Scotland and Ireland; (2) the Scandinavians; and (3) the Dutch and the German-speaking peoples of Germany, Austria, most of Switzerland, and other areas in Eastern Europe. Although these three groups of peoples speak related languages, their cultures cannot be considered particularly similar, and this is also true of the styles of their folk music. Of course, the folk music of the Germanic peoples is known in different phases and varying degrees. For the English-speaking peoples there exists a vast body of ballads, collected in America as well as in England; and the study of ballad variants, their interrelationship, structure, and origin, has been carried further for English material than elsewhere. Of German folklore we know best the songs that have come into the repertory rather recently. Swedish folk music happens to have available a large collection of fiddle tunes, because some Swedish collectors have concentrated on this aspect of music. Also, the Germanic peoples have been strongly influenced by their neighbors. For example, English folk song shows considerable relationship to that of the Low Countries and France, while German folk music is at times similar to that of its neighbors to the east, Czechoslovakia, Poland, and Hungary; Austrian folk songs have some common features with those of Italy. Thus, while we are treating the Germanic peoples as a unit in this chapter, it should not be assumed that their folk music is necessarily a stylistic unit. We should avoid the corresponding conclusion that the style of Germanic musics goes back to the time when all Germanic peoples were one and spoke one tongue, and the equally erroneous assumption that the Germanic-speaking peoples possess a psychic unity. The heritage of Germanic languages goes back much further than the style of present-day folk music, and whatever similarities are found are due almost certainly to cultural contact in recent times, that is, from the early Middle Ages on.

THE ENGLISH CHILD BALLADS

The most characteristic type of British folk song is the ballad, and the most famous ballads are the Child ballads. These have nothing to do with children but rather bear the name of Francis James Child (1825–96), who organized, published, and classified those ballads which he assumed were of popular (that is, rural and truly anonymous) origin. He avoided, in his classification, those ballads in the folk tradition which could be traced to the cities or to professional song writers, and those which he thought did not have high literary quality. It turns out, however, that many of the Child's ballads can now be traced; still, as a whole, these ballads are, textually and to an extent musically, a stylistic unit which contrasts with other bodies of English-language song. Because the different variants of each ballad do not bear identical titles or first lines, Child gave each ballad (or group of variants) a number, and for this reason the most famous ballads are known by their "Child numbers."

The stories of some of the most famous ballads are widely known to students of literature. Child 10, "The Two Sisters," deals with jealousy between two girls over a lover; the man chooses the younger sister, who is thereupon drowned by the older one, who in turn is punished for her crime. In an epilogue, various parts of a musical instrument are made from the younger sister's body. "Lord Randall" (Child 12) is perhaps the best known of the Child ballads and tells in a dramatic retrospective dialogue the story of a young man who is poisoned by his lady-friend.

This type of dialogue is also used in "Edward" (Child 13), in which a young man confesses that he killed his brother and that he will now leave his family. "The Maid Freed from the Gallows" (Child 95) finds that no one in her family is willing to rescue her from punishment by paying her fine, until her lover arrives.

Love ballads, especially tragic ones, are important among the Child ballads. "Mary Hamilton" (Child 173) is an historically founded story of a lady-in-waiting at the English court who is condemned to death because she becomes pregnant by the king. "Little Musgrave" or "Little Mathy Grove" (Child 81) is seduced by a noble lady; they are discovered by the husband, who kills Musgrave in a duel. In "The Gypsy Laddie" (Child 200) a noble lady runs off with a gypsy, and when her husband finds her, she tells him that she prefers to stay in poverty with the gypsy band. Some of the ballads have very simple stories. This is true of "Barbara Allen" (Child 84) in which a girl who has spurned her lover has second thoughts when she hears that he is sick with love, but arrives too late to save him from death. The eternal triangle is exemplified in Child 73, "Lord Thomas and Fair Elinor," in which a man jilts his fiancee to marry another; the unhappy girl comes to the wedding, kills her rival, and is in turn killed by her former lover, who ends the story by committing suicide. "Lord Lovel" (Child 75) is one of a number of ballads in which separated lovers are reunited in a meeting resulting from an outrageous coincidence.

Ballads of the sea are common. They can be exemplified by Child 286, "The Golden Vanity," in which a cabin boy is promised the hand of the captain's daughter if he will swim to and sink an enemy ship; but when his mission is accomplished, the captain leaves him to drown in the sea. "Lord Bateman" (Child 53) is imprisoned by the Turks but aided in his escape by a Turkish lady, whom he promises to marry; seven years later, she seeks him out just as he is about to marry another, and he finally keeps his word. In the "House Carpenter" (Child 243) we see remnants of the supernatural elements which once were common in ballad texts. A married lady is persuaded to run off with a former lover who, it turns out, has become a demon and destroys his ship and her when he finds that she wants to return to her husband and child. Remnants of medieval superstitions are also found, for example, in Child 155, "Sir Hugh," in which a young boy happens into the garden of a Jewish family and is sacrificed by the Jew's daughter in a satanic ritual. Humorous ballads are also known, as for example Child 277, "The Wife Wrapped in Wether's Skin," in which a man, afraid to beat his aristocratic wife, wraps her in a sheepskin, which he is able to whip. "Our Goodman" (Child 274) comes home drunk and finds his wife in bed with another man, but she insists that the evidence—the man's horse, hat, and

head—are ordinary things he should expect to find in the house, such as
a cow, a chamber-pot, and a cabbage.

A few of the ballads, as they are found in tradition today, consist
only of a vestige of the original story, or of a set of formulas which accompanied the story. Child 2, "The Elfin Knight," is a dialogue between
two lovers who ask each other to prove their love by committing extra-
ordinary feats, as making a Cambric shirt without any needle or needle-
work. Religious stories are also found. The best known is the "Cherry
Tree Carol," an apocryphal story in which the unborn baby Jesus com-
mands a cherry tree to bow down and to give cherries to his mother,
after which he announces his birth and identity from the womb.

There are about three hundred Child ballads, but for only about
two hundred has any music been collected; for the rest, only words survive. The famous ballads we have enumerated share some characteristics,
and they are representative of the whole Child group (with the exception
of a number dealing with Robin Hood), although most of the ones mentioned here are tragic, while the majority of the whole group of Child
ballads actually do not have unhappy endings. The stories of these ballads are easily available in most of the large array of folk song collections
made in the United States, and in Child's own collection, which dates
from the late nineteenth century.[1] The stories usually revolve around one
incident, names of places and characters change from variant to variant,
and setting and background are only briefly stated. The narrator does not
take an active part in the story but tells it dispassionately. There is some
dialogue, and there is also a tendency for whole verses to be virtually
repeated, as in the following excerpt from Child 200:[2]

(He says):	*Take off, take off those milk-white gloves,*
	Those shoes of Spanish leather,
	And hand you down your lily-white hand,
	We'll bid farewell together.
(Narrator says):	*Oh she took off those milk-white gloves,*
	Those shoes of Spanish leather,
	And she handed him down her lily-white hand,
	They bade farewell forever.

Other characteristics of ballads are also found in this example. We see
the use of conceits, that is, of descriptive phrases which appear re-

[1] Francis James Child, *The English and Scottish Popular Ballads,* 5 vols.
(Boston and New York: Houghton Mifflin Company, 1882–98); reprinted, New York:
Folklore Associates, 1956.

[2] Cecil J. Sharp, *English Folk Songs from the Southern Appalachians* (London: Oxford University Press, 1952), I, 235.

peatedly as if they were formulae. Thus hands are often described as "lilly-white" (as are gloves), horses are "milk-white," and so on. Many ballads have refrains, the origins of which are sometimes obscure. Flowers, plants, and spices are sometimes mentioned, as in Child 1,[3] which has been made famous in another variant, by the popular singers, Simon and Garfunkel.

> (*Verse*) *Go tell her to make me a cambric shirt*
> (*Refrain*) *Setherwood, sage, rosemary and thyme,*
> (*Verse*) *Without any needle or needle's work,*
> *And then she'll be a true lover of mine.*

Refrains, incidentally, are a feature of song shared by all regions of Europe. Some refrains mention dancing or movements that can be interpreted as parts of a dance. Here is an excerpt from "The Two Sisters" (Child 10):[4]

> *There lived an old lord in the North countree*
> (*Refrain*) *Bow down, bow down.*
> *There lived an old lord in the north countree*
> (*Refrain*) *Very true to you. . . .*

"Bow down" is thought to be derived from dancing. The reason for mentioning this is a theory that the ballad, narrative though it is, began as a dance song type. The name may, of course, be derived from the Latin *ballare* (to dance), and there is some evidence that ballads were once used as dance songs in medieval Scandinavia. On the Faeroe Islands, between Scotland and Norway, this tradition is still in existence, and lively group dances using the "Faeroe step" (two steps left, one right) may be performed while the dancers sing Norwegian ballads. We know of no ballad dancing in the English-speaking world, but this practice may once have existed there as well.

A look at the collections of Child or of some of the more recent great American collectors makes it obvious that the differences among variants of one ballad can be very great. Take Child 12, the popular "Lord Randall." Randall's name appears in all sorts of variant forms, Randall, Rendal, Lorendo, Durango, William, Tyranty, Nelson, Elson, King Henry, Willie Doo, etc. The person who poisons him may be his sweetheart, his grandmother, or his stepmother. It has even been estab-

---

[3] Sharp, *English Folk Songs*, I, 1.
[4] Sharp, *English Folk Songs*, I, 27.

lished that the children's song, "Oh where have you been, Billy boy, Billy boy?" which ends, "She's a young thing and cannot leave her mother" was derived from one version of the more dramatic "Lord Randall." Thus it would seem that formulae are very stable elements, while the details of a story are more subject to change. The lengths of the variants also differ greatly. A story told in one ballad with the use of fourteen stanzas may, in another version, be summarized in four, through elision, omission of events, and omission of stanzas giving background information.

Similar variety is found in the tunes. Bertrand H. Bronson[5] has assembled all of the tunes used for the Child ballads, and he finds that for each ballad story there seem to be two or three basic tune types to which all of the variants must be sung. For example, most of the tunes of "The Golden Vanity" (Child 286) are related to one of the two in Examples 4-1 and 4-2.

EXAMPLE 4-1. English folk song, "The Sweet Trinity," from Jan P. Schinhan, ed., *The Music of the Ballads* (Durham, N.C.: Duke University Press, 1957. *The Frank C. Brown Collection of North Carolina Folklore,* vol. 4), p. 120.

While ballad stories evidently moved from nation to nation in the Middle Ages, the tunes did not accompany them. For example, there is the ballad of "Lady Isabel and the Elf-Knight" (Child 4), in which a knight courts a lady but really intends to kill and rob her; when she discovers his false intentions, she foils him and causes him to drown. This ballad is known throughout Europe except for the Balkan area, but its tunes are largely national in provenience, and the tunes used with the English versions are evidently not related to those used in Dutch, Scandinavian, German, or other versions. On the other hand, variants of a tune used for one ballad in the English repertory may be found in other English ballads or songs.

---

[5] Bertrand Harris Bronson, *The Traditional Tunes of the Child Ballads* (Princeton, N.J.: Princeton University Press, 1958–).

EXAMPLE 4-2. English folk song, "The Little Cabin Boy," from Phillips Barry, Fannie H. Eckstrom, and Mary W. Smyth, *British Ballads from Maine* (New Haven, Conn.: Yale University Press, 1929), p. xxxiii.

BROADSIDE BALLADS

Besides the Child ballads, for which no written original can usually be found, the English-language repertory possesses other types, particularly a group of later origin, the broadside ballads. This type, so named because it appeared printed on large sheets of paper called broadsides, became popular throughout Western Europe. Written frequently by professional song writers, the broadside ballads tend to deal with historical events more than do the popular ballads, and they contrast with the Child ballads also in their concern for detail, in their more complex plots, and in the involvement of the narrator, who frequently appends a moral. The words are often shamelessly sentimental and usually do not have the literary value of the older ballads. But the broadside ballads (which were still being written in the twentieth century) functioned somewhat as newspapers in areas in which illiteracy was common. All of them did not, of course, pass into oral tradition, but a good many did and have thus become true folk songs. Some of our best-known songs originated as English broadside ballads: "The Foggy Dew," made popular by Carl Sandburg, "Brennan on the Moor," "Devilish Mary," and "Sam Hall." Some of the broadsides are even derived from the Child ballads. Thus a broadside ballad called "The Turkish Lady" is obviously just a variant of "Lord Bateman" (Child 53), in which a Turkish lady saves an English prisoner in her father's jail and marries him. The tunes of the broadside ballads are of diverse origin. Many of the printed broadsides did not include music but simply named the tune of this or that popular song, folk song, or hymn. Finally, the practice of printing broadside ballads and their dissemination into folk tradition is found not only in Britain but also in most European countries and, of course, in America.

THE STYLE OF ENGLISH FOLK MUSIC

As we have pointed out, the music of the English ballads does not differ greatly from that of English folk song in general; thus the discussion of ballad tunes below can be said to apply to English folk song at large. Many of the older tunes have, as one characteristic, a melodic contour which forms, roughly, an arc, starting low, rising in the second phrase, remaining on the higher level of tessitura in the third phrase, and moving down to the level of the first in the fourth phrase. Four phrases or lines are common, but five (usually through repetition of the fourth), six, and eight are also found, as well as two and three. Three examples of English folk song follow (Examples 4-3, 4-4, and 4-5); they may be considered representative of the whole style to an extent, but certain song types, such as dance songs, game ditties, children's songs, and humorous songs, are not represented. Example 4-3 is a Scots version of Child 76, as sung by Ewan MacColl, the well-known folk singer. Example 4-4 is a variant of the same song collected in Southern Indiana. It is essentially the same melody, but is sung in quite a different manner. Example 4-5 is the tune of a broadside ballad, "Girls of Newfoundland," of Irish origin, collected in Labrador. Perhaps we should point out here that much more British folk music has been collected in North America than in Britain, and that, for material collected in England itself, published collections with reliable transcriptions are difficult to come by. Thus we must rely to some extent on American versions for a picture of British folk music.

EXAMPLE 4-3. English folk song, "Lord Gregory." Reprinted from *The Traditional Tunes of the Child Ballads*, vol. 2, by Bertrand Harris Bronson by permission of Princeton University Press, Copyright 1962.

EXAMPLE 4-4. English folk song, "The Lass of Loch Royal," from Bruno Nettl, "The Musical Style of English Ballads Collected in Indiana," *Acta Musicologica* 27 (1955), 83.

She wet her cheeks——— with fallen——— tears   And then she kissed— my hand,   Said, Willie dear,   re - mem-ber me   When you're in——— some dis -tant   land.

Examples 4-3 and 4-4 use the so-called "ballad meter," that is, iambic lines alternating in four and three-foot lengths (- / - / - / - / ; - / - / - / ;) and so forth). This is common, though by no means universal, in British folk song and tends, in music, to be translated into one of three types of rhythm: $\frac{4}{4}$ ♩ |♩♩♩♩ |♩♩♩ or $\frac{3}{4}$ ♪|♫♩˙ ♪|♫♩˙ (with several variants, such as $\frac{5}{4}$ ♩ |♩♩♩ ♩ |♩♩♩ and $\frac{4}{4}$ ♪|♫♩ ♪♪|♫♩ ♪ or ♪|♩ ♪♩ ♪|♩ ♪♩). Example 4-3 uses the first of these, and Example 4-4 a variant of the second. There is, however, a tendency in those songs that are sung in the parlando-rubato singing style to include elongation and shortening of measures, and even a systematically heterometric structure. Thus, in Example 4-4, the measures have, respectively 3, 5, 5, 7, 5, 7, 6, 6, and 5 eighth-note equivalents.

Songs whose words are not cast in ballad meter nevertheless tend to use the same rhythmic types, with minor adjustments, in their tunes. Thus, Example 4-5 has a structure rather similar to that of Example 4-3, but the text has eight lines instead of four. This type of stanza is most frequently set to variants of the first or second rhythmic types given above, and is more common in the broadsides than in the Child ballads, and particularly widespread in the English-language ballads sung by the Irish.

British folk song is frequently said to be modal, but the great majority of the songs fall into the major or Ionian mode. (Our three examples are all major.) There are also many songs in the Mixolydian (major with lowered seventh) mode, in Dorian (minor with raised sixth),

EXAMPLE 4-5. English folk song, "Girls of Newfoundland," collected in Newfoundland by MacEdward Leach, transcribed by Bruno Nettl.

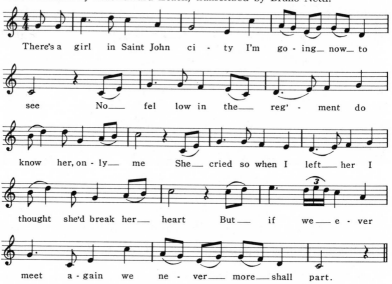

and in Aeolian (natural minor). The other modes are not common. Some modulation may occur (though this is often hard to identify because the music is monophonic) as in Example 4-3, in which the first two phrases seem to have G for a tonic, but the last one D.

Much has also been said of the pentatonic nature of English folk song. A rather large minority of the songs are pentatonic, while the majority (again, except for the old layer of children's and related songs) seems to be heptatonic or hexatonic. It is sometimes revealing to examine the functions of the various tones in a scale, however, for often it will be evident that the most important and most common tones are indeed five in number, while the other two are subsidiary or used only in ornaments. Also, the scale structure of the individual phrases or lines may be pentatonic. For instance, in Example 4-3, the first half of the song uses a common kind of pentatonic scale—D, F-sharp, G, A, B; the other tones, E and C-sharp, are brought in only later. Similarly, in Example 4-4 important tones are B, C (tonic), E, F, and G. Example 4-6, a version of Child 53, uses six tones, but one of them, F, appears only in ornaments. This song also is a good example of the kind of pentatonism found in English folk music.

The emphasis on pentatonic structure does not seem to be an ingredient of the newer layer of British song. The tunes that were introduced into the folk culture more recently, perhaps since the advent of music printing and the broadside ballad in the sixteenth century, are both more varied in style and more closely related to popular and art music. This is to be expected, of course, with regard to the broadsides, since their writers frequently set them to tunes of any sort that were widely current. Thus the later tunes are more frequently in major or harmonic minor, rarely pentatonic, and they do not deviate, as does Example 4-4, from a standard and consistent metric structure.

EXAMPLE 4-6. English folk song, "Lord Bateman," from Bruno Nettl, "The Musical Style of English Ballads Collected in Indiana," *Acta Musicologica* 27 (1955), 83.

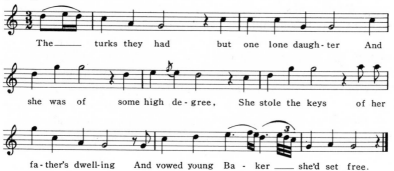

As we noted above (p. 48), Béla Bartók divided Hungarian folk singing into two types, which he called "parlando-rubato" and "tempo giusto."[6] The distinction between these two ways of singing does not always emerge from printed music, since it involves the singer's interpretation of rhythm and tempo. And although the distinction was derived for use in describing Hungarian folk music, it applies also to singing in other countries, especially those of Northern and Eastern Europe. Example 4-3 is a sample of tempo-giusto singing, while Example 4-4, a variant of the same song, exemplifies the parlando-rubato. In Hungarian folk music, parlando-rubato is used mainly for ballads and tempo-giusto for dance songs, but both styles are found in British ballad singing.

At this point we must mention also the Celtic-speaking inhabitants of the British Isles, particularly the Irish and the Welsh, peoples whose musical culture has played so important a part in their history that the Irish national emblem is the harp. Irish folk song today is almost entirely in the English language, and, indeed, the songs of Irish origin have contributed greatly to the English-language heritage of the United States,

[6] Béla Bartók, *Hungarian Folk Music* (London: Oxford University Press, 1931).

Canada, and Australia. On the whole, their musical style does not differ greatly from that of the English folk tunes of eighteenth- and nineteenth-century origin. Yet, certain minor traits characterize the singing of these ethnic groups. For example, Irish singers will take a conventional major ending (e.g.,) and change it to end on a repetition of the tonic ( ).

The Welsh have developed—partly through their folk heritage and partly because of the influence of hymn-singing—a tradition of choral singing of folk songs; this is done largely in the style of nineteenth-century hymns, with conventional chord progressions and triadic harmony. They also preserved, into the nineteenth century, an instrument that evidently was widespread in medieval art music, the *crwth* or *crowd,* a lyre with six strings—four over the fingerboard, two as drones—which was usually bowed. It evidently accompanied the songs of the bards, whose importance among the Welsh and Irish was very great. A similar instrument, the *tallharpa,* was used in Finland and Estonia, and today, Finland is the only country in which bowed lyres are still widely used.

SOME NETHERLANDISH FOLK DANCES

Of course, the ballads are not the only kinds of folk songs in the British Isles; we have chosen them as one representative group. The same sort of thing is true of the Dutch and Flemish folk dances, which are briefly discussed here because we have space to discuss only one of the categories of Dutch music, and because we must pay some attention to the dance music of the Germanic-speaking nations, despite the importance of ballads and lyrical songs.

Evidently folk dancing has indeed been a prominent activity in the Low Countries for centuries. An edict of Charlemagne outlawed dancing in churches and ceremonies, indicating the popularity of such activities. The practice of religious dance, including dances on the occasion of death, particularly by young girls, is attested by various documents from history, and appears to have remained in the folk tradition until relatively recent times. The religious dances are almost always round dances.

In other ways, also, Dutch folk music seems to have had a close relationship to the practices of Christian worship. There are many religious folk songs and carols of various kinds (Christmas and Easter), and the style of a great deal of Dutch folk music reminds us of the styles of Christian monophonic hymns and Lutheran chorales. To a considerable degree this is true of German folk music, as well, for in many instances it also adheres to the style of the hymn, with its typical lines consisting mainly of quarter notes except for the final long tone.

Many European folk dances have their origin in pre-Christian ritual dancing. An example from Holland is the "Seven Saults" dance, described by Kunst,[7] and known also in other parts of Western Europe. It was evidently once a sacrificial dance, but after the introduction of Christianity it was danced at harvest festivals, fairs, and wedding parties. These functions are, of course, residual of pre-Christian ceremonies involving the life cycle or changes in the year's cycle. Kunst reports seeing the "Seven Saults" still performed in the twentieth century on the Dutch island of Terschelling. The dance involves seven motions of a mildly acrobatic nature: stamping with each foot, touching the ground with each knee, then with each elbow, and finally with the nose. It was evidently performed—as are many European folk dances—with the accompaniment of group singing, such as that found in Example 4-7.

EXAMPLE 4-7. Dutch folk dance tune, from Jaap Kunst, "On Dutch Folk Dances and Dance Tunes" in *Studies in Ethnomusicology*, ed. M. Kolinski (New York: Oak Publications, 1961), vol. 1, 32.

The tune in Example 4-7 shows us some of the traits common in Western European folk dance music. Of course, since the music is used for dancing, and since it is sung by a group, it could not easily partake of the parlando-rubato singing style with its distortion of tempo and emphasis on words. It tends to be rigid in this aspect of music, to have simple

---

[7] Jaap Kunst, "On Dutch Folk Dances and Dance Tunes," *Studies in Ethnomusicology*, I (1961), 35.

rhythms consisting largely of two- or three-note values (as in this case, quarter, eighth, and sixteenth notes). The tune is in major, with an implication of harmony in the Western tradition, based on tonic, subdominant, dominant, and dominant seventh chords. Note also the repetitive refrain, whose words count off the "seven saults."

Holland, being near the center of the Germanic-speaking area, exhibits musical relationships to England, Germany, and Scandinavia. In both dance and dance music, some similarities between Dutch and Scandinavian folk music are striking. Variants of the same tunes and dance movements are found in both areas, as well as in Scotland, which was at one time under strong Danish and Norse influence.

SAMPLES OF SCANDINAVIAN INSTRUMENTAL FOLK MUSIC

The folk music of Scandinavia is of great interest because in some ways it seems to exhibit very ancient traits, and yet in other ways it has been very much under the influence of the cultivated tradition of the cities. An example of ancient practice frequently cited is the use of parallel fifths in Iceland, which has evidently preserved some traits of medieval Norwegian culture. For a long time there raged an argument, mentioned in Chapter Three, about the origin of Icelandic "organum," whether it represents a case of medieval church music practice which trickled down to the folk tradition or whether it is an example of ancient and generally forgotten folk practice which in the Middle Ages was taken up by the Western church. Similar historical arguments have been going on for decades about the relationship of other folk polyphony— that of Russia, the Ukraine, Yugoslavia, the Caucasus, the mountains of Italy—to that of medieval art music. The arguments have brought no conclusions, and today the interest in primacy has dwindled, especially as various kinds of polyphony have been discovered in many European folk traditions, but we may still marvel at what must surely be a musical tradition of great age. Aside from simple parallel fifths, Icelandic music seems to have used other forms similar to the earliest polyphony in Western church music, such as the so-called free and melismatic types of organum.

There is no doubt that many of the folk dances of Europe were originally dances of medieval and later towns and courts. This is true of the square dances, which grew out of quadrilles; of the polka, a more stately dance; and of the waltz, which originated in part in the slower and more dignified minuet. Frequently, of course, a dance almost completely changed character when it moved from court to countryside or vice-versa. Thus the sarabande, one of the slowest and most stately dances of seventeenth-century Western Europe, is thought to have been derived from a quick and violent Spanish folk dance which, in turn, had been brought from the Spanish-American colonies in the sixteenth century. More rarely, the music accompanying folk dances can also be traced to earlier forms of art music. In such cases we have musical instances of *gesunkenes Kulturgut*. Examples can be found in Sweden, where one of the important folk dances is the "polska," which is a form of the polonaise. Anyone familiar with Chopin's polonaises or with those of late Baroque composers such as G. Ph. Telemann or J. S. Bach will recognize the characteristic rhythm in Example 4-8, which is played by violins. Aside from rhythm, moreover, the melodic configurations are also definitely in a style reminiscent of baroque and pre-Classical music: note the arpeggios and the triad-like figures in the second section, reminiscent of the Alberti bass. The form, in which each phrase is repeated with first and second endings, is common in Western European instrumental music and similar also to the earliest known examples of medieval instrumental music, the *estampie* or *stantipes*. (Only the melodic line—not the accompaniment—is given in Example 4-8.)

EXAMPLE 4-8. Swedish "Polska" playel by two violins; melody only, transcribed by Bruno Nettl from recording issued by Sveriges Radio (Radio Sweden), RAEP 8. Collected in Halsingsland.

Tunes of various sorts, frequently more ornamented, are played in other Scandinavian countries on folk instruments such as the Norwegian "Harding fiddle." Typical of the multifarious forms of folk instruments in Europe, this is a violin with four or five sympathetic strings under the fingerboard (which are not played but are caused to vibrate by the vibrations of other strings activated by the bow). The four main strings are tuned in various ways, for example , , or .

Another instrument prominent in Scandinavia is the dulcimer, which in Sweden is known as the *Hummel* and exists in a great many forms. Unlike the dulcimer of the Southern United States, it is used more as a solo instrument than as an accompaniment to singing. It produces melodies with drone accompaniments, or tunes in parallel thirds. The dulcimer, basically, is a string instrument that lies flat on a table and is plucked or struck; it has anywhere from three to over a dozen strings, and usually one or more of them are fretted. The shape varies from that of an oblong violin to rectangular and irregularly triangular. Sometimes it is bowed as well as plucked. It seems likely that the American dulcimer was brought from Scandinavia or Northern Germany, though similar instruments do, of course, exist elsewhere in Europe, particularly in Hungary, whose Csimbalom (derived from the Persian *santour*) is something of a national instrument.

Throughout Europe, folk music enthusiasts are deploring the gradual disappearance of folk singing and the knowledge of folk music on the part of the rural population. Attempts to reintroduce folk music through schools and festivals have been only moderately successful. Nevertheless, there still seem to be many people who know and can sing folk songs from their family or village traditions. Denmark seems to be such a place, for we have available in a case study, made over a period of time by the Danish musicologist Nils Schiørring,[8] all of the songs known by one woman, Selma Nielsen. Mrs. Nielsen produced some 150 songs from memory, including material of every diverse origin—ballads from the Middle Ages, sea shanties, soldiers' songs, humorous ditties. It is possible to see throughout her repertory the close relationship between the development of folk and art music, for we find modal materials, jaunty songs in major and somewhat in the style of the lighter art songs of the pre-Classical period, and sentimental tunes obviously from nineteenth-century popular music. Scandinavia offers good illustrations of the interdependence of folk and art music in Europe.

---

[8] Nils Schiørring, *Selma Nielsens Viser* (Copenhagen: Munksgaard, 1956).

Swedish dulcimer.

GERMAN FOLK SONG

Nowhere, however, is the interrelationship between art and folk music stronger than in the German-speaking nations. The influence of the sophisticated musician on his rural counterpart has sometimes been so great there that the old practices of the German countryside seem to have disappeared and can be traced only through old documents or through the music of Germans whose ancestors emigrated from their homeland centuries ago. This is analogous, of course, to the study of British folk music through American folk song. The types of German folk song are similar, so far as text and function are concerned, to the English—medieval ballads, work songs, sailors' shanties, dances, year- and life-cycle songs, and so forth. In Germany proper, the vocal music seems to have developed much more strongly than the instrumental. But in Switzerland and Austria, instruments as well as special forms of singing have flourished. In the period since World War II, the emigrants from German-speaking communities in Hungary, the Balkans, and parts of Russia who returned to West Germany after centuries of isolation have produced singing informants with a knowledge of many older songs thought to have disappeared from the tradition.

The influence of the church on German folk song is of early medieval origin. Many of the German ballads with medieval themes have words of partly or entirely religious character. There are folkloric descendants of mystery plays in the modern moralities and in children's religious pageants. Much of the music fits in with the system of church modes as well as with the rhythmic structure of the early Lutheran hymns. The singing style is more frequently tempo-giusto than it is in the oldest British ballads.

German ballad texts remind us of the British ones, but the proportion of ballads with religious background is larger than in the English repertory. A greater dimension of tragedy seems to be present as well. Indeed, the historical and cultural differences between Germany and England can very well be illustrated by the differences in their ballad texts, although many of the story types used in these texts are identical in the two countries. For example, a German version of Child 95, "The Maid Freed from the Gallows," tells the story of a merchant who gambles away his son's life in a game of cards. The boy's sister is told by the judge that she can redeem him by running naked around the gallows square nine times, and she does this to save her brother. The dramatic impact of this detailed account is quite different from the formulaic recitation of the dialogue between the maid and her relatives in the English version, in which the listener never finds out how the maid came to be condemned in the first place, and in which ordinary payment of a fine, rather than humiliation of the sister, is the conclusion. German ballads contain more rape and seduction, more violence on the part of authorities than the English ones, and, generally, reflect the stormier and less isolated history of their country.

If the music of some of the old German ballads has medieval roots, the majority of extant German folk songs seem to stem from a later period, from the time—beginning in the seventeenth century—when the German countryside was dotted with minor courts, many of which had a sophisticated musical life, with court composers, orchestras, and opera. In this way even the smallest hamlets and the most remote farms began to have contact with art music, and the result seems to have been the assimilation of elements of the art styles into folklore. The folk music from that period, typically, is in major mode and has melodies making liberal use of triads with implied harmony. Tempi and meters are even and constant, and the singing style is definitely tempo-giusto. There is also a later layer of song, that of the German broadside ballads, mainly from the nineteenth century. Here the style is that of nineteenth-century popular music, with some chromaticism, modulation, instrumental accompaniment, and what we today feel is a sentimental quality.

A children's song still widely used is shown in Example 4-9. It is sung in autumn by children while walking in pairs or small groups, carrying lanterns. The structure, which consists essentially of one line

EXAMPLE 4-9. German children's song, "Laterne, Laterne," from pamphlet accompanying the recording, *Deutsche Volkslieder, eine Dokumentation des Deutschen Musikrates,* ed. Deutsches Volksliedarchiv, Freiburg (Wolfenbüttel: Moseler Verlag, 1961), p. 19.

repeated with variations, is typical of children's songs throughout Europe and may, historically, represent an archaic layer of style that preceded the various national folk styles, which are evidently mainly of medieval origin. Especially typical is the scale, which is tetratonic, but which emphasizes the tones, E, G, and A. The added C may be interpreted as a result of the importance of the triad in German folk song style.

In contrast to England and Scandinavia, polyphonic singing is common in Germany, Austria, and Switzerland. Canons are, to be sure, found throughout Europe, but a form of polyphony characteristic of Germany is parallelism, particularly parallel thirds. Whether this came about through the influence of art music or whether it originated as a folk practice cannot be said. Most likely it was once exclusively a folk practice that was reinforced by similar forms in art music. Much of the part-singing (which is concentrated in Southern Germany and the Alpine region) is definitely in the category of chordal harmony. This is surely the case in Example 4-10, a woodcutters' song from Bavaria. But at one point it leaves the widely accepted art music tradition: line 4 has several parallel fifths, which are performed consistently stanza after stanza. This song also, of course, indicates the importance, in German folk song, of triads in both harmony and melody.

EXAMPLE 4-10. German woodsmen's song, from pamphlet accompanying the recording, *Deutsche Volkslieder, eine Dokumentation des Deutschen Musikrates*, ed. Deutsches Volksliedarchiv, Freiburg (Wolfenbüttel: Moseler Verlag, 1961), p. 11.

M.M. ♩ = 132

Im Fruah jahr, wann der Schne e weggeht, gehn Holz-knecht mir an Wald; An Ko - bi, der aus Rin - d'n ist, da bleibn ma jung und alt. Mir hak - ka Baam die gros - cht'n her, fur so an Holz - knecht ist's an Ehr, wann er im Schlag is nit da letzt, und ar - bet frisch und gsetzt.

Ho la - ro, ho la ro, rü - di - rü ru dl ja,   rü - di - rü - ru - dl ja, ru - di - ru ru dl - ja,   rü!

rü - di - rüru - dl - ja

GERMAN FOLK MUSIC IN THE ALPS
AND EASTERN EUROPE

The Alpine region of South Germany, Austria, and Switzerland has developed a regional body of folklore and folk music, including certain unique practices, which contrast with those of Germany proper. It is sometimes thought that the extreme isolation of the mountain dwellers as well as their exceptional physical environment are responsible for this regional peculiarity, and some scholars have tried to draw parallels between Alpine folklore and that of other mountain regions in the belief that geography plays an important role in determining the nature of a people's traditions. Two characteristic aspects of the Alpine musical heritage are the *alphorn* and yodeling.

The *alphorn* is a Swiss instrument, a wooden trumpet from four to twelve feet long, used to call cattle and to signal across valleys; it is played also at sunset rites. Similar instruments are found in other countries, including Estonia, Poland, and Rumania. Its repertory is mostly short calls, but there are also a few traditional tunes. Since its sound can be heard for miles, especially with the help of echoes, its presence in the Alps can be explained, at least partly, by the geographic environment. The fact that the player uses the higher partials has caused its music to make use of a peculiar scale—C-D-E-F sharp-G (transposed, of course, to various pitches when the instrument varies in size)—which has also been used as the basis of some Swiss folk songs.

Yodeling, the rapid alternation between chest and head voice while singing meaningless syllables, is also a practice due partly to the possibility of communicating over long distance from one mountainside to another. While we do find the use of falsetto in various continents, true yodeling is rare outside the Alpine region. Yodeling usually appears in the refrains of songs, although there are also some songs which consist entirely of yodeling. There is in the Alps also some polyphonic yodeling with parallel thirds or triads, for polyphonic singing of the type described for Germany is particularly strong in the Alps. The practice of yodeling has led to the emergence of a class of semiprofessional musicians in the Alpine region, for certain individuals achieve fame as yodelers and give paid performances.

Brief mention of European Jewish folk music is perhaps suitable here. The Yiddish folksongs are related to German folklore, for Yiddish is essentially a German dialect of the late Middle Ages that has been penetrated by words borrowed from Hebrew, Polish, Russian, and other languages. During the late Middle Ages, the Jews were driven out of Germany and sought refuge in Eastern Europe, keeping their special brand of German folk culture. Thus the songs of the Yiddish-speaking Jews have retained some of the German medieval character. But to a greater degree their songs partake of the styles of the nations to which they moved—Russia, Poland, Rumania, and elsewhere. And there are also traces of Hebrew liturgical music in their folk songs. Thus the styles of Yiddish folk song have great variety, and the whole corpus of Yiddish folk music is not a homogeneous one. A similar development, incidentally, occurred among the Sephardic Jews who, during the Middle Ages, lived in Spain but were driven out in 1492 and carried with them a Spanish-derived language, Ladino, and songs partially Spanish in style. (For a discussion of Israeli folk music, see William P. Malm's book in this series, *Music Cultures of the Pacific, the Near East, and Asia.*)

There are—or there were, before World War II—many enclaves of German population in various parts of Eastern Europe (Russia, Hungary, Yugoslavia, Rumania), in South America (particularly Brazil and Argentina), and in the United States and Canada. These consist largely of descendants of individuals who left Germany in quest of religious freedom between the sixteenth and the nineteenth centuries. Their folk music has occasionally been collected. As we might expect, it has sometimes been influenced by their new surroundings; German-Americans have, for instance, incorporated English tunes into their repertory. But, more important, these groups tended to keep intact some of the styles and many of the songs that were evidently once current in Germany proper, but that have disappeared in the original center of their distribution.

There is much variety in the music of the Germanic-speaking peoples of Europe, but their styles stand together when compared to those of the Slavic and Finno-Ugric speaking peoples of Eastern Europe, or to those of Italy, France, and the Iberian peninsula. No doubt peoples who speak related languages very frequently share other aspects of culture such as music, but it is not always so. And while we can perhaps speak of a Germanic style of folk music, we must also be aware of the interchange of materials and styles between these and neighboring peoples—the impact of German and Austrian music in Czechoslovakia and Poland, the similarity between Dutch and Belgian songs and styles, the impact of Italy on Austria, and the relationship between Scandinavian and Russian music.

BIBLIOGRAPHY AND DISCOGRAPHY

Cecil J. Sharp is the author of a number of fundamental works on British folk music. One of the important ones is *English Folk Song, Some Conclusions*, 3rd ed. (London: Methuen, 1954). A readable survey of the British ballad is Evelyn Wells, *The Ballad Tree* (New York: Ronald Press, 1950), and a very useful introduction to both texts and tunes is a book by Roger D. Abrahams and George Foss, *Anglo-American Folksong Style* (Englewood Cliffs, N.J.: Prentice-Hall, 1968). The most comprehensive collection of British ballad tunes, because it reprints the tunes in many other important collections, is Bertrand H. Bronson, *The Traditional Tunes of the Child Ballads* (Princeton, N. J.: Princeton University Press, 1958–1970). Bronson's article, "About the Commonest British Ballads" *J-IFMC*, IX (1957), 22–27, is important reading. Donal J. O'Sullivan, *Songs of the Irish* (New York: Crown Publishers, 1960), is a standard collection. A number of Bronson's important studies are reprinted in his *The Ballad as Song* (Berkeley: University of California Press, 1969).

A short survey, with examples, of Dutch folk music is Jaap Kunst, "On Dutch Folk Dances and Dance Tunes," *Studies in Ethnomusicology*, I (1961), 29–37. For Norwegian folk music, a monumental set of volumes covering the entire repertory is being published under Olav Gurvin, *Norwegian Folk Music* (Oslo: Oslo University Press, 1958–   ).

An interesting collection of Danish folk music collected from one informant is Nils Schiørring, *Selma Nielsens Viser* (Copenhagen: Munksgaard, 1956). Many collections of German folk music are available. A classic is Ludwig Erk and Franz Magnus Boehme, *Deutscher Liederhort* (Leipzig, 1893–1894, reprinted by Olms, Hildesheim, 1962). A more recent publication, still incomplete but with comprehensive notes, is *Deutsche Volkslieder mit ihren Melodien*, edited by John Meier and others (Freiburg: Deutsches Volksliedarchiv, 1935–). Many publications by German scholars on German folk song are worth reading; those by Walter Wiora and Erich Stockmann are particularly to be noted. In the field of musical instruments, Stig Walin, *Die schwedische Hummel* (Stockholm: Nordiska Museet, 1952) is an excellent, profusely illustrated study of the Swedish dulcimer.

The number of records of British folk song, both field collections and artistic interpretations, is enormous. To be mentioned especially is a set of Child ballads produced by British traditional singers, A. L. Lloyd and

Ewan MacColl, for class and other educational use: *English and Scottish Popular Ballads*, Washington Records 715–723. Also worth hearing are *Sussex Folk Songs and Ballads*, edited by Kenneth Goldstein, Folkways FG 3515; *Songs and Pipes of the Hebrides*, Folkways P 430; *The Art of the Bagpipe* (with elaborate annotations), Folk-Lyric Records FL 112; and, as a selection of Gaelic songs, *Songs of Aran*, Folkways P 1002. Child ballads as sung by American informants are available on many recordings published by the Library of Congress. See particularly *Child Ballads Traditional in the U. S.* (AAFS 57–58).

Songs and Dances of Holland, Folkways 3576, and *Songs and Dances of Norway*, Folkways FE 4008, are both educational and entertaining selections. For German folk song, a set produced by the famous Freiburg archive is to be recommended: *Deutsche Volkslieder*, Deutsche Grammophongesellschaft 004–157 to 004–160 (2 disks), with a pamphlet giving texts, notes and complete transcriptions.

It must be noted, however, that most recordings of the European music discussed here are not field recordings sung by rural singers, but by professional folk singers; the tunes are thus authentic, but the singing style is frequently not.

FIVE

EASTERN EUROPE

If the area east of Italy, Germany, and Scandinavia has any internal unity in its folk music style, this must be due to the fact that on the whole this area has been much less under the influence of art music than has the western half of Europe. Peoples as diverse as the Greeks, the Russians, and the Finns can hardly be expected to have one style of folk music. For many centuries, parts of Eastern Europe have repeatedly been conquered and re-conquered from several peoples from the outside —Mongols, Turks, Romans, Germans. Its culture has many roots, among them Hellenistic, Islamic, Oriental, and North Asian. It is inhabited by peoples speaking languages of several distinct families and groups: Slavic, the largest group; Finno-Ugric (Finnish, Hungarian, Estonian, and several minority languages in Russia); Turkic (the Turks, the Chuvash of the Russian interior, etc.); Romance (Rumanian); Albanian; and Caucasian. Musical influences have come from sources as diverse as the chants of the Byzantine Church, the pentatonic tunes of Mongolia, and the complex rhythms of the Arabic and Hindu spheres. And certainly there are important links between Eastern and Western Europe, tunes found in both areas, identical uses and functions of music in the culture.

In view of this great diversity, this chapter makes no attempt to discuss these individual nations one by one. Some, indeed, are entirely omitted. Instead, we discuss certain techniques of composition and certain types of song which are found in several of the cultures. But let us bear in mind that each of the Eastern European countries, from gigantic Russia to tiny Albania, has a rich folk music heritage; each has enough songs to fill a multi-volume anthology and a musical culture of sufficient wealth to keep scholars busy for several lifetimes. It is also important to bear in mind the fact that while there is a common flavor to East European folk music, there is probably more variety of practices and styles in each of its nations than there is in the typical Western European country.

MELODIC SEQUENCE:
HUNGARIANS, CZECHS, CHEREMIS

East European scholars have studied intensively their native musical traditions, and nowhere has this been more true than in Hungary. For decades in the nineteenth century it was thought that the folk music of Hungary was the music of the gypsies who supplied ethnic entertainment in the cities, but in the twentieth century the great wealth of true Hungarian peasant music (which has little in common with the gypsy tunes) was discovered, largely by Béla Bartók and Zoltán Kodály. Since the Hungarians are linguistically related to the Finns, it was thought that the styles of these two peoples would have something in common. This turned out to be only partially the case, but other Finno-Ugric speaking peoples living for centuries in isolation from the Hungarians, inside Russia, do have music somewhat similar to that of Hungary. The most important of these groups is the Cheremis, who live in a semi-autonomous republic of the Soviet Union some five hundred miles east of Moscow.

These peoples have something in common that is also found far to the east, among the Mongolians, and even to some extent further on, in American Indian music; and this strengthens our belief that the essential features of the oldest Hungarian folk music are very old, and that they were brought by the Finno-Ugric tribes when they moved westward in the early Middle Ages. The most striking of these features is the practice of transposing a bit of melody, once or even several times, to create the essence of a song. Many Hungarian songs have the form $A^1A^2A^1$(a fifth lower)A^2(a fifth lower), for example. Transposition is usually up or down a fifth, perhaps because this interval is an important one in the series of overtones, or perhaps because this practice may have originated long ago, in the Far East, where fifths are also significant, or for any of several other possible reasons. In Hungarian folk music, and even more in that of the Cheremis, pentatonic scales composed of major seconds and minor thirds predominate. Such scales have sometimes been called "gapped scales" on the assumption that they are simply diatonic scales in which gaps have been made. Of course such a label is not really justified, for there is nothing any more "natural" about a scale made up of seconds (of two sizes) than there is about one made up of seconds and thirds, or, for that matter, one made up of quarter tones or augmented fourths. To demonstrate the integrity of the kind of pentatonic scale we have mentioned, let us examine a Cheremis song that makes use of the principle of transposition, (Example 5-1).

EXAMPLE 5-1. Cheremis song, from Bruno Nettl, *Cheremis Musical Styles* (Bloomington: Indiana University Press, 1960), p. 37.

The song consists of three lines, the last two of which are identical. The first consists of two halves, the second of which is derived from the first (and is therefore designated as B_a). The first half of the second line is a downward transposition of the first half of the first line, by a fifth (and is therefore designated as A_5). But there are further ramifications of this notion of transposition, as the analysis in the next paragraph indicates.

First we assign to each of the notes in the scale a number: beginning with the lowest tone, B–1, C sharp–2, E–3, F sharp–4, G sharp–5, B–6, C sharp–7, E–8. Then we compare the section labeled A with that labeled A^5. Obviously their melodic contours are similar, but at some of the points at which A has a minor third, A^5 has a major second, and A^5 begins a minor sixth below A but ends on a perfect fifth below A. Now, if we translate the tones into the numbers we have assigned, and compare musical lines A and A^5, we have the following sequences:

Line A^5 5 5 4 5 4 3 2 3 3 2 3 2 1
Line A   8 8 7 8 7 6 5 6 6 5 6 5 4.

The relationship between the number sequences is constant because the principle involved in this transposition is not a constant relationship of the frequencies (which would occur if the method of transposition were an exact one), but that of tonal transposition. Presumably the scale used in this song existed, in an unconscious sense, in the mind of the composer when he was making up the song, and when he began transposing he did so within the framework of the scale, which is made up of both thirds and seconds.

To some degree, the use of transposition as a structuring device is found in a great many cultures throughout the world, and certainly everywhere in Europe. It takes on special significance in parts of Eastern Europe because of its greater frequency there. The practice of transposing as an integral part of the composition process seems to have radiated from Hungary to its neighbor countries. The Slovaks and, to a small extent, the Czechs make use of it also. The Slovaks transpose sections largely in the manner of the Hungarians (up or down a fifth), the Czechs more frequently up or down a third or second. Perhaps the difference between the Czech and Hungarian practice is due to the greater frequency of diatonic, especially major, scales among the Czechs. Or the influence of neighbor nations may be at work, for the Czechs have lived in an area surrounded by Germans and they participated, more than their neighbors to the east, in the development of art music. Thus their songs sound more like Western cultivated music, and they have variants of many tunes found also in Germany. Example 5-2 is a Czech song using transposition.

EXAMPLE 5-2. Czech folk song, "Vrt sa devca," learned by the author from oral tradition.

WORDS, MUSIC, AND RHYTHM:
THE BALKANS AND CZECHOSLOVAKIA

It is natural to look to the characteristics of a language to explain the characteristics of the songs sung by its speakers. Indeed, the structure of folk songs is frequently determined by the form of their texts, and the rhythmic, even the melodic, quality of a musical repertory may be substantially influenced by the stress, length, and the patterns of the words to which it is sung. Of course we could not claim that the rhythmic structure of a folk music style automatically comes from the language, and we could easily find examples in which the rhythm of folk songs contravenes that of their language. However, there is no doubt that the nature of a language has much to do with shaping the style of the folk songs for which it is used.

It is interesting, in this light, to compare the rhythmic structure of Czech and German folk songs. That of the Czech songs frequently is more accented, while the German flows more smoothly. The German songs more frequently have an anacrusis—a pickup or up-beat, as it is popularly called—while the Czech ones rarely do. These distinctions may come from one of the major phonological differences between the two languages. Czech speakers tend to accent their stressed syllables heavily, and the Czech language automatically places an accent on the first syllable of each word. Also, Czech has no articles such as "a" or "the" that would be unstressed. As a result, Czech utterances begin with accents, and so do Czech songs and instrumental folk compositions. German, with its accents coming on any syllable, and with its unstressed articles preceding nouns, has given rise to a musical structure in which an unstressed beat in the music often precedes the first measure.

The rhythm of Czech and Slovak songs is relatively simple, with the meter typically an isometric duple or triple. Hungarian folk songs are frequently in similarly simple meter, but there are also many Hungarian songs with irregular metric patterns, and some that move steadily in 5/4 or 7/4 meter. One of the common features of Hungarian rhythm is the use of dotted figures— ♩. ♪ or, even more typically, ♪♩. —with heavy stress on the first note. Perhaps, again, the rhythmic structure of the language is evident here, for in Hungarian, as in Czech, there are no articles, and the first syllable is automatically accented. Also common in Hungarian and some other Eastern European folk styles is the use of isorhythmic structure. This means that a rhythmic pattern is repeated for each line. The meters may vary and the measures may have irregular numbers of beats, but the sequence of note values remains the same from line to line in this type of song. The following rhythmic patterns appear in some of the Hungarian as well as the Rumanian folk songs with isorhythmic structure:

① 𝅘𝅥𝅮𝅘𝅥𝅮𝅘𝅥𝅮𝅘𝅥𝅮𝅘𝅥𝅮 𝅘𝅥𝅮𝅘𝅥𝅮 𝅘𝅥𝅮𝅘𝅥𝅮   ② 𝅘𝅥𝅮𝅘𝅥𝅮 𝅘𝅥   𝅘𝅥𝅮𝅘𝅥𝅮𝅘𝅥𝅮

③ 𝅘𝅥𝅮𝅘𝅥𝅮 𝅘𝅥𝅮𝅘𝅥𝅮 𝅘𝅥 𝅘𝅥   ④ 𝅘𝅥 𝅘𝅥 | 𝅘𝅥𝅘𝅥 𝅘𝅥 | 𝅘𝅥𝅘𝅥 𝅘𝅥 | 𝅘𝅥𝅘𝅥 𝅘𝅥 |

The reason for the frequency of this kind of structure in some Eastern European styles may lie, again, in the structure of the poetry. In Western Europe, it is the number of metric feet (iambic, trochaic, dactylic, anapestic) which are constant. Each foot corresponds to one or to a half measure of music. The actual number of syllables per line may vary, since a line consisting of iambic feet may suddenly be broken by a foot of anapest:

"Thĕre wăs ă youth ănd ă jól-lў youth" ("ănd ă jól-" is the anapest foot).

But in most Eastern European styles of poetry it is not the number of accented syllables that is constant, but the number of syllables in toto. Thus an isorhythmic arrangement, even if each phrase has several measures of different lengths, is better for accommodating the kind of line sequence that makes up the poetry.

On the whole, the Balkan countries have in common an unusual degree of rhythmic complexity. It appears in three forms: (1) freely declaimed melodies, which can only with difficulty be classified as to meter, and which are performed with extremes of the parlando-rubato technique; (2) tunes with few different note values, but with frequently changing meter; and (3) tunes with a single dominant meter which, however, is based on the prime number of beats—5, 7, 11, 13, and so on. The first type is well exemplified in the Yugoslav epic, which is discussed further on in this chapter. The second and third types are especially common in the Rumanian and Bulgarian traditions, so much so that songs in 11/8 or 7/8 have been called tunes "in Bulgarian rhythm" among Balkan folk song scholars. Example 5-3 gives some of the rhythms found in these songs.

Example 5-4 is a Rumanian Christmas carol with the meter of 10/16 kept consistently throughout the song. Actually it might be possible to divide the song into measures of different lengths, but in spite of the rather complicated relationship between such note values as eighths and dotted eighths, or sixteenths and dotted sixteenths, there is a steady rhythmic pulse which is followed throughout: 𝅘𝅥𝅮 𝅘𝅥𝅮. 𝅘𝅥𝅮. 𝅘𝅥𝅮 . The curious

EXAMPLE 5-3. Examples of metric patterns found in Bulgarian folk songs.

EXAMPLE 5-4. Rumanian Christmas Carol, from Béla Bartók, *Die Melodien der rumanischen Colinde* (Wien: Universal Edition, 1935), p. 68. Reprinted by permission of Boosey and Hawkes, Inc., New York, and Universal Edition, Ltd., London. Copyright 1918 by Universal Edition, Renewed 1945. Copyright and renewal assigned to Boosey and Hawkes, Inc., for U.S.A.

thing is that the pulse is not regular. It alternates between eighths and dotted eighths. Perhaps this is the key to the rhythmic complexity of some Balkan songs as, for instance, the one given in Example 5-4. There is a meter—10/16 in this case—but the denominator of the fraction does not indicate the length of the beat, as it would in most Western European music, because the length of the beat varies, depending on its position in the measure.

It would seem almost that ♪♪. ♪. ♪ is another version of ♪♪♪♪ and that ♪.♪.♪ is simply an elongation of a simpler figure, ♪♪♪ . We should point out, incidentally, that there is a vast body of Christmas carols in the Rumanian folk repertory. Bartók collected several hundred tunes, and they seem to be particularly archaic, being short, with forms that do not correspond to the simple line organization of Western European, Czech, or Hungarian songs and are irregular not only in the structure of the measures but also in the number of measures and phrases per song.

One might expect the dances of the Balkan countries to be based on simple metric schemes; after all, people have two legs and two arms, to which movement in duple meter lends itself; no one has seven feet. Nevertheless, among the five most important folk dances of the Bulgarians, only one is in duple meter. The Bulgarians have (1) the *Pravo Horo*, a simple round dance, in 2/4 meter; (2) the *Paiduška*, in quintuple meter, with two beats— ♩ ♩. ; (3) the *Povărnato Horo*, a back-and-forth round dance, in 9/16, with four beats— ♪ ♪ ♪ ♪. ; (4) *Račenica*, danced by couples in 7/8 meter, with three beats— ♩ ♩ ♩. ; and (5) *Eleno mome* ("My Helen"), a more recent introduction, also in 7/8, with four beats— ♩ ♩ ♪ ♩. The metric structure of these dances, once established, is quite consistent.

The tunes with frequently changing meter are illustrated by Example 5-5, a simple Rumanian Christmas carol with the range of a sixth, with alternation of 3/8, 4/8, and 5/8. The simple yet irregular rhythmic structure of many Balkan songs is illustrated by the fact that the rhythm of the first three measures reappears in the last three. The transcription by Béla Bartók gives the way in which the first stanza was sung, and

EXAMPLE 5-5. From Béla Bartók, *Die Melodien der rumänischen Colinde* (Wien: Universal Edition, 1935). Printed by permission of the copyright owner, Dr. Benjamin Suchoff, Successor-Trustee, The Estate of Béla Bartók.

then, by means of numbered references, indicates the ways in which subsequent stanzas differ from the first. There are seven stanzas, and the variants are given in the order in which they appear.

We are not able, in this short book, to discuss the words of folk songs to any significant extent, especially as far as their content is concerned. In general, however, it must be pointed out that there are broad but recognizable differences between Eastern and Western European folk song texts. Thus, for example, the widespread importance of the ballad in Western Europe, particularly in the Germanic-speaking countries, is balanced by the greater importance in Eastern Europe of lyrical songs, particularly of songs involving activities of and feelings about tilling of the land. Both types of songs are found throughout Europe, but it is in Eastern Europe that songs truly reflective of a peasant economy are found in large number. Possibly this reflects the earlier and greater urbanization of the Western part of the continent. As samples of Eastern European lyrical songs, we present here a few Czech folk song texts, in English translation,[1] from the many that deal with agricultural life and are among the most popular. They are usually not real work songs, but lyrical poems sung after work.

> *Around Trebon, around Trebon*
> *Horses are grazing on the lord's field.*
> *Give the horses, I'm telling you,*
> *Give the horses oats.*
> *When they have had their fill*
> *They will carry me home.*

Often the songs concern love among young peasants. For example:

> *Come, young man, to our house in the morning.*
> *You shall see what I do.*
> *I get up in the morning, I water the cows,*
> *And I drive the sheep to pasture.*

The fruits of agriculture may be used as special symbols in the text:

> *Under the oak, behind the oak*
> *She had one or two*
> *Red apples; she gave one to me.*
> *She did not want to give me both,*
> *She began to make excuses,*
> *That she hasn't, that she won't give, that there are too few.*

[1] Czech folk song texts quoted from Bruno Nettl and Ivo Moravcik, "Czech and Slovak Folk Songs Collected in Detroit," *Midwest Folklore*, V (1955), 40–48.

Many of the Czech lyrical songs deal with or mention music, such as this—

In the master's meadow I found a ducat.
Who will change it for me? My sweetheart is not at home.
If she won't change it I'll give it to the cimbal (dulcimer) player.
The music will play until dawn.

FORM IN BALKAN FOLK SONGS

The forms of Balkan songs exhibit similarities to, but sometimes also considerable differences from, those of Western Europe. In the latter area, we are overwhelmed by a large number of four-line stanzas, in which there is either progressive development (ABCD, each line a new melody with no repetition) or some recurrence of the first line. As we have seen, AABA is very common in German folk music, in British broadside ballads, and in modern popular and popular-derived songs. ABBA is common also in the older British ballads, especially in relationship to the curved melodic contour. The reverting forms—AABA and ABBA—are common also in the western part of Eastern Europe, in Czech, Polish, and Hungarian song. AABA especially is found in Czech and Polish music, perhaps because of strong German influence. ABBA is found in Hungarian and other Finno-Ugric groups, but more common is a variant of this form, A A(5) A(5) A, indicating transposition of the first section up or down a fifth for the second and third sections. The use of three sections, such as ABA, with the middle section longer or shorter, and sometimes at a tempo different from the first, is sometimes found in the Balkans and sometimes among the Czechs. (Example 5-5 has a shorter middle section, for instance.) Songs with two, five, and six or more lines are found throughout the Balkans and in the Baltic area. Often these can be subdivided into asymmetrical units (like the measures in Bulgarian rhythm). Simple general principles may govern the development of greatly varied groups of forms. Many Rumanian Christmas songs can be divided into two parts, the first longer than the second, with both having common material. The second part is often a condensation of the first (e.g., ABC-AC; A^1A^2B-A^1B).

An area of the world as rich in both folk tunes and folk song scholars as the Balkans was perhaps bound to produce pioneer work in the classification of musical forms. Bartók devised a system which he used for his collections of Hungarian, Slovak, Rumanian, and Serbo-Croatian songs. In his Slovak collection, the songs are first divided according to the number of melodic lines (normally two, three, or four) without counting repetitions of material. Thus a tune with the form ABBA has two different melodic lines, but the form ABCD has four. Each class is then subdivided according to the position of the final tones of the lines in their relationship to the last tone of the song. For example, a song in which all lines end on the same pitch is in one class; one in which the sequence of final tones of lines is GAAG would be in another; and so on. Beyond this, each of the categories is then divided according to rhythm—dotted rhythms are separated from even rhythms. Finally, each of these groups is subdivided according to the number of syllables per line, distinguishing the songs that have the same number of syllables in each line from those in which the number varies from line to line. Bartók's scheme of classifying melodies differs greatly from that used by most students of British folk song, such as Cecil Sharp, who classified tunes according to mode. The reason for this difference is probably related to the fact that there is in the British (and other Western European) styles less formal variety than there is in East European folk music, for the former, being based on poetry with metric feet, relies on more or less constant meter and length of line.

Folk song scholars in Eastern and Central Europe, particularly in Hungary and Czechoslovakia, have followed Bartók's lead and continue to work with great energy to find more adequate methods of classifying folk tunes, now frequently using computers to process the vast amounts of data at their disposal as a result of the wealth of collected tune material. The purposes of classification are (1) to make it possible to find tunes by the musical characteristics; (2) to show that tunes are related genetically, that is, that they are members of one tune family; and (3) to provide a basis for broad analytical and descriptive surveys of the style of a folk music repertory. The folk music scholars who are most involved in questions of classification have made great strides, but their methods still do not easily and automatically provide solutions for these problems.

EPIC SONG:
YUGOSLAVIA, FINLAND, RUSSIA

Traditions of epic poetry are important in a number of European folk cultures, but especially in those of Eastern Europe. An epic is a narrative poem, distinctly longer than the ballad, usually sung, with a main character who is usually a national hero, and who has many adventures in war and love. Its basic unit of organization is usually the individual line of poetry rather than a stanza consisting of several lines. In the Middle Ages the epic was fairly widespread in Western Europe; the French "chansons de geste" and such famous works as the "Song of

Roland" are examples. In Western Europe, the epic tradition was evidently one in which folk and sophisticated traditions shared and mixed,
for it was presumably carried by professional minstrels who at least occasionally used written texts. In Eastern Europe the epic tradition is today
much more alive and much more closely associated with the genuine folk
culture. We find epic material in the Slavic world, and also in Albania
and Finland, where the main body of folk epics, the *Kalevala*, consists of
songs dealing with the Finnish mythical culture hero, Väinemöinen. The
Kalevala is structured in couplets, and the songs were performed by pairs
of bards who would alternate, which is probably responsible for the
peculiarly repetitive form of the text, as shown in this excerpt:[2]

> *O thou wisest Väinemöinen,*
> *O thou oldest of magicians,*
> *Speak thy words of magic backwards,*
> *And reverse thy songs of magic.*
> *Loose me from this place of terror*
> *And release me from my torment.*

Of course the reader will recognize the style as that also used in Longfellow's "Song of Hiawatha." The influence of the *Kalevala* on nineteenth-
century poets was certainly considerable. The Finnish bards sang to the
accompaniment of the *kantele*, a psaltery with 20 to 30 strings.

The Russian tradition of epic poetry is, typically, unaccompanied.
The Russian poems are called *byliny;* they are slow-moving, unrimed,
and performed in a rhythmically free style. Their stories—in contrast to
the mythical past of the Finnish *Kalevala* cycle—deal with historical or
semihistorical events of eleventh-century Russia and of the wars against
the Tartars which took place for the next two hundred years. Of course
there are literary motifs that are found in many nations: for instance, the
poor and neglected prince who becomes a hero, found in all European
folklore but perhaps without historical foundation. The practice of singing *byliny* seems to have reached a peak of artistic perfection in the
seventeenth century, when like the epic tradition of Western Europe in
the Middle Ages it was penetrated by professional minstrels. The
Ukrainian version of the epic is a body of songs called *Dumy*, dealing
largely with the struggles of the Ukrainians against the Tartars and Poles
in the late Middle Ages.

One of the most interesting folk song types of the Greeks is the
"Klephtic song." The Klephts (meaning bandits in Turkish) were the men
who fought against the Turks from the fifteenth to the nineteenth centur-

---

[2] From the book *Kalevala: or, The Land of Heroes*. Trans. from the Finnish
by W. F. Kirby. Everyman's Library Edition. Published by E. P. Dutton & Co., Inc.
Used by permission of E. P. Dutton & Co., Inc., and J. M. Dent & Sons Ltd.

ies for Greek independence. Klephtic songs deal with these fighters, who have become folk heroes, in a way somewhat similar to that of the Yugoslav epics. The songs are performed in a rubato manner, with much ornamentation and complex metric arrangements. They do have a strophic structure, but the melodic and poetic forms do not coincide; in fact, the musical line ordinarily covers one and a half textual lines. Thus, in a sense the modern Greeks share in the epic traditions of Eastern Europe.

The most accessible body of epic singing today, however, is that of the Yugoslavs (mainly the Serbs, but also the Croatians and Montenegrans whose style is also found in Bulgaria and Albania). Their songs deal mainly with the struggles against the Turks from the thirteenth to the seventeenth centuries. Some of the epics are told from the Christian point of view, others from the Muslim. The songs deal mainly with the rulers and the leaders in war. That the tradition is still alive is attested to by the mention of modern appliances such as the telephone, and by the existence of an epic about the shooting of Archduke Ferdinand at Sarajevo at the beginning of World War I. That it is also ancient is proved by the songs' musical structure. There have been attempts to link the Yugoslav tradition to that of the Greek Homeric epics, and certainly we can learn a great deal about the possible genesis of the *Iliad* and *Odyssey* and about the way in which these great epics must have been performed from the structure and cultural context of the Yugoslav epics.

The Yugoslav epics take from less than one to perhaps ten hours to perform; they are performed by semiprofessional minstrels in cafes, and they are sung only by men. They are accompanied on the *gusle* (which the singer himself plays), a simple fiddle with one string made of a strand of horsehair, a belly of stretched skin, and a crude bow. The *gusle* usually plays a more ornamented version of the singer's melody, or it performs a drone and plays ornaments between the singer's lines.

It would be surprising if songs of such length were sung exactly the same way by any two singers, or even twice alike by the same one. To a considerable extent they are improvised, re-created each time. Thus the process of creation and performance are to a degree united.

There are points where adherence to a norm is required, of course; a particular epic has certain themes, certain motifs, and certain formulas —similar to the "conceits" of the British ballads—which recur. In the structure, one of the typical arrangements is the ten-syllable line, which remains constant throughout the hours required to complete the poem. Just how a singer who is partly improvising can consistently and undeviatingly produce lines of exactly ten syllables is one of the mysteries of this ancient tradition. We know that he must learn to sing in accordance with certain patterns, mastering first the stories and the formulas, then singing single episodes, and only later being permitted to sing full-blown songs. Even more exacting than the overall structure is the requirement of a "word boundary" after the fourth syllable in some of the Yugoslav styles; that is, the fourth syllable always ends a word, and no word occupies both fourth and fifth syllables. Here is a sample of this kind of poetry:[3]

> Beg sad priđe|đamu do penđera,
> Pa dofati|knjige i hartije,
> Kaljem drvo|što se knjiga gradi,
> A mastila|što se knjiga piše,
> Pa načinje|knjigu šarovitu,
> Sprema knjigu|ljičkom Mustajbegu.

(*Translation*): Now the bey went to the window
And he took letter paper,
A quill with which letters are made,
And ink with which letters are written,
And he prepared a well-writ letter;
He directed the letter to Mustajbey of the Lika.

Example 5-6 gives a short sample of the music, showing its very ornamental style of singing and playing, and its use of some small intervals. The scale could not be notated without the use of additional marks; arrows indicate slight (quarter-tone) raising or lowering. The notes played by the *gusle* include, consistently, a tone between C-flat and C, and one between G and G-sharp. Several possible reasons for this use of microtones have been advanced: the influence of Turkish and Arabic music; the ancient Greek tradition, with its enharmonic genus; and the use of the *gusle*, which, when fingered by the human hand in natural position of tension, produces such intervals.

The rhythm of Yugoslav epics is also worthy of discussion. If the many vocal ornaments were disregarded, we would find two main types of line:

♩ ♩ ♩ ♩│♩ ♩ ♩ ♩ │♩ ♩ ♩ ‖   and   ♩ ♩│♩ ♩ ♩ ♩ │♩ ♩ ♩ │♩ ♩ ♩ ‖ .

But near the beginning of a song or an episode (usually preceded by introductions played on the *gusle*) the rhythm varies more, the first note of each line is elongated, and the singing has an even more dramatic character than it does in the remainder of the song.

Finally, we should point out that regional and individual styles of

[3] Albert B. Lord, *The Singer of Tales* (Cambridge, Mass.: Harvard University Press, 1960), p. 84.

EXAMPLE 5-6. Sample of Yugoslav epic song (transcribed by Béla Bartók), from Milman Parry and Albert B. Lord, *Serbo Croatian Heroic Songs,* vol. 1 (Cambridge, Mass.: Harvard University Press, 1954), p. 440.

singing are very highly developed in Yugoslav epic poetry. Two singers will sing the same song with many points of difference. Albert Lord narrates an incident of great interest which affords unusual insight into the relationship of tradition and individual creativity:

> When [the epic collector and scholar Milman] Parry was working with the most talented Yugoslav singer in our experience, Avdo Mededović in Bijelo Polje, he tried the following experiment. Avdo had been singing and dictating for weeks; he had shown his worth and was aware that we valued him highly. Another singer came to us, Mumin Vlahovljak from Plevlje. He seemed to be a good singer and he had in his repertory a song that Parry discovered was not known to Avdo; Avdo said he had never heard it before. Without telling Avdo that he would be asked to sing the song himself when Mumin had finished it, Parry set Mumin to singing, but he made sure that Avdo was in the room and listening. When the song came to an end, Avdo was asked his opinion of it and whether he could now sing it himself. He replied that it was a good song and that

Mumin had sung it well, but that he thought he might sing it better. The song was a long one of several thousand lines. Avdo began and as he sang, the song lengthened, the ornamentation and richness accumulated, and the human touches of character, touches that distinguished Avdo from other singers, imparted a depth of feeling that had been missing in Mumin's version.[4]

SCALES AND INTERVALS: BULGARIA, GREECE, POLAND

If we measured the intonation of genuine folk singers anywhere we would probably find that their intervals do not coincide as well with those in Western music theory as our notations indicate. Especially in Eastern Europe, and perhaps more in the Balkans than elsewhere, would we find intervals smaller than the minor second, thirds which are neither major nor minor, and the like. The Balkans have for centuries been under the cultural influence—now strong, now weaker—of the Near East, where small intervals are common. But they have also conformed to a degree with the diatonic system found in Western folk and art music, and with the widespread pentatonic modes which use minor thirds and major seconds and can be derived from the circle of fifths. Thus we find a great deal of variety in the melodic material used in Balkan folk music.

The use of small intervals—some microtones, but more frequently minor seconds—is an important feature of some Balkan styles outside the epic tradition. The importance of ornamentation seems to have contributed to this predilection, for vocal ornaments as well as instrumental ones seem especially made for the use of small intervals. Thus a Macedonian song uses a scale with the tones E-flat, D, C, B, and A-sharp. The fact that the ranges of Balkan songs are, typically, small may also be a contributing factor. According to Kremenliev,[5] Bulgarian songs rarely exceed an octave in range, and a great many of them are within the compass of a fifth. Occasionally one even finds two-tone melodies with only a minor second between the tones. Ornaments in Bulgarian folk song are improvised; they vary from stanza to stanza and, in any single song, from singer to singer. Their purpose may be that of pleasing the audience through vocal virtuosity, of calling attention to the song or to particular words (this is evidently the purpose of melismatic passages preceding a

---

[4] Lord, *The Singer of Tales*, p. 78.
[5] Boris Kremenliev, *Bulgarian-Macedonian Folk Music* (Berkeley and Los Angeles: University of California Press, 1952), p. 78.

song, a practice common also in the Yugoslav epics), or of imitating instrumental passages.

Greek folk music, like that of some other Balkan countries, seems to be a combination of archaic and more recent melodies and contains a great diversity of styles. It is possible to find traces of the ancient Greek modes, and many Greek songs fit perfectly into the system of the diatonic modes. Many other songs, however, are more chromatic. Perhaps the combination of these two concepts—diatonic modes with small, chromatic steps—is responsible for the existence of heptatonic scales that have four minor seconds, such as the so-called Gypsy scale: C-D-E flat-F sharp-G-A flat-B. In most ways, however, Greek folk music seems to show the influences of centuries of Turkish and Muslim occupation. What remains of the ancient Greek traits seems best preserved in Asia Minor and the islands of the Aegean.

Polish folk music is quite different from that of the Balkans and is quite distinctive, but in some ways it is close to that of Russia, while in others it is obviously related to the music of Western neighbors, the Czechs and the Germans. It is also similar to the folk song style of two Slavic-speaking peoples, the Wends and the Jorbs, who lived in Eastern Germany, first as a numerous group and, by the nineteenth century, as a small minority, eventually becoming completely absorbed by the Germans. The folk songs of these peoples were collected in the middle of the nineteenth century; they form something of a link between the German and Polish styles.

The oldest layer of Polish songs is pentatonic, but the majority make use of seven-tone scales, which can be classed as church modes. Those modes similar to the modern minor mode, with lowered sixth and seventh or lowered third, are the most common; that is true also of Russian folk music. But both Poland and Russia also have many songs in major. In contrast to Russia, Poland has little polyphonic folk music and what part-singing there is seems to be of recent origin and emphasizes parallel thirds. The range of the songs is relatively small. A peculiarity of the singing style—typical perhaps of many and varied peculiarities of singing through Europe that never seem to appear in the printed collections of folk songs—is the practice of holding the final note of a song for several seconds, or of trailing off with a downward glissando.

MUSICAL INSTRUMENTS

Perhaps the most characteristic feature of East European folk music is its wealth of instruments and instrumental music. There are far too many instrument types to enumerate or describe, so again we must be content with a sampling. Instruments may serve as clues to the musical past of a nation or region. For example, the association between ancient Greek and modern Near Eastern and Slavic cultures is evident in their use of similar instruments. The ancient Greek *aulos* was a reed instrument with two tubes; similar instruments are today found among the Persians, Arabs, Turks, and Southern Slavs, and in India and Central Asia. In Yugoslavia, an instrument of this type is the *dvojnice* which is, in effect, a double recorder or plugged flute. The right-hand tube has, typically, four or five finger holes and is used for playing simple, embellished melodies; the left-hand side has three or four holes and is normally used to play an accompanying drone. Sometimes the two pipes are played in unison.

The Czechs, Slovaks, and Hungarians all have a large number of instruments. One of the most widely used is the bagpipe, which (perhaps to the surprise of some) is by no means limited to the British Isles; on the contrary, it is found throughout Europe and parts of Asia, and evidently it was brought to Scotland from the East. The kinds of bagpipes found in various countries differ, of course, from the very simple kinds found among the semiliterate tribes in Russia (such as the Cheremis) to the beautifully fashioned and sonorous instruments with three and four pipes found in Western Europe. In Scottish and Irish piping, the tunes are most frequently unrelated to the vocal music, and complex compositional forms, such as *Pibroch*—a kind of theme with variations—make up the repertory. In Eastern Europe, however, much of the bagpipe music consists of the same tunes as are used in vocal music, and some Hungarian folk songs, for instance, appear—with richer ornamentation—in the bagpipe repertory.

In Czechoslovakia and Hungary we also find many instruments related to those of other areas; for example, the Hungarian Csimbalom, a large, hammered ducimer; many kinds of flutes; the ordinary violin, especially prominent in Bohemia; and the accordion.

Folk music instruments seem to be especially numerous in Poland. Many forms of several basic types—flutes, fiddles, bagpipes—exist, each with regional variants. For example, among the stringed instruments, there is a one-stringed *diable skrzypce* (devil's fiddle); a musical bow with three strings; several types of *gensle* (fiddles in various shapes with four and five strings, some held on the knee, some under the chin); the *suka*, with four strings tuned in fifths; the *mazanka*, a small fiddle with three strings tuned in fifths; and the *maryna,* a very large fiddle, also with three strings tuned in fifths, a form of the medieval Western European *tromba marina.*

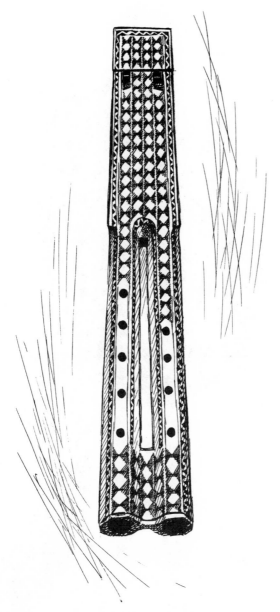

Yugoslav double recorder.

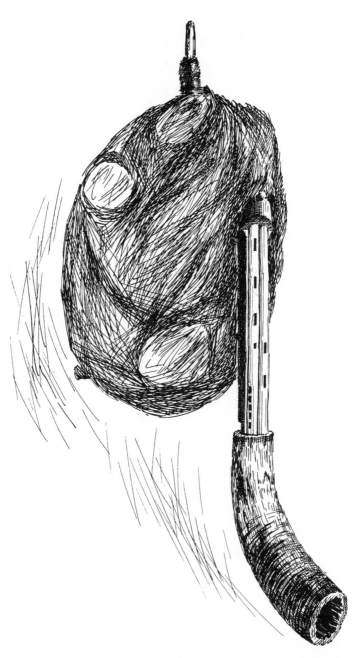

Cheremis bagpipe.

Perhaps because of the proliferation of instruments, Polish folk music is dominated by instrumental tunes, most of it used, of course, for dancing. There is an immense number of dance types, each with regional provenience. Some of these have been taken over into art music by composers such as Chopin—the polonaise, the mazurka, the polka, the krakowiak. Typically, the Polish dances are quick, and the majority use triple meter.

While many Eastern European peoples have instruments that are derived from art music, or closely related to it, one finds pockets in which the instruments closely resemble some of those in the world's simpler cultures. This is the case among the Cheremis of Eastern European Russia, where we find long, wooden trumpets without finger holes, simple bagpipes and flutes, horns made of bark, a one-string fiddle, a simple drum, and whistles made of fired clay.

POLYPHONY:
THE SLAVIC COUNTRIES AND THE CAUCASUS

Polyphony is one type of music that characterizes all of Eastern Europe. It seems to exist everywhere except among the Finno-Ugric and Turkic peoples; its development has been greatest in Russia and the Caucasus. The existence among the Georgians of polyphonic songs similar to the *organa* of medieval Europe has long tantalized the historian of Western art music, who can hardly assume that the Caucasus could have had an influence on Western European practices and who finds the East too remote to have received stimuli of such a specific nature from the medieval West, but who also believes that the two forms are too similar to have been invented independently twice. This is one of the riddles of historical ethnomusicology that may never be solved. The existence of organum-like folk music in Iceland and of other polyphonic types in Spain, Italy, and elsewhere (sporadically) indicates a possible solution: that polyphonic singing was once widespread in folk practice but receded to the marginal areas of Europe. Example 5-7 is a song of the Gurians, a tribe in the Caucasus, in three voices. The solo phrase at the beginning is typical also of Russian and Ukrainian polyphony. The first part of the song makes liberal, though not consistent, use of parallel triads. The second part also uses the principle of the drone, above which parallel thirds appear.

The role of Eastern (Orthodox) Church music in the development of this kind of polyphony may have been considerable. Polyphony was

EXAMPLE 5-7. Gurian polyphonic folk song, from Robert Lach, *Gesänge russischer Kriegsgesangener* Band 3, 1. Abt. (Wien: Wiener Akademie der Wissenschaften, 55. Mitteilung der Phonogrammarchivs Kommission, 1928), p. 108.

officially adopted by the Eastern Church in the seventeenth century, and its style was strongly influenced by Western European polyphony, with its absence of parallel fifths or triads. Russian folk polyphony must have felt the impact of this polyphonic singing in the churches, for while there are occasional parallel fifths and fourths, the tendency is to have four voices which sing harmony largely in the Western tradition. In Russia and the Ukraine, the practice of polyphonic singing is extremely important. Singing is typically a group activity, except in the case of narrative poetry, and even in the 1950s we hear of young people in Russian cities walking in groups and singing informally. The polyphonic songs are traditional, but some improvisation in the lower parts seems to be acceptable. In the

Russian songs, the upper voice is definitely the melody; but in the Ukrainian ones, the two or three voices seem to be roughly equal in importance. Parenthetically, we should point out the rather unusual developments in Russian folk music since World War I. The Soviet government has attempted to preserve the folk heritage not only of the Russians but also of some of the many minority populations in the Soviet Union, at the same time making their songs servants of the communist ideology. The result is a large body of folk song in the traditional musical styles—although the traits of Russian songs per se have to an extent penetrated the domain of some of the minority groups—with words of recent origin, often mentioning the leaders of the Soviet Union and the communist ideology.

The Cossacks of the Don River basin (who have produced the famous professional Don Cossack choruses) have developed the art of polyphonic singing to especially great heights; evidently even the epic *byliny* were sometimes sung by them in chorus. Another area of Russia in which polyphony flourishes is the North, especially the area around the monastery of Pečory. The Ukrainians also have a polyphonic style of great interest; Example 5-8 is typical of those Ukrainian songs which make use of parallel fifths. The polyphony of the Eastern Slavs, while

EXAMPLE 5-8. Ukrainian polyphonic song from Poltava, collected by Ossyp and Roman Rosdolsky, transcribed by Bruno Nettl.

essentially relying on parallel movement, does not follow this principle throughout. There is occasional oblique and contrary motion, use of the drone and even of imitation. Nor does the interval between the voices remain constant in one song. Example 5-8 contains parallel thirds as well as parallel fifths, with an occasional fourth and seventh. The beginning by a soloist is typical, and the choral parts may be doubled at the octave when both men and women sing. Tonality, in the case of the parallel fifths, may be difficult to identify, for each voice retains its own distinct tonality in order to preserve strict parallelism. But a common closing formula that establishes the final tonality proceeds from a third or triad built on the second degree of the scale to an octave on the tonic.

As we move westward, polyphony decreases in prominence, and the vertical intervals become smaller. Poles, Czechs, and Slovaks use parallel thirds (and occasionally sixths), perhaps under the influence of the Alpine style with its emphasis on triadic harmony and melody. In the Balkans we also find vertical seconds and, occasionally, parallel seconds.

In Yugoslavia, there are also various types of polyphony, the most distinctive emphasizing major and minor seconds not only as passing intervals but as the main supports of polyphonic structure. For example, there are vertical and even parallel seconds in the type of singing called "Ojkanie," whose melodies are sometimes similar to the melodic lines of the epics. The members of the Balkan folk cultures evidently do not consider the parallel seconds complex or difficult to perform, for in Bulgaria even children's songs may contain them.

Although polyphony is not common in the Baltic area, it does occur in some interesting forms also using vertical seconds. Example 5-9 is a Lithuanian round, sung by three groups, in which only two tones are sung simultaneously. The reason is that one of the three groups is always resting. Thus, the tune, consisting of phrases A and B and the rest, X, has the following form when sung as a round:

Voice 1	A B X A B X
Voice 2	A B X A B
Voice 3	A B X A.

Our examples have shown that Eastern Europe possesses one of the richest traditions of folk music. Variety and regional diversity are tremendous, but if we had to divide the area into geographic subdivisions with some stylistic homogeneity, it would have to be into four groups: (1) the Western Slavs—Czechs, Slovaks, Poles—who tend to show Western European characteristics and the influences of Western art music; (2) the Russians, Ukrainians, and Caucasians, whose main characteristic is highly developed polyphony; (3) the Balkan peoples, with music of small intervals and a strong influence of the Near East; and (4) the Hungarians and other Finno-Ugric peoples who, in spite of their isolation from each other, have retained some elements of their common heritage, such as the prominence of the pentatonic scale without half tones and the practice of transposing phrases as an essential part of song structure.

EXAMPLE 5-9. Lithuanian round in three parts, from pamphlet accompanying the recording *Lithuanian Folk Song in the United States* (New York: Folkways Records P 1009), pp. 4–5.

BIBLIOGRAPHY AND DISCOGRAPHY

The folk music of some of the Western nations in Eastern Europe is a field that was thoroughly studied by Béla Bartók and Zoltán Kodály, and their publications are to be recommended, among them the following. Bartók's *Slovenske l'udovne piesne* (Bratislava: Slovakian Academy of Sciences, 1959–) is a monumental collection of Slovak folk song which also shows Bartók's method of classifying the songs. Zoltán Kodály, *Folk Music of Hungary* (London: Barrie and Rockliff, 1960) is an important discussion. Bartók's *Melodien der rumänischen Colinde* (Vienna: Universal Edition, 1935) includes the melodies of hundreds of Rumanian Christmas carols.

Among the many good readings on Yugoslav folk music, we suggest Bartók and Albert B. Lord, *Serbo-Croatian Folk Songs* (New York: Columbia University Press, 1951); Albert B. Lord, "Yugoslav Epic Folk Poetry," *J-IFMC*, III (1951), 57–61 and *The Singer of Tales* (New York: Athenaeum, 1965); and George Herzog, "The Music of Yugoslav Heroic Epic Folk Poetry," *J-IFMC*, III (1951), 62–64. Two important discussions of Greek folk music are Solon Michaelides, *The Neohellenic Folk-Music* (Limassol, Cyprus: Nicosia, 1948) and Rodney Gallop, "Folksongs of Modern Greece," *Musical Quarterly*, XXI (1935), 89–98. A detailed discussion of one Balkan style is Boris Kremenliev, *Bulgarian-Macedonian Folk Music* (Berkeley: University of California Press, 1952). *Treasured Polish Songs with English Translations*, published by Polanie Club, selected by Josepha K. Contoski (Minneapolis: Polanie, 1953), is a collection for practical use, as is Rose Rubin and Michael Stillman, *A Russian Song Book* (New York: Random House, 1962). Polyphonic Russian songs are collected in A. Listopadov, *Pesni Donskikh Kazakov* (Moscow: Musgys, 1949–). Aspects of Caucasian folk music are discussed in Victor Belaiev, "Folk Music of Georgia," *Musical Quarterly*, XIX (1933), 417–33. The music of one special ethnic group in the USSR is presented in Bruno Nettl, *Cheremis Musical Styles* (Bloomington: Indiana University Press, 1960).

The following records give samplings of Eastern European folk music: *Czech, Slovak and Moravian Folk Songs*, Monitor MF 389; *Czech Songs and Dances*, Apon 2473; *Folk Music of Hungary*, collected under the auspices of Béla Bartók, Folkways P 1000; *Folk Music of Yugoslavia*, Folkways 4434; *Folk Music of Rumania*, collected by Béla Bartók, Folkways 419; *Folk Dances of Greece*, Folkways FE 4467; *Folk Music of Greece*, Folkways FE 4454; *Polish Folk Songs and Dances*, Folkways FP 848; and *Russian Folk Songs*, Vanguard VRS 9023, a recording performed by professional interpreters.

SIX

FRANCE, ITALY,
AND THE IBERIAN PENINSULA

The area comprising France, Italy, Spain, and Portugal is distinguished by its particularly long and close association with art music. This is especially true of France and Italy, the nations which, since the Middle Ages, have perhaps more consistently than any others had a tradition of urban civilization, of learned courts and monasteries, and of the trappings of art music such as notation and written theory. It has often been thought that these countries, as a result, now have little folk music except for a residue of earlier art music which has somehow trickled down to the rural communities. Indeed, certain song and dance types now part of folklore turn out to have originated in the art music tradition of the Middle Ages; for that matter, this art music tradition (for example, that of the Troubadours and Trouvères) certainly had more in common with folk traditions than did later art music traditions in Europe, such as the symphony orchestras of the nineteenth century and their music. Some of the forms of contemporary folk music, such as that of the French *branle* in Example 6-1, are pointedly similar to forms found in medieval instrumental music—in this case the *stantipes,* which also consists of a series of repeated musical lines with first and second endings. Whether this form originated in folk or art music, it is obviously an example of the close relationship between the two traditions. But recently, folklorists have also uncovered enclaves in which folk music seems to have developed with much less influence from the cities, and styles which appear to have grown with an amazing degree of independence.

FRENCH FOLK MUSIC AND ITS TIES
TO ART MUSIC OF THE PAST

In France, the main areas preserving old traditions are in the South, near the Pyrenees, and Brittany—relatively isolated regions, as one might expect. On the whole, the French folk songs have the same kinds of functions and uses as those in England, Germany, and the Low Countries. Ballads are not quite so numerous, nor are songs involving religion, while lyrical love songs, humorous songs, and dance music are among the most prominent types.

A large number of dances—whether they were used in the peasant culture, in the towns, or at the courts we don't always know—are described in Thoinot Arbeau's *Orchésographie* (1589); and a number of these dances are still alive in folklore today. Notable among them is the above-mentioned *branle,* performed either as a round dance or by two lines of dancers facing each other, in moderately quick duple meter.

Example 6-1 is a *branle* performed on a hurdy-gurdy. The tune exhibits some interesting characteristics. It is in straight duple meter. (Most French folk music is in duple or triple meter, with little evidence of the parlando-rubato style in either instrumental or vocal music.) The tune is heptatonic and, if it made use of the note A, could be considered as alternating between the major and Lydian modes. It contains a tritonic tetrachord (e.g., C-D-E-F♯), which is also common in several styles of instrumental folk music, particularly in the Alps, and which composers of art music have sometimes consciously introduced to impart a folk flavor.

The form of this piece is related not only to Western European medieval forms, but also to instrumental folk music forms found throughout Europe, even as far away as the Cheremis in interior Russia.

EXAMPLE 6-1. Excerpt from "Branle carré," French instrumental piece, played on the hurdy-gurdy. Transcribed by the author from the recording, *Folk Music of France*, edited by Paul Arma, with introduction and notes on the recordings by Paul Arma (New York: Ethnic Folkways Library P 414, 1951), Side A, Band 1.

The hurdy-gurdy performing Example 6-1 is not to be confused with the barrel organ also known by that name, for it is a stringed instrument. It has a number of strings, all but one of which are used only as drones. Instead of fingering the instrument, the player uses a kind of keyboard with mechanical stops which shorten the melody string. And instead of a bow, a rosined wheel is cranked; this touches all of the strings and automatically produces a melody with drone accompaniment. The unbroken character of the music gives it a bagpipe-like effect. The hurdy-gurdy is known in France as the *vielle*, but this should not be confused with the simple medieval fiddle also known by that name. Indeed, known by a Latin name, *organistrum*, the hurdy-gurdy was important in the Middle Ages, and was evidently used (probably in a somewhat larger form, played by two men) in churches. It was evidently once much more widespread in Europe, and variants of it appear in corners of the continent as, for example, in Sweden, whose *Nyckelharpa* is almost identical with the French hurdy-gurdy except that it is played with a bow instead of a wheel.

The importance of melodies accompanied by drones is remarkable in European folk music, perhaps sufficiently so to make this one of the special characteristics of Europe. However, the drone is of great importance in Middle and Near Eastern music as well. A number of other-

French hurdy-gurdy (eighteenth century).

wise unrelated instruments seem fashioned especially for use as drones. Besides the hurdy-gurdy there is, of course, the bagpipe (which, known as *cornemuse*, is common in France and has evidently been popular there for centuries, as is attested to by the many pieces entitled "Musette" in seventeenth- and eighteenth-century art music). The double flutes or clarinets of the Balkans, such as the Yugoslav *dvojnice*, use one pipe for melody, the other for drone. The dulcimer is frequently used in similar fashion. But even in the music of instruments that because of their structure are not especially suited to drones, the drone principle is often present. Thus Anglo-American fiddle players and the performers on the Norwegian Hardanger fiddle often strike open strings in addition to the melody tones, producing a kind of interrupted drone effect. And the chordal accompaniment on instruments such as the banjo and the guitar frequently revolves around a single chord, which gives an effect related to the drone.

In spite of regional diversity and even though archaic styles of French music exist in isolated pockets, the predominant style of French folk music shows the powerful impact that art music through the centuries must have had. The typical tunes are isometric, they have major or (much less commonly) melodic minor tonality, they are monophonic or accompanied by chord or drones, and they move briskly in strophic forms. Singing is with relaxed voice and with little ornamentation. The fact that some of the French forms can be related, whether through the etymology of their names or through their structure, to some of the genres of music (such as the dances) of the Renaissance and Middle Ages should prove to us the close contact that exists between art and folk music. In the last three or four centuries, this relationship can also be shown in the diffusion of the quadrille and its relative, the square dance. This type of dance evidently originated in France some time before the eighteenth century and was a sort of transition between round and couple dances. It became a dance popular in the cities and at the courts, had a period of being stately and dignified, and then was again accelerated. In the nineteenth century it gradually declined as a dance of city folk but found its way again into rural folk culture, eventually becoming the typical folk dance of the English-speaking world. Similarly, remnants of medieval forms of troubadour song seem to have found their way into contemporary folk culture. Thus Carlos Vega[1] believes that he has found variants of medieval troubadour melodies from Provence in Argentine folk tradition.

[1] Carlos Vega, in a paper read at the First Inter-American Conference on Musicology, Washington, D.C., May, 1963.

ITALIAN FOLK MUSIC—
THE ANCIENT AND THE MODERN

For several decades in the twentieth century it was widely believed that Italy had no folk music, that the country had been in the grip of musical sophisticates for so long that no folk heritage with its characteristic traits—oral tradition, communal re-creation, and the like—still remained. In the 1950s, however, through the collecting efforts of several scholars including Diego Carpitella and Alan Lomax, a great treasure of folksongs quite different from art music and exhibiting great variety of style and forms was uncovered. Carpitella[2] believes that a rather sharp division exists between an ancient style, which is found largely in lullabies, work songs, and funeral laments, and a modern style, found largely in lyrical songs. The ancient style is characterized by the church modes and, occasionally, by scales with five and fewer tones. The later style (which evidently really did come about through the growth of art music) is characterized by the use of major and of harmonic and melodic minor scales, as well as by the use of harmonic accompaniment and of melodies constructed on a latent harmonic background. The ancient style is found mainly in those regions of Italy which have remained relatively undeveloped and unmodernized, and which, even after 1950, had a noticeably lower standard of living than did the rest of the nation; these regions are the mountains of South and Central Italy, and the islands of Sicily and Sardinia.

Among the most interesting finds of the recent upsurge in ethnomusicological research in Italy is a rich tradition of polyphony. Among the simpler instances is Example 6-2, a kind of duet recitative. A beginning by a soloist who is joined by a second voice is typical of this style, though not found in this example (see Example 5-8 for a Ukranian example of this feature which is found in many European countries and in Africa). In Example 6-2, the movement is largely in parallel thirds, which is a feature also common in Italian popular and light classical music. Of special interest is the divergence of the two voices from unison to fifth in the second half of the first line, the parallel fifths in the middle, and the ending on a unison: these are reminiscent of medieval *organum*.

A characteristic of some of the more complex Italian polyphony is the alternation of melodic movement among the voices. While one voice

[2] Diego Carpitella, "Folk Music: Italy," *Grove's Dictionary of Music and Musicians*, 5th ed. (New York: St. Martin's Press, 1960), X, 137.

EXAMPLE 6-2. Italian polyphonic folk song, from Alberto Favara, *Corpus di Musiche Siciliane* (Palermo: Accademia de Scienze, Lettere e Arti, 1957), vol. 1, 225.

Mas - sa - ru Ma - ri - a - nu, mi vog- ghiu spi - a - ghè,

Se suo ch'a vi 'na fig - ghia, se'a vu - li— ma - ri - è.

sings a bit of melody, the other one is sustained; in the next phrase, the previously sustained voice becomes the carrier of the melody, and so on in alternation. The use of different kinds of rhythmic structure in each voice is also typical; one voice may carry the main tune, another may sing sustained notes supplying harmony, while a third may sing a rapid rhythmic figure with meaningless syllables on one tone perhaps imitating a drumbeat. Polyphonic singing is found in various kinds of Italian song—shepherds' songs, songs of dock workers and sailors. Some of the polyphony makes use of instruments as well as of voices; in such cases the singers are often accompanied by instruments that can produce a drone, bagpipes, a small organ, or the *launeddas*, which is discussed below.

The influence of cultures outside Italy on Italian polyphony may explain some of the regional differences. The north of Italy, which is dominated by the more modern style of folk song and by singing in parallel thirds and sixths, has had close contact with the Alpine musical cultures with their love of triadic structures. The South has had less contact with Europe and has preserved older forms. Influences from Africa and the Near East can perhaps also be felt in the South. According to Carpitella,[3] a type of song sung in the tunny-fishery areas near North Africa is characterized by the kind of call-and-response patterns common also in Black African music and found sometimes in North Africa as well. If he is correct in his belief that this song type actually came from Africa, he has come upon an interesting early example of the kind of influence on Western music that African music has come to exercise so strongly in the last two centuries, for it is precisely this call-and-response pattern which has been one of the cornerstones of the various Afro-American styles in folk and popular music.

The instruments most evident in Italian folk music are those which

[3] Carpitella, "Folk Music: Italy," p. 140.

have been taken over from the cultivated tradition: violin, guitar, mandolin, clarinet, accordion. But there are also much older instruments, some of which seem to have remained relatively unchanged since classical times, in the more isolated parts of the nation: various percussion instruments (clappers, rattles), conch trumpets, the Jew's harp, panpipes, simple bagpipes with up to three drone pipes, recorder-like plugged flutes, reed pipes, and ocarinas made of fired clay. One of the most intriguing, found mainly in Sardinia, is the *launeddas,* which consists of three reed pipes. The longest and shortest of these are fastened together and held in the left hand (these are called *tumbu* and *mancosedda,* respectively); the middle-sized one, *mancosa,* is held in the right hand. The *launeddas* is used for polyphonic music of the drone type, similar to that played on the Yugoslav *dvojnice.* One of the problems faced by the player is the need to keep blowing without pausing for breath; it is solved by a technique of blowing air out of the mouth while inhaling with the nose, called "circular breathing," also found in distant parts of the world such as Australia, whose aboriginal *didjeridu* players use the same technique. A boy learning to play the *launeddas* learns circular breathing, as have Mediterranean musicians since Egyptian antiquity, by blowing through a straw into a pail of water. The teacher can see whether the pupil is succeeding by observing the bubbles in the water.

The close relationship between Italian folk and art music during the past few centuries is also illustrated by the sources of the words of some of the songs. In Central Italy, a type of song (or perhaps a sequence of songs) known as *maggio* is sung during May. Its words are frequently taken from the works of famous poets, Ariosto, Tasso, Dante, even Classical poets such as Virgil and Ovid. Its structure is evidently related to some of the earliest manifestations of opera around 1600. The form of the *maggio* consists of a choral or instrumental introduction, recitatives, and instrumental or choral interludes which recur, functioning rather like refrains or *ritornellos* (instrumental refrain-like pieces in early opera). In thematic content the various parts of a *maggio* are not necessarily related; the recitative may be in the modal style of ancient Italian folk music, the choral section may have some features found in the part-songs of Renaissance Italian art music, and the instrumental sections may be popular dances such as polkas or tarantellas.

THE BASQUES—EUROPE'S OLDEST FOLK CULTURE?

Legend has it that the Basques are the oldest people in Europe, but they seem to have retained little of their ancient heritage of folklore.

On the contrary, they seem to have partaken of the traditions of Northern Spain and Southwestern France, and their culture is a repository of archaic forms of that region, both French and Spanish. For example, young Basque men have a custom, also found in other parts of Europe, of going from house to house on the last Saturday of January, wishing the inhabitants good health and a good life, and singing songs to them. Elsewhere, this may be done before Christmas and even at Easter, and the singers may be young boys and girls. Another custom shared by the Basques with some other areas of Europe is the singing of "rough music" around the house of people who have engaged in some presumably immoral act.[4] An adulterous couple, an old man who marries a young girl, or a wife who beats her husband may be visited by a group who use pots, pans, cowbells as rhythmic accompaniment to improvised, insulting songs. In Germany and other countries, similar "music" is performed on a wedding night or on the night before a wedding.

We know very little about the ways in which European folk songs were composed. This applies to words as well as music, although we realize that some of the material is composed by sophisticated song writers and then passed into oral tradition. Among the Basques, improvisation is particularly important; it is even thought that most of the Basque folk songs originated on the spur of the moment. Evidently the Basque language (which is said to be so difficult that not even the devil can learn it) lends itself easily to improvisatory riming. Many improvised poems of the Basques have a humorous or satirical character and deal with recent events of village interest, politics, and the church. Many are anticlerical in sentiment. Evidently the improvised text was sung to a traditional tune, and most Basque men participated in the practice of improvising words. A few of them gained preeminence, and some of their songs still carry their names after years and decades. This is one of the few examples in a folk culture of a composer's being recognized and associated with works years after he composed them. The most famous Basque improviser, or *kolaris,* was known as Etchahoun and was born in the valley of Soule in 1786.

Like a large proportion of the Spanish and French songs, Basque songs are frequently in 6/8 meter and make use of the church modes; the latter is true of the ballad in Example 6-3, which is Dorian. More complex meters, such as 5/8, are also common, as are songs without ascertainable metric structure. The most famous illustration of quintuple meter in Basque folk music is the *zortziko,* a type of melody used mainly for dance tunes. The forms of Basque songs consist of from four to six

---

[4] Rodney Gallop, "Basque Songs from Soule," *Musical Quarterly* XXII (1936), 461.

EXAMPLE 6-3. French singing game, "Yan petit," from Violet Alford, "Dance and Song in Two Pyrenean Valleys," *Musical Quarterly* XVII (1931), 253.

phrases, interrelated in various ways. Lullabies frequently consist of varied repetitions of a single musical line (A¹ A² A³ . . .), while love songs and dance songs have forms such as ABCC, ABCB, AABCD, AABB, and AABCDC.

Instrumental folk music among the Basques features a three-holed flute (*chirula*) and the *ttun-ttun,* an instrument with six strings, similar to the dulcimer but held in the arm. The same player uses both instruments, accompanying the tunes of the *chirula* with a drone on the *ttun-ttun.* Instrumental music is used in dances and for "mascaradas," processions accompanied by dances performed at carnival time. This custom is one found throughout Europe, but it is preserved in very elaborate form in the Basque country. Ceremonial dances are performed by certain stock characters—the hobby horse, which is surely a remnant of the tournaments of the Middle Ages, the fool, the sweeper, and the lord and the lady. Similar practices are found among the Negroes of Uruguay, where the *candombe,* interestingly enough, features a broommaker analogous to our "sweeper" (see Chapter Nine). There is a sword dance which, like those of France, Spain, and England, was probably originally a representation of the century-long struggle between Christians and Moors. There is also an acrobatic dance in which dancers leap and turn in complicated steps around and over a tumbler of wine without upsetting it. Basque instrumental music is similar in style to the songs, but the song tunes themselves do not normally seem to be used by the instrumentalists.

The Basques have also retained a form of the medieval mystery play, called *Pastorales*. These folk plays make use of interpolated songs which appear at particularly important points in the plot. The themes of the *Pastorales* are biblical or legendary and frequently hark back to the battles of Christians against Moors in the Iberian peninsula. No matter what the plot, the characters are divided into Moors or Turks dressed in red costumes, and Christians, in blue. The battles for national or cultural survival in Spain and France have evidently had just as great an impact on the development of folklore as have the struggles against the Turks in Yugoslavia, with its epic tradition, or as did the fights between Christian and Tartar in Russia.

SPAIN AND PORTUGAL—
A REGION OF GREAT DIVERSITY

There is great variety in the folk music of the Hispanic peninsula. Particularly, there is a great difference between the North, which is closely related to France and Italy, and the South, which bears much resemblance to North Africa and the Middle East, and, thus, also to the Balkan peninsula (due to the importance of Arabic influences on Spanish culture throughout the Middle Ages and to a smaller degree ever since). Beyond this major difference, each area has its own folk music repertory and styles. Nevertheless, there is also considerable unity: few listeners would fail, after some experience, to recognize a Spanish folk melody. Of course, the many kinds of folk songs have also spread to Latin America, where together with Afro-American and, to a smaller degree, American Indian elements, they form the basis of a huge wealth of folklore.

It is difficult to identify and separate those traits which make Spanish or Portuguese folk music sound Hispanic. Triple meter abounds: slow triple meter, usually noted as 3/4, and quicker, compound meters such as 6/8 and 9/8 are very common. But songs in duple meter are also found, as are some in quintuple. There is also a great deal of recitative-like singing, without metric structure, and with considerable ornamentation, similar to types of song found in the Eastern Mediterranean. Scales tend to be diatonic and the tonality major, natural minor, or characterized by the

use of augmented and minor seconds, thus: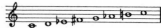
Intervals are small, and large leaps are rare, as with the anhemitonic
pentatonic scales so common in England and Eastern Europe. The forms
of the songs are often strophic, like those of Italy and France but in
many cases somewhat less regular as far as the relative length of the
lines is concerned. But other kinds of formal organization, less tight and
less standardized, are also found. There is a good deal of polyphonic
singing, mainly in parallel thirds or sixths or with the accompaniment of
a drone.

Ĺ The influence of Arabic music on Spanish folk song seems to have
been considerable, which is not surprising when we remember the
long period of Arab rule over the peninsula (ninth through fifteenth
centuries). Specific tunes from the Arabic tradition do not seem to have
remained in any large numbers, however. The scales with augmented
seconds may have been introduced by the Arabs, or they may have developed as a result of Arabic influence, since such intervals are a typical
feature of much Arabic music. The great amount of ornamentation found
in some of the melodies that have no metric structure may also ultimately
be of Near Eastern origin, for singing of a related sort is found in some
Arabic music of today. Example 6-4 is such a melody from Santander.

Perhaps a more important feature common to both Spanish and
Arabic music is the manner of singing, which is rather tense, nasal,
and harsh-sounding. Again, similarities to the Balkan styles of singing
may be noted. Ornaments of a modest sort are found in many songs; the
mordent and the turn are particularly common. The tempo of Spanish
songs may be rapid, vigorous, and downright driving, or, on the other
hand, slow and stately.

Among the many kinds of song in Spain and Portugal we should
mention the *copla,* which is a short, lyrical type, usually with only one
stanza. Ballads are also found in Spain; they deal, frequently, with the
heroism of medieval warriors such as Charlemagne and El Cid, and
their content has more in common with the epics of Eastern Europe than
with the old tragic ballads of Britain, impersonal as the latter usually are.
The arrangement of a group of ballads around a hero is rather like the
clustering of epic tales around a leader such as the Serbian Kraljevic
Marko (Prince Marko), and it has something in common with the cycle
of Robin Hood ballads, which were once sung throughout Great Britain.
Some of the themes of Spanish balladry are of wide provenience, however; the same stories have been found, on occasion, in French and
Scandinavian songs.

When one thinks of Spanish folk music one perhaps thinks
automatically of dancing, and, of course, there are many Spanish folk

EXAMPLE 6-4. Spanish folk song, from Kurt Schindler, *Folk Music and Poetry of Spain and Portugal* (New York: Hispanic Institute in the United States, 1941), song no. 530.

dance types: the *jota*, the *gitana*, the *seguidillas*, the *bolero*, the *fandango*, the *murciana*, and others too numerous to mention. Each district has its own version of the dance types of national provenience. The *jota*, a combination of song and dance, is one of the most interesting. In rapid triple meter, it is danced by a couple—originally it was probably a dance of courtship—whose complicated footwork and tricky castanet rhythms are especially fascinating.

The *flamenco* tradition of Andalusia in Southern Spain is perhaps the most widely known aspect of Spanish folk music. It is not typically Spanish, for it is particularly the music of the Spanish gypsies, although it probably did not originate with them but was simply taken over by them. The gypsies, who inhabit many countries of Southern and Eastern Europe, have a tradition of entertaining and, evidently, a talent for emphasizing and exaggerating the most characteristic elements of the folk music in each country in which they live (in addition to continuing their native tradition). Thus, for example, the Russian gypsies have developed a style out of the Russian folk tradition, and the Spanish gypsies have fashioned the *flamenco* style out of elements already present in Spain.

One type of *flamenco* music is the *cante hondo*, which means "deep" or "profound song." The words are frequently tragic, sometimes verses of complaint against injustices. The range of these songs rarely exceeds a sixth, and the structure is not strophic but consists of irregular repetitions and alternations of two or more phrases with variations. The singing is highly ornamented, non-metric, and contains occasional microtones. It is often accompanied by the guitar, which performs simple repetitive chord sequences in rapid triple meter and dominated by figures such as

♪ ♫♫ . The words of *flamenco* proper are usually erotic, and the dance is performed by a soloist or a couple, with the audience participating with encouraging shouts of *olé*.

In order to give the reader a somewhat more intimate insight into one aspect of Spanish folk music culture, let us consider briefly the performers on the *dulzaina* (*dulzaineros*) in the province of Léon, in Northwestern Spain.[5] The *dulzaina* is an oboe-like instrument that has evidently been widely used in the area for centuries, but is not necessarily known in all of its villages. In earlier times, the *dulzaina* was used by shepherds in order to help pass the time. It was also played in various social situations—dances, serenades, and spontaneous gatherings, such as feasts held after a hunt. Furthermore, it was also used on semireligious occasions, such as the dances performed on Epiphany or certain

---

[5] The material on the *dulzaina* is based on field research carried out by Martha E. Davis, graduate student in anthropology at the University of Illinois.

saints' days, and it was even used as part of the liturgy, playing pro-
cessionals and recessionals in church, and even parts of the mass. The
dulzaineros were evidently professionals who performed without pay in
their own villages, but were paid when asked to perform elsewhere. The
dulzainero was frequently accompanied by singing (sometimes his function was to stimulate people to join in and to sing), and by a drummer
(who was the junior partner of a rather stable combination), and sometimes by tambourines and castanets. There was usually one *dulzainero*
per village, and, clearly, he occupied an important role in village life.
Today, the instrument is used far less. Most of the *dulzaineros* are elderly
men, some of them reluctant to play because their music is regarded
as backward by more modern-minded villagers, and restricting their
music to their own homes and to the late evenings. One reaction to the
dwindling of *dulzaina* playing and the modernizing trend has been
the establishment of *dulzaina* competitions with prizes. Shepherds no
longer play the instrument, and in social gatherings it has been replaced
by accordion and saxophone. Priests have forbidden its use in certain
churches. But the instrument has not disappeared, having been adapted
to new repertories such as popular songs from the cities, and having been
changed to resemble, in appearance and sound, the modern clarinet.

Throughout these discussions of European folk music, we have
pointed out the close relationship of this body of music with musics elsewhere. Despite the fact that European folk music turns out to be a rather
homogeneous unit, contrasting markedly with the musics of other cultures such as China, India, Africa, and aboriginal America, those parts
of Europe which are near other continents exhibit influences, moving in
both directions, which testify to the mobility of music. Spanish folk music
is perhaps the best example of this kind of mobility. The music of Spain
has received much of its character from Asia, by way of North Africa;
and it has, in turn, passed on this material to the Americas, where it was
in turn combined with elements of yet other cultures, to form new and
characteristic styles. At the same time, Spain and Portugal partake of the
general character of European folk music through their similarity to the
musics of France and Italy, the nations to whom they are historically and
linguistically most closely related.

BIBLIOGRAPHY AND DISCOGRAPHY

An interesting collection of French folk song is Émile Barbillat and
Laurian Touraine, *Chansons Populaires dans le Bas-Berri* (Paris: Gar-
gaillou, 1930–1931, 5 vols.). The best discussion in English of French

folk music is in the fifth edition of Grove's *Dictionary of Music and Musicians*, under "Folk Music" in the subdivision on France (by C. Marcel-Dubois). Rodney Gallop, "Basque Songs from Soule," *Musical Quarterly*, XXII (1936), 458–69, and Violet Alford, "Dance and Songs in Two Pyrenean Valleys," *Musical Quarterly*, XVII (1931), 248–58, are interesting readings on the area common to France and Spain. A large and comprehensive collection of Spanish and Portuguese music is Kurt Schindler, *Folk Music and Poetry of Spain and Portugal* (New York: Hispanic Institute, 1941). The best discussion, in English, of Italian folk music is in Grove's *Dictionary of Music and Musicians*, fifth edition, the supplement volume (1960)—not the section on Italian folk music in the body of the fifth edition. Alberto Favara, *Corpus di Musiche Popolari Siciliane* (Palermo: Accademia di scienze, lettere e arti, 1957, 2 vols.) is a comprehensive collection from Sicily. Discussion of one song type appears in Wolfgang Laade, "The Corsican Tribbiera, a Kind of Work Song," *Ethnomusicology*, VI (1962), 181–85.

For selections of French, Hispanic, and Italian folk music, the appropriate disks from the *Columbia World Library of Folk and Primitive Music* are especially useful. Also to be recommended are *Folk Music of France*, Folkways P 414; *Folk Music from Italy*, Folkways F 4220; *Songs and Dances of Spain*, Westminster WF 12001–5, with notes by Alan Lomax; *Flamenco Music of Andalusia*, Folkways 4437; and *Music of Portugal*, Folkways 4538 (2 disks).

SEVEN

MUSIC OF BLACK AFRICA

The music of Black Africa has been regarded as an essentially homogeneous mass, despite the many inhabitants and the large number of distinct cultures, and despite the many contacts that Africa has had, over the centuries, with peoples of other continents. It is true that hearing a few records of African music will probably give the listener a fairly good overview of the mainstream of the African styles. But it has become increasingly clear that the total picture of African music is a very complex one, that there is a large variety of sub-styles, that cultures vary greatly in the nature of their music, in its quantity and significance, and in the attitudes that people hold towards music. As in other chapters, we must here confine ourselves to a few examples of the kinds of things that are found, realizing that the world of African music is still largely unknown to scholars, and that generalizations can be made only with great caution.

We are considering the music of Africa, south of the Sahara only, in this volume. The area north of the Sahara and the Sahara itself have music which is very closely related to that of the Middle East and is thus discussed in another volume in this series, William P. Malm's *Music Cultures of the Pacific, the Near East, and Asia.* But there has, of course, been a great deal of exchange between the North Africans and the inhabitants of Black Africa. Instruments, such as harps and drums, have evidently been carried from one area to the other; similar formal types and certain techniques, such as responsorial singing, are held in common. There are some peoples, at the boundary between the two areas, who have music in both the distinctly Black African and the North African styles. On the other hand, while North African music has ties with the Middle East, the music of Black Africa has had, in the past two or three centuries, an enormous impact on the musical development of Europe and the Americas.

The part of Africa discussed here—and, for the sake of brevity, we will call it simply "Africa" from now on—is composed of (or was, before parts of it became thoroughly modernized) four culture areas, each of which has considerable homogeneity, and each of which contrasts in some rather specific ways with its neighbors. The western part of the very tip of Southern Africa is called the Khoi-San area; it is inhabited by the Bushmen and Hottentots. The Bushmen are a somewhat different group, racially, from Negroes, shorter and lighter skinned; the Hottentots are evidently the result of a racial mixture between Bushmen and Negroes. The Khoi-San area has a simple culture dependent mainly on nomadic gathering of food.

The eastern part of our Africa, from Ethiopia southward, is called the Eastern Cattle Area. Its cultures are complex and revolve about cattle, one of the main sustaining forces of life and also the symbol of wealth. Some of the tribes are warlike; some, such as the Masai and Watusi, are very tall and rule over neighboring tribes of smaller stature, living near them and maintaining a caste-like relationship.

The southern coast of the western extension of the continent, which includes Ghana, Nigeria, Ivory Coast, and Liberia, is known as the Guinea Coast. This area lacks cattle and is characterized by elaborate political organization which, before the imposition of European rule, gave rise to powerful kingdoms. Carved masks of great beauty are also typical here. The Congo area, north of the Khoi-San area and centered in the Congo republics, has to some extent a combination of Eastern Cattle and Guinea Coast traits. It includes a number of Pygmy and Negrito tribes who live in relative isolation in the jungle. The Congo area probably has the most highly developed visual art tradition in Africa.

A fifth area that properly belongs to sub-Saharan Africa consists of a strip immediately north of the Guinea Coast, and includes the northern sections of such nations as Ghana and Nigeria. Its cultures are related to those of the Guinea Coast and the Congo, but many of the peoples who inhabit it are Muslims.

There are several characteristics, found in a majority of African musical cultures, that give African music its distinctiveness. Several of them are discussed in some detail further on, but here is a brief listing: (1) Instruments are numerous; they are used individually, as accompaniment to singing, and in small ensembles. (2) There is a tendency to have at least two things going on at a time. Thus polyphony is widespread; polyrhythms performed by percussion ensembles are common; and even the players of simple instruments, such as the musical bow or the flute, may find ways, by manipulating the overtones produced by the bow, or by humming along with blowing, for example, to have two musical entities produced simultaneously. (3) The percussive sound is evidently an ideal; percussion instruments such as drums, xylophones, rattles, etc., are important, but even in the use of wind instruments that are played in groups, with each producing only one tone, the percussive principle seems to be present, and plucked string instruments greatly outnumber those played with a bow. (4) Variation of and improvisation upon short melodic motifs dominate melodic structure. (5) There is a close relationship between language and music. (6) Melodies are built of major seconds and minor thirds. (7) Even more than elsewhere, music is associated with dance. (8) Perhaps most significant, there is a tendency toward dualism: thus melodies often consist of two phrases; performance is often by a leader and a chorus; polyphony is usually structured so that there are two parts or two groups of vocalists or instruments; and in various other obvious or subtle ways, one can detect the essentially binary nature of this music.

However, almost the opposite of these characteristics is found in the northernmost part of sub-Saharan Africa, where Middle Eastern influences are strong. Thus solo performances, monophony, nonpercussive instruments, such as fiddles and oboes, and smaller intervals, such as minor seconds, are more prominent. Some peoples, such as the Hausa of northern Nigeria, have music in both the typical African and the Middle East-influenced styles.

THE USES OF MUSIC IN AFRICA

In Africa, music has many uses. It functions as accompaniment to all sorts of activities, but also for entertainment. Some of the general characteristics usually given for music in nonliterate societies do not appear strongly in Africa. For example, the idea that participation in music in a primitive society is quite general and that all persons participate equally cannot be accepted. In contrast to many tribes elsewhere, there are professional musicians who actually make their living from music, or who are regarded as trained specialists. There are so many instruments that it would be ridiculous to think that all members of a tribe could perform on all of them and know all of the tribe's music. But it cannot be denied that Africans, on the whole, do participate in musical life much more—and more actively, in singing, playing, composing, dancing—than do members of Western civilization.

In at least some of the African cultures, elaborate classification of types of musicians exists. According to Merriam,[1] the Basongye of the Congo have five classes of male musicians: (1) the *ngomba*, the professional instrumentalist; (2) the performer of slit drums; (3) the player of rattles and double-bells; (4) the song leader; and (5) the member of a singing group. These are listed here in the order of their prestige; only the first is a full-time musician, the second and third also receive some pay, while the lowest two classes are never paid. Despite this evidence of concern with the relative status of various kinds of musicians, the Basongye generally do not regard musicians highly; and in this they reflect a tendency found in the majority of the world's cultures. Rather, they regard musicians as being of low status. Musicians are said to be heavy drinkers, debtors, unreliable, impotent, adulterers, poor marriage risks, and they are the butt of many jokes. People do not want their children to become musicians, but the musicians are nevertheless tolerated because they are essential to the life of the whole group. The picture presented by Merriam appears to be roughly similar to that of some other African cultures.

Obviously, also, Africans think about music a good deal. For example, some tribes recognize many different types of songs and have elaborate terms for them. Thus, according to Merriam, the Bahutu of Ruanda-Burundi have at least twenty-four different types of social songs, including "those played by professional musicians for entertainment, songs for beer drinking, war homage to a chief, hunting, harvesting, and general work; songs sung at the birth of a child or to admonish erring members of the society, to recount a successful elephant hunt, to deride Europeans; songs of death, vulgar songs, and others."[2] These categories are separate from the other large group of ceremonial or religious songs. Some of these types are again sub-divided by the Bahutu, who, for example, distinguish among different kinds of songs associated with

[1] Alan P. Merriam, *The Anthropology of Music* (Evanston, Ill.: Northwestern University Press, 1969), pp. 129–30.

[2] Merriam, "African Music," in *Continuity and Change in African Cultures*, ed. William Bascom and Melville J. Herskovits (Chicago: University of Chicago Press, 1959), p. 50.

canoes: different songs are used when paddling against a strong current, when paddling with the current, and so forth.

Also of Ruanda-Burundi, the Watusi, whose lives center about their cattle, have many song types involving them: "songs in praise of cows, songs to indicate the importance of having cows, songs for taking cattle home in the evening . . . for drawing water for the cattle,"[3] and the like. There are special children's cattle songs, songs to praise the royal cattle, and songs that recount historical events in which cattle have played a part. There are two points to remember here: This classification of songs is one developed by the Africans themselves; and the music is a part of those activities which are most fundamental in the culture. In this sense, perhaps, music in African life can be said to have a greater or more important role than it does in Western civilization.

It would be useless to attempt to catalogue all the uses of music in Black African music. In many ways they parallel those of European folk music. Religious and ceremonial music is an ever-present category whose importance evidently increases as we move from complex to simpler cultures. The large amount of music for entertainment, such as the playing of xylophones at markets, is remarkable. Social songs, such as those mentioned above, are a larger category than in most folk and nonliterate societies. The use of music for political purposes of various sorts should be noted. Examples of the association of music with political strata and with the ruling individuals or classes abound. Among the Hausa of Nigeria, elaborate fanfares are played for ruling chiefs. The "royal drums" of the Watusi signal the appearance of the ruler in public. And among the Venda of South Africa we find an elaborate system (by no means unique in its general character but similar to systems found elsewhere in Africa) of classifying musical types in accordance with the level of political leadership permitted to sponsor it. Evidently in some of the African cultures it is easier to indicate discontent with employers or with the government if the discontent is sung than if it is spoken. We therefore find many songs expressing criticism of authority, but also songs composed especially to praise chiefs and wealthy men. Songs are used also to spread information on current events of interest and gossip, and to perpetuate knowledge, much in the way that broadside ballads functioned as newspapers in eighteenth-century England and America. Work songs—songs not only dealing with labor but also accompanying rhythmic work by groups and making it easier—are prominent in Africa. In the Western Congo, song-like passages appear in the litigations of clans and individuals who may argue about ownership of territory, wives, or honorific titles.

---

[3] Merriam, "African Music," p. 53.

INSTRUMENTS OF AFRICA

One of the characteristics of Negro Africa is its enormous variety of musical instruments. Far from being a land only of drums, as it is pictured by some early sources, it is an area in which varied instruments and instrumental music play a role equal to that of the voice and vocal music. There is in all areas a great deal of music for solo instruments, and there are instrumental ensemble groups consisting of unrelated instruments, or of several instruments of the same type. Also, accompanied singing is widespread.

The importance of rhythm in African music can be seen in the percussive quality of much of the instrumental sound. As we have noted, percussion instruments—drums, rattles, and melodic percussion instruments such as the xylophone—occupy a major role. Among the wind instruments, those in which each pipe performs only one note (panpipes or *hocket*-type performance on flutes or horns) are important. Among string instruments, those that are plucked are more prominent than the bowed ones. The percussive nature of much of the instrumental sound as well as the absence of the possibility of *legato* in the playing of most of the instruments is probably caused by the desire for strong rhythmic articulation.

It is impossible to describe or even to name all African instruments; but some of the most important ones are discussed briefly in the next few paragraphs. Among the idiophones (instruments whose bodies vibrate in order to produce sound), the xylophone is one of the most widespread. Consisting of anywhere from seven to twenty-five slabs of wood, it varies greatly in size. The largest ones lie on the ground, supported by small tree trunks; the smallest hang around the player's neck. In Central Africa, xylophones are frequently built with calabashes, gourds, or other hollow bodies attached to the slabs in order to add to the resonance. They are frequently played in groups; in parts of Central Africa, three players will entertain at a market together. In the Eastern part of Southern Africa, among the Chopi, orchestras of six and more xylophones of various sizes are used. This point is of great interest, since there is some evidence for the belief that xylophones were brought to Africa from Indonesia, perhaps a thousand years ago. The people of Madagascar speak Malayo-Polynesian languages which must have originated near Indonesia. And for centuries the Indonesians have had a very complex musical culture with instruments made of metal, of the xylophone type. It seems possible that the xylophone was brought to

Africa, or that the musical culture of Indonesia influenced the particular direction in which xylophones and xylophone playing developed in Africa. Xylophones of the simplest type—one or two slabs of wood which are struck—are found throughout the world, including indigenous Latin America; this has evidently given rise to an erroneous belief that the xylophone (or rather, its form with resonators, the marimba) came from Central America and was brought thence to Africa.

One instrument that apparently originated in Africa, and which is related to the xylophone, is the *sansa* or *mbira*, which is sometimes also called the "thumb piano" or "kaffir harp." Its provenience is largely East and Central Africa, and, except for some Negro cultures in the Americas, it is not found outside Africa. It consists of a small board or wooden box on which is nailed a bridge. Tied to this bridge are a number of "keys," made usually of iron pieces pounded flat, but occasionally of reeds. These are gently plucked by the thumb or the fingers to produce a soft, tinkling sound. The number of keys varies from eight to about thirty. Frequently a calabash resonator is attached to the instrument; sometimes beads, which produce a rattling percussive accompaniment, are also attached. The *sansa* is played as a solo instrument or in groups. It is frequently used to accompany singing, and in some African music of recent origin it is used to play an ostinato accompaniment not too different from the piano accompaniments of certain Western popular songs. The tuning of both xylophone and *sansa* varies greatly. The keys of the *sansa* may be tuned by moving them forward or backward in relationship to the bridge, or by adding some pitch or tar to them in order to increase their weight.

Other idiophones include rattles, bells, and the misnamed log drums. There are many types of rattles—pebbles enclosed in small woven containers (West Africa) and in antelope ears (the Hottentots); rattles made of fruits, nuts, reeds, or cocoons strung together (South Africa); and so on. Sometimes they are tied to the ankles of dancers. One characteristic of these idiophones is the importance evidently placed on distinctions in pitch. Rattles and bells (there are both metal and wooden bells) often appear in pairs, with one smaller than the other so that two pitches can be distinguished. This is also characteristic in the playing of the log drum idiophone, a hollowed log with one or two slits, which is most frequently used for signaling. Thus, while the rhythmic element seems to be pronounced in the melodic aspects of music and its instruments, we may also say that the melodic aspects of music are developed in that music and those instruments whose main function is rhythm.

There are several types of true drums, that is, drums with skin heads. The most common kinds have one head and are relatively tall; they are usually closed at the bottom. Two-headed drums and drums

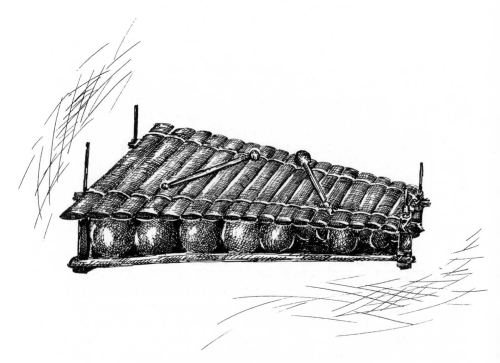

West African xylophone with gourd resonators.

Sansa or mbira.

with an open end are also found. The drums are beaten with sticks, or with the hands, or both. Hand beating is characteristic, however, and the complex rhythms are often the results of intricate manipulation and alternation of fingers, thumb, and heel of the hand. Techniques somewhat similar to those of Africa are found in India, and there is a possibility that the rhythmic intricacies of India and Africa have a common origin. Typically drums are played in groups of three or more. They may stand on the ground, hang from a strap around the player's shoulder, be held in the player's arm or between his legs, or be sat upon when they are played.

The types of drums and of drumming may be intimately associated with different activities. Among the Yoruba of Nigeria, different types of drums are used for the various cults associated with the numerous gods in the Yoruba pantheon. For example, the *igbin* drums are upright drums with a single head, open-ended, with small wooden legs; *dundun* are kettle-drums with the skin stretched across a small bowl; *bata* drums are long truncated cones with two heads, one head being appreciably smaller than the other and producing a higher pitch; and there are several other types. Each type is used for one or several deities, and each deity has its distinctive rhythms, a practice carried over into parts of the Americas such as Haiti. Thus, as Bascom notes,[4] the *igbin* drums are sacred to *Orishanla* ("the great deity") and are played by members of his cult, among whom are albinos, hunchbacks, and cripples. *Bata* and *dundun* drums are played by professional drummers. *Dundun* are used for signaling—they are the "talking drums"—they are also used by the cult of *Egungun*, younger brother of the powerful *Shango* (the thunder god). *Bata* are sacred to the god *Shango* and his wife *Oya*, but may be played for other deities as well.

Several types of aerophones (wind instruments) are of great interest. Horns are common in various parts of Negro Africa. They are made of natural horn, wood, or ivory, and are used for music as well as signaling. They usually have no finger holes or valve mechanism, and only the open or natural tones can be played. In recent times, however, finger holes seem to have been introduced. One characteristic of African horns is the position of the mouthpiece or hole used for blowing, which is frequently on the side of the instrument rather than at the small end as is common in European horns. One use of horns that produce only one pitch is in the *hocket* technique, in which each horn plays only when its note is supposed to appear in the melody.

---

[4] William Bascom, notes accompanying the record, *Drums of the Yoruba of Nigeria*, Folkways P441.

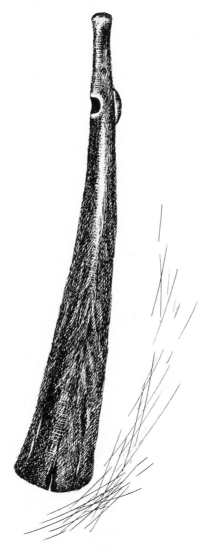

West African ivory horn.

Flutes are also frequently without finger holes; they are some-times used for performance in the *hocket* technique in a fashion similar to horns. This is done particularly by Negro tribes of South Africa. En-sembles of flutes with finger holes are also found, as among the Mambuti pygmies of the Congo, who use as many as six flutes, each of which varies its own short ostinato figure. The flutes are most commonly true flutes rather than the plugged flutes like the recorder. Both end-blown and transverse flutes are found, the former being held vertically. Pan-pipes are also present in most of Black Africa, but little is known of the music that they produce.

Many instruments have very specific and restricted uses. Thus the *epudi*, a kind of ocarina used by the Basongye of Kasai, is associated with hunting. It accompanies hunters' songs before and after the hunt, and it is used as a signaling device during the hunt. It has one finger hole and produces two tones, about a major second apart. Its major use in sig-naling is for reproduction of the tones of the language in ways similar to drum and horn signaling techniques.[5]

Africa has developed a large number of chordophones, or string instruments. The simplest is the musical bow, which normally has only one string but sometimes produces fairly complex music. It is found through Black Africa, but evidently has more forms in Southeast Africa than elsewhere. It is shaped essentially like a hunting bow whose string is plucked or struck with a stick, and its sound is soft. Thus a resonator is almost always required. It may be attached to the end of the bow or to its middle. In the latter case, the string is usually stopped at the point at which the resonator is attached, so that in effect two strings, with con-trasting pitch, are used. If the resonator is not attached, the bow may be held against an inverted pot. A third way of producing resonance is for the player to hold the end of the bow in his mouth, which then acts as the resonator. If he changes the configuration of his mouth, different over-tones can be heard. The bow is used as a solo instrument as well as an accompaniment to song.

There has evidently been a development from the musical bow, through single-string fiddles and lutes, to more complex stringed instru-ments; the most important ones among African Negroes are zithers (with several strings stretched across a board of hollowed block), harps (usually with four to eight strings), and fiddles (with one to five strings). The shapes, arrangements, and tunings of these are almost innumerable. For example, the Ganda of Uganda tune their harps into five roughly equal intervals, each of about 240 cents (100 cents equal a tempered semitone)

[5] Alan P. Merriam, "The Epudi, a Basongye Ocarina," *Ethnomusicology* VI (1962), 175–77.

or five quarter tones. The *lulanga* of the Bashi (Congo), a trough zither in which eight strings are stretched along a concave block of wood between two and three feet long, has a tuning using mainly major and minor seconds. Frequently the tunings and thus the music produced seem to have little relationship to the intervals and scales of vocal music. The harps of East Africa bear a close resemblance to those of ancient Egypt.

Instrumental ensembles in Africa exhibit enormous variety. Ensemble playing on a single instrument is found, as in the zither-playing of the Bashi, in which one man plays the strings and another, opposite him, raps rhythmically on the instrument with his knuckles, or in the playing of large xylophones by two men next to each other or opposite each other, in West Africa and the Congo. At the other extreme are the xylophone orchestras of the Chopi of South Africa; these consist of some thirty men who play in a heterophonic style, with a conductor. Between these extremes there are ensembles of many sorts. Some consist of several instruments of the same type, such as xylophones, *mbiras*, or drums. Others are heterogeneous, consisting, for example, of drums, rattles, and bells (West Africa) or *mbira*, zither, and rattle (Congo), and a great many other combinations.

The distribution of instrument types in Africa is broad. Many instruments are found in almost all parts of the continent south of the Sahara. Drums, xylophones, the *mbira*, are practically universal. Musical bows are widespread. Nevertheless, there seems to be a great variation in the specific instruments, and in their number, used in individual tribal groups, and even neighboring peoples sometimes exhibit substantial differences. Thus the Ganda of Buganada have an enormous store of instruments: many kinds of idiophones, from the simple percussion beam to rattles, bells, and xylophones; several types of musical bows, lyres, a tube fiddle and a harp; flutes, animal horns, gourd trumpets; and many kinds of drums. On the other hand, the Bashi of the Congo area have only a few instruments: two types of zithers, two types of *mbiras* or *sansas*, a flute, and one kind of drum.

MUSIC AND LANGUAGE IN AFRICA

All over the world, music and language interact; but in Africa, this interaction appears to be more intense than elsewhere. In addition to music in the proper sense of the word, the use of musical sounds for signaling purposes is common in Africa. The relaying of drum signals over a long distance is legendary; horns are also used for this purpose, and also, for more conversational ends over short distances. In some tribes, signaling takes on the character of Morse code, that is, arbitrary signals are used to indicate words or concepts. More frequently, however, the system of signaling is tied to the pitch structure of the language.

The languages spoken in Black Africa belong mainly to three families: Khoi-San, characterized by clicks in the throat and mouth, which is spoken by the Bushmen and Hottentots; Niger-Congo (including the Bantu group), which occupies most of the area through the Congo region and the Guinea Coast, and which is a closely knit group of languages clearly related to each other; and Sudanic, which is spoken in the northeastern region of Black Africa. Most of the Bantu and many of the Sudanic languages are tone languages; that is, the relative pitch at which a syllable is spoken helps determine the meaning of the word. Thus, in Jabo, a language spoken in Liberia, there are four "tones"; that is, four different relative pitch levels of speech are distinguished for purposes of meaning, which we can number from 1 to 4, highest to lowest. In Jabo, the word *ba* may mean four different things, depending on the pitch. *Ba* (1) means namesake, *ba* (2) means "to be broad," *ba* (3) means "tail," and *ba* (4) is a particle expressing command.[6] In signaling, the pitches of the words—or rather their internal relationship, for of course the language tones are not fixed pitches but are relative to the pitch of the surrounding syllables and the speaker's voice range—are transferred to the drum. Jabo signaling is done with two drums made of hollowed logs with slits, one large, the other smaller. They are not true drums, of course, but idiophones. The pitch on each drum varies according to the place at which it is struck. And, interestingly, the two lower tones of the language are combined into one tone on the large drum. The fact that many words or sentences have the same sequence of tones, and that in the drum language tones 3 and 4 are indistinguishable, would seem to make deciphering of messages difficult. Only a few men are qualified to signal, and only certain things may be said in signal language. Understanding must come from knowledge of the kinds of things likely to be signaled, and evidently the Jabo restrict themselves to expressing thoughts, such as, "Our neighbors are on the warpath," or, more appropriately in this period of modernization, "Hide! The tax collector approaches!"

Just what happens when words in a tone language are set to music for the purpose of creating song? Does the melody slavishly follow the pitch movement of the words? Or is there free melodic movement which violates and to some extent obscures the meaning of the words by ignoring the linguistic tones? Not too much is known about this intricate relationship between music and speech, but it is obvious that no simple

---

[6] George Herzog, "Speech-Melody and Primitive Music," *Musical Quarterly*, XX (1934), 453.

rule describes it. And it may well be that each tribal culture has evolved its own accommodation between language and music in song. It is evident, however, that melody does not slavishly follow speech, but that the tones of the words do have an influence on shaping the melody.

The Ibo in Nigeria, according to one kind of analysis, use two tones, high and low. If it were possible to formulate a rule for Ibo on the basis of a small sampling of songs, we would have to say that the musical pitch sometimes moves up and down in the same direction as the pitch in speech, and that it sometimes remains the same while the speech tones change, but that pitch movement in the music is hardly ever contrary to that of the language. On the other hand, an example from the Chewa in Central East Africa, where the language also has two tones (marked in Example 7-1 by acute and grave accents, respectively), indicates very

EXAMPLE 7-1. Chewa song, from George Herzog, "Speech-melody and Primitive Music," *Musical Quarterly* XX (1934), 457.

close correspondence. These samples are intended only to show some of the kinds of things that may be found; they should not be used to draw conclusions regarding the way tone languages are set to music throughout Africa.

Another example of the close relationship among music, language, and other activities appears in some of the xylophone music of the Jabo in Liberia. According to Herzog, one form of evening entertainment is the repeated playing of short phrases on large xylophones which consist of big slabs laid across banana tree trunks.[7] These phrases are ordinary music to most listeners, but to a few who have inside knowledge they are musical versions of the tone patterns of sentences commenting on current events or mocking a member of the tribe. The person being mocked may not realize it, and the audience may burst into laughter when a piece that makes fun of an oblivious bystander is played. Sometimes this music is performed by two players sitting on opposite sides of the xylophone. They may perform a single melody together, they may play a canon, or they may repeat a tiny contrapuntal piece based on the speech tones of two sentences or phrases.

[7] George Herzog, "Canon in West African Xylophone Melodies," *Journal of the American Musicological Society,* II (1949), 196–97.

GENERAL CHARACTERISTICS OF AFRICAN FORMS

The most striking thing about the forms of African music is their dependence on short units, and in many cases on antiphonal or responsorial techniques. Most African compositions do not have units as long as the stanzas of typical European folk songs. They consist of short phrases that are repeated systematically, or alternated, or on which are based longer melodies in which a motif reappears repeatedly in different forms. Typical of the brevity of the phrases is Example 7-1, which in actual performance was probably repeated many times.

In instrumental music, short forms of this type are also found distributed over a large part of Africa. Example 7-2, recorded in Johannesburg and performed on the musical bow, consists of a systematic repetition of a rhythmic phrase that uses only two fundamental pitches. The upper voice in Example 7-2 is produced by overtones, and it, of course, is varied; but the piece consists of the manifold repetitions of this phrase.

EXAMPLE 7-2. South African musical bow melody, from Charles M. Camp and Bruno Nettl, "The Musical Bow in South Africa," *Anthropos* L (1955), 75.

Solo performance is common enough in Africa, but the most characteristic African music is performed by groups with alternating performance techniques of various kinds. We say "characteristic" because this kind of performance is more developed in Africa than elsewhere, and because it is this element which, more perhaps than any other, has been retained in the Negro cultures of the New World. The simplest of these alternating techniques is responsorial singing, the alternation between a leader and a group which is sometimes also called the "call-and-response" technique. Example 7-3, from the Republic of the Congo (Brazzaville), shows what may frequently happen in such a form. Drums and an iron bell provide a constant rhythmic background whose general outline and meter remain the same, but whose accent patterns and specific note values vary somewhat. A female soloist sings a two-measure phrase alternating with a two-measure monophonic phrase sung by a group of women. The two phrases are different in content, but are similar at the cadence.

Improvisation is an important feature in many African styles. Evidently there is some real improvisation—that is, the creation of music without the use of pre-existing models as the basis—but this seems to be rare. More common is improvisation in which a tune is varied as it is being performed. The forms, consisting of short phrases that are repeated many times, lend themselves especially well to this kind of improvisation, since it is possible for a singer to begin with the standard version of a tune and then to improvise variations that depart increasingly from the standard. This is what happens in the successive repetitions of the soloist's phrase in Example 7-3. The members of the chorus also improvise variations, but they do not depart as much from the original.

A further result of improvisation, presumably, is the creation of polyphonic forms. One of the characteristics of African music is har-

EXAMPLE 7-3. Kuyu (Congo) women's dance, from Rose Brandel, *The Music of Central Africa* (The Hague: M. Nijhoff, 1962), p. 197.

mony and polyphony, which are discussed below. Here it is relevant to point out that improvisation in choral and ensemble performance adds to the number of pitches heard at one time. Thus the fact that improvisation and variation are encouraged in some African cultures seems to have influenced the degree to which polyphony is accepted. Actually, variation by improvisation seems to be considered the mark of good musicianship in some African cultures. We should mention also a feature found in some African music that involves both form and polyphony, namely the tendency, in some pieces, for a number of apparently unrelated things to be going on at the same time. Some of this is due to the development of complex rhythmic polyphony, the simultaneous presentation of several rhythms which seem, to the Western listener, to have little in common. It is hard to say whether the African listener feels all of these rhythms to be part of one overall rhythmic structure (as a Westerner can conceive all of the voices in a Bach fugue to be independent yet united), or whether the African conceives of music as consisting of the simultaneous presentation of unrelated phenomena. At any rate, it is possible, in such a piece, to have phrases and other units of varying lengths appearing in different voices or instruments.

The performances are at least in some cases intricately structured, despite the fact that they may consist only of repetitions and variations upon a short theme. In the music performed on the *mbira*, or *sansa*, in Southern Africa (as illustrated and described in detail on the recording, *Mbira Music of Rhodesia*) the repetitions and variations on a basic theme are grouped into nine steps or stages. The *mbira* player begins by playing the basic chords of the underlying harmony; then, in the second section, he varies them slightly; and in the third step, he takes the basic chords and creates an accompanying melody out of them, playing their tones in alternation rather than together. This third step is considered the basic pattern which dominates the piece. In the fourth step, we find more and faster separation of the notes, rhythmic changes, and the addition of the singing voice. There is a climax at the end of this section, which is followed by variations on the vocal melody in the fifth and sixth steps. In the fifth, the singer introduces a yodel-like technique. Steps 7, 8, and 9 are more or less identical with the first three steps, presented in reverse order. Each of these stages has a name. The details of the sections, their length and specific content, may be improvised, but the form of the performance is essentially set.

Thus forms rivaling in sophistication those of European art music and the Far East are found in Africa, and they are built upon the basic formal principles of brevity, repetition and variation, binary structure, and improvisation. The amount of repetition and variation may be determined by the performer's interaction with his audience or by the needs of the activity which the music accompanies. Composite forms, consisting of series of pieces, are particularly common in ceremonial situations, where a large group of pieces, which may take a day or longer, must be performed in correct order. Perhaps the most complex forms are the suites performed by the xylophone orchestras of the Chopi, for here we find structures of six to eight related movements, each of which is cast in a mold similar to that of the *mbira* pieces described above.

MELODY

So far as the melodic elements of music are concerned, African music seems generally rather intelligible to the Western listener; it does not really have the exotic sound that some Oriental and some American Indian music has at first hearing. The conclusion we may tentatively draw from this fact is that African music, on the whole, fits more or less into the diatonic scheme that is also the basis of most Western art and folk music.

There have been attempts to identify a truly "African" scale. Ballanta-Taylor, an early West African scholar, believed that the basic scale of West African music has sixteen tones per octave, and statements regarding the importance of pentatonic scales in Africa have been made. But the consensus of scholars is that there is no single system, that exact measurement of intervals would produce—at least in vocal music—a clustering about the intervals found also in diatonic scales, and that in many ways the kind of melodic structure in Africa corresponds to that of European folk music. As in Europe, so in Africa, we find songs with few tones (ditonic and tritonic scales). There are pentatonic tunes with minor thirds and major seconds, and there are pentachordal ones as well. There are heptatonic songs, and there are occasional chromatic pieces. There are, moreover, intervals that do not fit into the diatonic scheme, such as neutral thirds (as are found also in Europe). There is, finally, a reported tendency in the heptatonic songs to use the intervals of minor third and minor seventh above the tonic. Our interest in this feature stems from certain phenomena of jazz (the lowered seventh is one "blue note"), but it seems doubtful that these intervals constitute a special feature common to all African music. The fact that glides and ornaments are common in some African singing techniques also adds to the difficulty of defining a specific scale structure. Thus we must content ourselves with the generalization that African scales are varied but that as a group they seem to be closely related to those of Europe.

Types of melodic movement also exhibit great variety. In one area, Central Africa, we find the following kinds described by Brandel:[8] melodies clustering around a nucleus of one or two tones; melodies based on the perfect fourth, either descending directly from one tone to another a fourth below it, or making use also of the intervening tones; melodies built on the tones of the triad, and others using a whole string of thirds with only occasional use of intervening tones; melodies built on the triad with an added sixth (♪); melodies with the augmented fourth predominating, sometimes made up of three major seconds in a row (♪); and melodies with the range of an octave or more, in which the lowest tone and its upper octave are the most important.

The melodic contours also have various types. Rather large ranges seem to be characteristic of Africa. Europe has many songs with a range of less than a fifth, relatively few (except for what appears to be recent material) with a range much larger than an octave. In African Negro music the number of pieces with a large range seems to be somewhat greater. Melodies move predominantly in three ways: (1) in a mildly undulating fashion, beginning on a low tone, rising gradually to a somewhat higher level, and returning to the low tone; (2) beginning on a high tone and descending; and (3) tracing a pendulum-like movement, swinging rapidly back and forth between high and low tones. Example 7-4 illustrates this pendulum-like movement; it also exemplifies the melodies made up largely of strings of thirds, discussed above.

EXAMPLE 7-4. Batwa Pygmy song (Ruanda), from Rose Brandel, *The Music of Central Africa* (The Hague: M. Nijhoff, 1962), p. 70.

Tone systems in African music are sometimes very restricted. The music of the Xhosa, a large group of people living at the tip of South Africa, lies almost entirely within the framework of a pentatonic scale, with minor thirds and major seconds. The melodies are almost always rather sharply descending. The tunes very frequently consist of two phrases, which are similar, identical, or analogous, the second phrase centering about a tone a major second below the tonal center of the first phrase.

[8] Rose Brandel, *The Music of Central Africa* (The Hague: Martinus Nijhoff, 1962).

The music of the Mbuti Pygmies of the Congo is largely built on a pentatonic scale consisting again of major seconds and minor thirds, but with the two thirds adjacent (e.g.,). On the other hand, in some other African cultures there appears to be a wide variety of scale types and a rather complex tone system. In instrumental music, of course, melodic movement is more specialized, for each instrument invites certain kinds of movement, range, and interval. Thus melodies played on the musical bow are likely to have a small range and use a melodic type clustering about one or two notes that are close together; horn music is likely to use larger intervals, while pendulum-like melody is more easily suited to the xylophone. We should also mention in this connection the great variety of tone colors achieved by the human voice. Yodeling, growling, raucous tones, and tense as well as relaxed singing are found. The imitation of animal cries and sounds of nature are also a part of vocal music in Africa. In general, Black African singing is relaxed, open-throated, and full-bodied, very much in contrast to the tense and tighter sounding Middle Eastern singing style found in the North. It is also usually unornamented and straightforward.

RHYTHM

The feature of African music that has been most widely discussed is rhythm, and obviously it has indeed been more highly developed in Africa than have some other features or elements of music, such as melody and form. To some extent we may say that African rhythm is also more highly developed than the rhythm of other cultures. The latter statement must be made with caution, of course, for certainly it would be possible for a composer of Western music to put together a piece with a rhythmic structure much more complex than that of any African piece. He could do this because he can use notation. It is, however, very difficult for a Western musician to reproduce or even to comprehend the more complex African rhythmic structures with the use of his ear alone. The level at which African music seems to be rhythmically more developed is that of listener and performer perception. It is doubtful whether a Western listener could, without special training, perceive and reproduce the most complex structures in Western music, especially without a score, simply from sound. With training he might, of course, learn to match the performance and perception of African musicians. But this sort of training is not present in our culture, while it is—though not always formally—a part of African Negro musical training, for both the listener and the performer.

The rhythm of African music must be approached from two points of view. First, we are interested in the rhythmic structure (and its complexity) in a single melodic line. Here the rhythm and meter are usually not too difficult to understand. Metric structure with regular beats appears to be the rule. Once beats are established it is possible to identify that widely discussed element, syncopation, which results from the regular articulation of notes at points other than the beginnings of beats. A distinctive feature of West African music that seems to have been carried over in Negro music of the New World is the ability of musicians to keep the same tempo for minutes and hours. Waterman refers to this ability (which no doubt is learned, not inherited) as the "metronome sense." We will never know, of course, whether such strict adherence to tempo has ever been practiced in Western music. Certainly in Western cultivated music in the twentieth century it is not found, something one can easily prove by playing a symphony recording and keeping time with a metronome. Rigid adherence to tempo may have made possible the considerable variety of rhythmic motifs and patterns in African music, for the musician who has a steady beat in his mind, and who does not deviate from it, can perhaps more easily elaborate the details of the rhythm. The compelling nature of rhythm is recognized in West African terminology, where the term "hot," applied to rhythmic drumming, evidently originated.[9] "Hot" rhythm in West Africa is particularly important in ceremonial music, and the more exciting the rhythm, the "hotter" the music is said to be.

The more spectacular rhythmic complexity of African Negro music appears, however, in the rhythmic polyphony, the superimposition of several rhythmic structures. Its most obvious manifestation is found in drumming, but of course it is also present in the combination of several voices or, more frequently, of instruments with voices. There is a great deal of drumming, but in other ways also, the music seems to be dominated by a percussive quality. Individual tones in singing are attacked strongly without a semblance of *legato*. There are few instruments on which one can slur notes together, and generally the music is vigorously accented. Thus the importance of drumming can perhaps be traced to the need for strong rhythmic articulation.

The perception of various simultaneous meters seems to be widespread among Africans. Rhythmic polyphony of a rather complex type

---

[9] Richard A. Waterman, " 'Hot' Rhythm in Negro Music," *Journal of the American Musicological Society,* I (1948), 25f.

can be performed by a single person who may sing in one meter and drum in another. The superimposition of duple and triple meters, one type of hemiola rhythm, is evidently a basic ingredient of much West and Central African rhythmic polyphony.

In music using three or more drums, the rhythmic polyphony is developed to its most complex level. While such music can be mechanically notated in a single meter, the various drummers are actually performing with independent metrical schemes; one drum may use duple, one triple, a third quintuple meter. Moreover, if the several drums or other instruments use the same basic metric scheme (such as 3/8), the beginning of the unit or measure may not come at the same time in all of the drums; thus we may have the following combination: 3/8, 5/8, 7/8, as in Example 7-5, which is a sample of Yoruba drumming with the pitch variations of the individual drums omitted.

EXAMPLE 7-5. Yoruba drumming in honor of Ogun (god of war). The top part is the smallest and highest drum, the lowest part, the largest and lowest drum. From Anthony King, "Employment of the 'standard pattern' in Yoruba Music," *African Music II*, no. 3 (1960), 53.

Percussion ensembles of various types are important in the Guinea Coast area of Africa. Typically, they consist of drums, rattles, and bells. Let us examine, as an example, the Abadja rhythm, used in social songs of the Ewe people of Ghana. Three drums of various pitches (each with one skin), several large gourd rattles, and two double-bells are used. The instruments enter in order, each playing its own rhythmic pattern without change, beginning with the bells, followed by the rattle, and finally by the drums. The last to enter is the master drum, which improvises against the consistent rhythmic background produced by the others, using motifs from their patterns, combining and rearranging them. The first bell is regarded as having the fundamental rhythm. The rhythms could be reduced to a common 12/8 meter, but the Ghanaian listener is more interested in the interaction of the various rhythms and hears them as individual entities rather than as "rhythmic chords." Thus the various instruments begin their patterns at various points, not simultaneously, and there is tension between those which are essentially in 6/8 and those that appear to be in 3/4 meter. Example 7-6 gives the patterns of all but the master drum (which does not play only a single pattern in its performance).

The melodic element in drumming, as illustrated by the "royal drums" of the Watusi, which accompany the supreme chief whenever he emerges from his tent, is also important; drums used together always contrast in size and thus in pitch, and it is possible to follow each drum individually. In music using several melodic instruments, or voices and instruments, the structure of the rhythm is as complex as it is in the drumming, and the various voices often perform in different meters. To what extent the performers are listening to each other cannot always be ascertained, and to what degree an African listener perceives the total rhythmic structure is also unknown. An important feature of West African rhythmic polyphony, and perhaps a major key to its understanding, is the hemiola concept. The juxtaposition of three beats against two, and of more complex rhythms composed of these units, both simultaneously and in alternation, is the basis of a great deal of this music; it can be found, for instance, in Example 7-6, in which the *kidi* drum performs a rhythm that can be reduced to 3/4, and the *kagan* drum another in 6/8, while the rattle alternates these two meters in its short repeated phrase.

EXAMPLE 7-6. Abadja rhythm, used in Ghana. After William K. Amoakn.

POLYPHONY

Closely related to rhythmic polyphony and to the problem of perception of a group of individual rhythmic lines as a unit is the field of polyphony at large, and the question is whether in Africa several voices are perceived independently or as a single vertical harmonic structure.

Whether it is polyphony or really harmony, it is very well developed in African Negro music. And it appears in many media. There is choral singing, usually in the responsorial form. There is instrumental music of an orchestral nature, with a number of instruments of the same type playing together. And there is something similar to chamber music —instruments of different types playing together, alone or along with singing. Drumming and other percussion may of course act as accompaniment. Finally, there is also the concept of accompaniment for singing. There is polyphony of many types, and it seems to be present throughout the African Negro area, although concentrated in the Eastern cattle area and the Congo or Central Africa.

The fact that many kinds of polyphony are present in Africa, and that this also seems to be the case elsewhere in the world where polyphony is found, strengthens our belief that polyphony is a unified concept. When a culture discovers or learns to perform polyphony it seems to learn several different kinds. There are cultures with no polyphony at all, but there are few, if any, that use, for example, only parallel fifths and nothing else.

Most African polyphony belongs to two types: that in which all of the voices use the same melodic material, and that which comes about through the peculiarities of the instruments. In the former category we find, of course, parallelism. There are parallel thirds, fourths, fifths, and occasionally sixths, but other intervals seem to be rare. In the case of parallel thirds, alternation between major and minor thirds is usual, made necessary by the diatonic seven-tone scales which, as we have said, are common in Africa. Parallel fourths and fifths seem to be more common in East Africa, while thirds and sixths seem to dominate in the Congo and Guinea Coast areas. Parallelism is rarely completely exact, for the tendency to improvise seems to militate against slavish following of one voice by another.

Example 7-7 illustrates parallelism among the Thonga of South Africa. A chorus of men and women is led by a female soloist and accompanied by a musical bow, which also plays interludes between the stanzas. The player of the musical bow, which is evidently limited to the

EXAMPLE 7-7. South African choral song with musical bow, from Charles M. Camp and Bruno Nettl, "The Musical Bow in Southern Africa," *Anthropos* L (1955), 80.

tones D, E, and F, plays the melody along with the soloist and with the second part of the chorus, but switches to an approximation of the highest part of the chorus when his range permits it.

African music also possesses rounds, which often seem to have come about through antiphonal or responsorial singing. For example, if leader and chorus use the same tune, the chorus may become overanxious and fail to wait for the leader to finish his turn, and a round of sorts is born. The fact that many African rounds do have the entrance of the second voice near the end of the first voice's rendition of a tune points to this matter of origin; so also does the fact that most known African rounds have only two voices. Also resulting from the antiphonal technique is the kind of polyphony in which one voice sustains a tone, perhaps the final tone of its phrase, while the other voice performs a more rapidly moving melody, at the end of which it, in turn, holds a long note while the first voice performs a moving part. This gives rise to a sort of drone relationship between the voices.

In Southern Africa, where polyphony appears to be most wide-spread, we find a type of relationship among the voices that appears to be similar to the Western harmonic system in its eighteenth- and nineteenth-century manifestations. The compositions are, as one might expect, in two sections, each consisting of a melody, sometimes accompaniment as well, and sometimes of several intertwined melodies. In most cases, however, the material in each section revolves about one triad, and the relationship of the two triads is analogous to the relationship between a dominant and a tonic chord, although the roots of the two African chords are separated not by a fourth or a fifth but by a major second. The consistent harmonic movement, however, justifies the hypothesis that here we have a harmonic system that dominates the music much as harmony dominates Western music.

There is also a relationship between the voices that could be called real counterpoint, but this seems to appear most frequently in instrumental music, where the structure of the instrument may in itself be conducive to certain melodic patterns and devices. Thus the accompaniment of singers on a harp, a xylophone, or a *mbira* (see page 131) may have nothing to do melodically with the tune of the singers. In the case of accompaniment, an "ostinato" relationship between voices and instruments is frequent. A short bit, perhaps a two-measure phrase, is repeated (with variations) by the instruments, while the singer or singers perform a longer melody which, however, is also repeated with improvised variations. This sort of structure is similar, of course, to that of much Western music, especially of popular or folk provenience; and Africans in the cities, who have come under the influence of Western popular music, have composed songs in which the African sort of accompaniment by an ostinato figure, with a very short stanza by the singer, is used. We will have occasion to discuss the results of combining Western and African elements in the New World; but here is an example of the same sort of things in modern Africa. In both places, those features in African music which are highly developed but which have a European counterpart seem to be preserved in the acculturated music of Africans and Afro-Americans.

REGIONAL VARIATION IN BLACK AFRICAN MUSIC

We have noted the fact that each African tribe has its own songs and music, and that each tribe may differ in its musical style from its

neighbors. On the other hand, we have also cited a number of characteristics present in Black African music as a whole. These characteristics are
not equally pronounced in each tribe or each area. Just as there are culture areas in Africa, there are also music areas, regions in which the
musical style is more or less homogeneous, and which contrast with their
neighboring areas in some specific way. The music areas coincide, on the
whole, with the culture areas, and this is not surprising when we consider
the essential roles of music in the culture as a whole. Thus Merriam[10]
recognizes the following music areas: the Khoi-San area (Bushmen and
Hottentots), East Africa, Central Africa (mainly the Congo region), and
the West Coast (plus several areas in the northern part of the continent
that are largely under the influence of Islamic musical culture). The four
areas we have mentioned comprise the main body of Black African music.
To them should be added the music of the Pygmies, who live in various
isolated parts of central Africa surrounded by Negro groups but whose
music is a distinctive unit. The differences among these groups are expressed not in clear-cut dichotomies but rather in statistical terms. What
may be found in one area is also present in another, but with a markedly
different degree of frequency or complexity.

The main characteristics of the West Coast are the metronome
sense and the accompanying concept of "hot" rhythm, the simultaneous
use of several meters, and the responsorial form of singing with overlap
between leader and chorus. The Central African area is distinguished by
its great variety of instruments and musical styles and by the emphasis,
in its polyphony, on the interval of the third. East Africa has, for centuries,
been somewhat under Islamic influence, though by no means to as great
an extent as the northern half of Africa. Vertical fifths are more prominent here, and rhythmic structure is not so complex, nor are percussion
instruments so prominent. The development of a sense of harmony seems
likely. The Khoi-San music area is evidently similar in style to East
Africa, but has simpler forms and instruments. It contains a good deal of
music performed with the *hocket* technique, as does the Pygmy sub-area
of Central Africa, which is also characterized by the presence of a vocal
technique similar to yodeling.

We have been describing those aspects of African Negro music
which seem to have developed without influence from other cultures, or
of which Africans have made a specialty. But outside influence is not
just a recent phenomenon in African music. Thus it shares some traits
with European folk music, indicating perhaps a period of contact many
centuries ago. Also, contact with Indonesian music seems likely, and the
influence of the Near East and possibly of India is ancient and has in-

[10] Alan P. Merriam, "African Music," p. 77.

Central African musical, bow, played with mouth of resonator.

creased greatly in the last few centuries. Western culture has also played a part for centuries and has grown especially in the last hundred years. Thus we find African music now—and it has probably always been this way to a degree—in a state of change, and it is both difficult and perhaps useless to try to single out unchanged elements. On the contrary, it behooves us to observe the changes as they take place, for this is the way to study music as a living phenomenon. We find that some tribes have almost completely changed to music in a Near Eastern style. We find that others have retained, in part, a repertory of "pure" African music but have added to it songs in an Arabic style; this is true of the Watusi, who have solo drumming of a kind unknown in the Near East but also songs strongly reminiscent of Arabic music, and of the Hausa. We find North and Latin American popular songs known in tribes that otherwise perform aboriginal songs. And we find that because of the improvement of communication and transportation as well as through the growth of unified African nations on a supratribal level, African tribal groups are learning more from each other, musically and otherwise, than they did before.

Like music everywhere, African music has changed rapidly in the twentieth century, particularly because of the increased contact with Western music and musical thought, and with Western technology such as is exhibited in the mass media. Africans hear much of their music on records and on the radio, and the degree of general participation in musical activities appears to be declining. They hear the music of different tribal groups, and they have created popular musical styles by combining their resources and mixing them with Western elements. The very popular high-life style of West Africa is such a combination, and throughout Africa one can find music which is essentially Western, but which retains those elements of African music that are most developed and most prominent. There have also been attempts, sometimes resulting from the increasing nationalism of the various new nations of the continent and sometimes from an antiquarian attitude, to preserve old forms, and the interest in African music has been stimulated by institutions of recent origin, such as contests among xylophone orchestras among the Chopi of South Africa. Thus African music continues as a lively and ever-changing art; but its most important features seem to remain relatively constant even in the face of the onslaught of Westernization.

We should not leave a discussion of African music without mentioning its enormous impact on much of the world's music in the last hundred years. Its chief characteristics have been brought to the Americas and form the basic elements of all types of Afro-American performance practice. It is less well known that Africans who were brought to various parts of the Old World over the past several hundred years also brought with them much musical material. Thus, for example, the folk music of the Persian Gulf area has many African characteristics, and their origin is attested to by the presence of many individuals of African racial type. Most important, however, the main distinguishing features of the popular musics of the Western world, and of jazz, are ultimately of African origin.

BIBLIOGRAPHY AND DISCOGRAPHY

Several publications by Alan P. Merriam discuss sub-Saharan African music as a unit: "African Music" in *Continuity and Change in African Cultures,* edited by William J. Bascom and Melville J. Herskovits (Chicago: University of Chicago Press, 1958); "Characteristics of African Music," *J-IFMC,* XI (1959), 13–19; and 'The African Idiom in Music," *Journal of American Folklore,* LXXV (1962), 120–30. George Herzog, "Speech-Melody and Primitive Music," *Musical Quarterly,* XX (1934), 452–66, is an excellent discussion of tone languages and their relationship to music. Regional studies of African music are not numerous. As samples we might mention J. H. Kwabena Nketia, *African Music in Ghana* (Evanston, Ill.: Northwestern University Press, 1963), for West Africa; and Rose Brandel, *The Music of Central Africa* (The Hague: M. Nijhoff, 1962), for Central Africa. Sir Percival Kirby, *The Musical Instruments of the Native Races of South Africa* (London: Oxford University Press, 1934) is a classic on the instruments and their musical styles in one area. A book profusely illustrated, dealing with instruments, in Bertil Söderberg, *Les Instruments de Musique au Bas-Congo et dans les Régions Avoisinantes* (Stockholm: Ethnographic Museum of Sweden, 1956).

Many excellent records of African music are available. A survey is presented on *Africa South of the Sahara,* edited by Harold Courlander, Folkways FE 4503 (2 disks). South and East Africa are represented on a constantly growing set of records, now already over 200 disks in number, published by the International Library of African Music, Johannesburg: *The Sound of Africa.* It is accompanied by detailed notes on a large set of catalog cards. The Central African area is well represented on *Voice of the Congo,* edited by Alan P. Merriam, Riverside RLP 4002; *Music of Equatorial Africa,* Folkways P 402; *Folk Music of the Western Congo,* Folkways P 427. West African drumming in its many varieties is illustrated in *Drums of the Yoruba of Nigeria,* Folkways P 441. The music of Madagascar is illustrated on *Valiha, Madagascar,* Ocora OCR 18. *Mbira* music of South Africa is found in *Mbira Music of Rhodesia,* performed by Abraham Dumisani Maraire, University of Washington Press 1001. The area which combines Black and North African elements is exemplified on *Ethiopia,* Anthology Records AST 6000, and *Nigeria-Hausa Music I,* Unesco Records BM 30 L 2306. *Voice of the Congo* also includes examples of modern African music that combine traditional and Western elements.

EIGHT

THE AMERICAN INDIANS

This and the following chapters discuss the folk and traditional musics of the Americas. The American continents possess a great wealth of traditional music. That of the American Indians has been in existence for a long time, though no doubt in constantly changing forms. Other repertories have been brought from other continents, mainly Europe, and preserved more or less intact. Still other musics of the Americas began as offshoots from these imported traditions, then developed into independent styles with their own character and internal dynamics; this is true particularly of the various Afro-American traditions. Some musical repertories in the Americas came about through interaction and fusion of older musics which were found here or brought from elsewhere. And finally, although it would be difficult to state unequivocally that there are traditions in the Americas that grew up entirely without influence from older, Indian, African, or European musics, there are some styles that can be said to be in real essence American.

It seems logical to discuss the music of the Americas in three categories; (1) the music of the Indians, which is a tradition relatively undisturbed by the influx of other music; (2) the Afro-American musics, whose main characteristic is the combination of styles which were originally widely separated and highly distinctive; and (3) the folk music of peoples of European origin—Spanish and Portuguese, English, French, German, and Eastern European—which is characterized by the retention of archaic forms no longer known in their original home as well as by the development of distinctive offshoots of the European models.

There is little doubt any more that the American Indians came from Asia, across the Bering Straits, in several or many separate waves, beginning some 50,000 years ago; that they are Mongoloid in race; and that the simplest tribes were pushed to the edges of the area (Tierra del Fuego, for example) and into relatively undesirable spots such as the jungles of Brazil and Bolivia, the Great Basin area of Nevada and Utah, and the tundra of North Canada and the icy wastes of the Polar area. While we realize that in 50,000 years there must have occurred a great deal of change in the styles and uses of Indian music, and while we know practically nothing about the music of East Asia of thousands of years ago, it is still possible to discover certain similarities between Indian and Oriental music, and especially between the musics of the Eskimos and of the Paleo-Siberian tribes living in easternmost Siberia. These similarities involve emphasis on melody rather than on polyphony, some use of relatively large intervals (thirds and fourths) in the melodies, and, possibly, a rather strained, tense-sounding vocal production. On the other hand, there are many different styles and style areas in North and South America, and music of the simplest sort as well as musical cultures of great complexity are found. The latter had largely disappeared by the time ethnomusicologists became competent to deal with them and they can be studied only by archeological techniques; but some of the simplest styles are still with us. The size of the Indian population seems always to have been small; north of Mexico there were probably never more than one or two million, while South and Middle American Indians apparently never exceeded about five million. That such a small number of people developed so varied and intensive a musical culture is a fact that should inspire in the modern reader a good deal of respect. Except for the similarity among the simplest tribes in both continents, there is today a great difference between South and North American Indians as a whole: The South American tribes, for the most part, have been absorbed into the Hispanic-American cultures, to which they have contributed greatly, and whose music they have to a large degree adopted; thus, for knowledge of their aboriginal music, we must depend on a few isolated tribes. The North American tribes have generally remained more separate from their white and Negro compatriots and seem to have preserved earlier musical styles to a much greater degree. For this reason, and because South American Indian music is not yet well known, our emphasis in this chapter must be on the North American Indians.

THE SIMPLEST STYLES: EXAMPLES FROM BOLIVIA AND CALIFORNIA

Among some Indian tribes we find music as simple as any in the world. Melodies with only two or three tones, and with a single phrase which is repeated imprecisely many times, can be found in several areas. The Sirionó of Bolivia are an interesting example,[1] for they contradict one of the truisms often repeated about the "earliest" music: rather than fulfilling ritual functions, it seems to be used mainly for entertainment. The Sirionó have no instruments and only a few simple tunes. They sing in the evening after dark, and in the morning, in their hammocks, before beginning the day's activities. The words of the songs are evidently improvised and deal with all kinds of events, past and present, assuming in a way the role of conversation. The songs usually have descending melodic contour and are sung with a "decrescendo" as the singer's breath runs out. Curiously, it seems that each member of the tribe has one tune that is the basis of all the songs he sings. He makes up different words but uses one and the same tune, possibly throughout his life. Even in such a simple musical culture there are some individuals who are said to be superior singers and who teach the young people to sing. Example 8-1 illustrates a Sirionó song.

Similarly simple styles are found in the music of some tribes of

EXAMPLE 8-1. Sirionó Indian song, from Mary Key, "Music of the Sirionó (Guaranian)," *Ethnomusicology,* VII (1963), 20.

repeats many times

[1] Mary Key, "Music of the Sirionó (Guaranian)," *Ethnomusicology* VII (1963), 17–21.

Northern California. Detailed analysis of the songs in such a repertory may reveal, however, that within the severe limitations that the composers in a tribe place upon themselves there is a great deal of variety and sophistication. The last "wild" Indian, Ishi, who was discovered alone in 1911, the last living member of the Yahi tribe, and who sang all of the songs that he knew for anthropologists at the University of California Museum of Anthropology before he died in 1916, provides an interesting example. The songs of Ishi are all extremely short—five to ten seconds of music, repeated many times—and they use two, three, or four tones (in very rare cases, five) within a range of a fourth or fifth. Most of the songs consist of two or three short phrases, related to each other in various ways. The second phrase may be a variation of the first, an inversion, an extension, a condensation. A large number of different kinds of relationship between two or three short bits of music are exhibited; the composers had done everything possible, as it were, to provide musical variety and interest within the strict limitations that tradition had placed on them. Example 8-2 illustrates two of the songs of Ishi.

EXAMPLE 8-2. Two Yahi Indian songs, sung by Ishi, from Bruno Nettl, "The Songs of Ishi," *The Musical Quarterly* LI (1965), 473, 474.

USES OF INDIAN MUSIC:
AN EXAMPLE FROM THE PLAINS

In their traditional culture, Indian tribes with more complex kinds of musical culture usually had several types of songs, each of which was associated with different activities. For example, the Arapaho Indians of the North American Plains had ceremonial and secular songs. Among the former, the most elaborate are the songs of the Sun Dance, a ceremony performed in the summer, when the various bands of the tribe came together after being separated all winter. The Sun Dance involves the search for a vision in which the individual warrior receives a guardian spirit. The vision is brought on by self-torture and by dancing around a pole while looking at the bright sun for hours. With the exception of the Ghost Dance and Peyote songs which are discussed below, all of the

Arapaho songs are very much alike; they consist of two sections, each descending in a terrace-like contour; they have a range greater than an octave and scales of four, five, or six tones; and they are sung with great tension on the vocal chords and with rhythmic pulsations on the long notes. Even though they sound much alike, the various types of songs have certain individual characteristics. Thus the Sun Dance songs are a bit longer than the rest; have a slightly larger average range (about a twelfth); and their final phrase, in the last repetition at a performance of a song, is sung by the women alone. Songs learned in visions are another type, and songs belonging to the various age-grade societies, a third. (Each man was a member of one of seven age-grade societies, with elaborate initiations and with particular duties in war; as he aged he was promoted from one society to the next.) Among the secular songs, we may mention various types of social dance songs—the snake dance, turtle dance, round dance, and rabbit dance. Each has minor characteristics distinguishing it: The round dance songs are usually in rollicking triple meter; the rabbit dance—danced by couples and evidently introduced after contact with the whites—has songs that ordinarily begin with descending fourths. There are war songs intended to inspire warriors, and others used to recount events in recent battles. There are also songs said to be taught by the guardian spirit, which the recipient is to sing only when he is near death. Also, there are children's songs, lullabies, and love songs.

Finally we must mention two types of songs recognized as separate genres by the Arapaho and by other Plains tribes, the Ghost Dance and Peyote songs. The Ghost Dance is a religion that was introduced in the 1880s by tribes further west, in the Great Basin of Nevada; it was a cult, outlawed by the United States in 1891, which preached war and annihilation to the encroaching whites, a last-ditch stand against the inevitable. The Ghost Dance movement brought with it, from the Great Basin, a musical style different from that of the older Plains songs. Typically its songs had a smaller range and a form in which each phrase is repeated once, for instance, AABB or AABBCC. Among the Plains Indians, such as the Arapaho, these songs came to be associated with the Ghost Dance religion, and when the dance was outlawed, the songs continued to be sung. Their style was also associated with hand games and gambling games.

Another musical style was brought to the Arapaho and to many other tribes throughout the United States and particularly to the Northern Plains, by the Peyote religion. Peyote, a cactus indigenous in Mexico, has buttons which when chewed have a mild narcotic effect, producing euphoria and eventually pleasant hallucinations. The Aztecs already had a cult built around Peyote, but a religion of a different sort, preaching conciliation with the whites and including some superficial elements of Christianity, was based on this drug in North America. Peyote reached some of the Apache tribes after 1700 and spread from them to the majority of tribes in the United States during the nineteenth and early twentieth centuries. The style of Peyote music is essentially the same among all of the North American tribes that use the Peyote ceremonies; and it differs uniformly from the older musical styles of those tribes. Its form is similar to that of the older Plains songs, but its rhythm is characterized by the fact that it is rapid and composed mainly of only two note values which can be notated by quarter and eighth notes; also it is accompanied by rapid playing of the drum and rattle. Special kinds of meaningless syllables and a particular closing or cadential formula are used. Peyote songs are definitely considered as a special type by the Arapaho.

The Arapaho culture did not have as many uses of music as did some other Indian tribes. For example, the Pueblo Indians had much more complex and numerous ceremonial songs. They also used music to accompany work, something unusual among Indians. The Navaho had elaborate curing rituals accompanied by several series of songs, and a large body of corn grinding songs. The Indians of the Southeastern United States had many kinds of social dances. Throughout, music was associated with religion, and no description of a ceremony would be complete without a discussion of the songs. In most tribes, the most significant musical creations were those in the ceremonies. Among the Eskimos, some songs were used to settle disputes and to relieve the resulting tension.

MUSIC IN INDIAN THOUGHT

We have only little knowledge regarding the musical aesthetics of Indian tribes. Ability to sing many songs, and to sing high, is the mark of a good singer on the Plains; the Pueblo Indians, on the other hand, prefer singers with low, growling voices. Songs are judged according to their "power" rather than their beauty. Various ideas regarding the origin of songs are found among the North American tribes. According to some, all songs were given to the tribe "in the beginning," and the idea that new songs can be made up is not accepted. Among the Yuman tribes of the extreme Southwest, songs are thought to be "dreamed," that is, made up or given to a person while he is asleep.[2] Curiously, Yuman persons who

[2] George Herzog, "Music in the Thinking of the American Indian," *Peabody Bulletin*, May, 1933, pp. 1–6.

are disturbed or emotionally maladjusted retire for a few weeks to a secluded hut, there to meditate and to "dream" songs, eventually to emerge much improved. Among the Pima of the Southwest, we find the idea that songs already exist, and that it is the job of the composer simply to "untangle" them. Among the Plains tribes, the idea that songs come in visions is prevalent; of course all songs do not come in this way, but those which are ceremonially most significant do. The possibility of learning songs from other tribes is accepted variously; Herzog found that the Pima, who sang songs with Yuma words, would not admit that these songs could have been imported. On the other hand, Plains tribes regularly label the songs borrowed from other tribes; thus the Cheyenne Indians have "Kiowa songs" and "Comanche songs."

The degree to which songs retain their form from year to year and from generation to generation also varies. Some tribes, such as those of the Northwest Coast, consider it important to keep a song intact. Change or error might invalidate its purpose in ritual or rob it of its power. Thus organized rehearsing was instituted and errors were punished. The attempt to retain the cultural heritage intact and the resistance to change in general is also felt, of course, in the musical culture. The Pueblo Indians, who have tended to resist change in all areas, have also kept their musical culture away from Western influence more than have some other tribes. The Plains Indians, who had a rather loose and informal political and ceremonial structure, evidently did not adhere to such standardized forms; one Arapaho informant, upon hearing a recording of one of his tribal songs, performed what he considered "the same song" by singing what seemed to the investigator a totally different melody.

MUSICAL INSTRUMENTS

The instruments of the North American Indians are relatively few in number, but the Middle and South American tribes had a considerable wealth of them. In North America, flutes and various sorts of percussion instruments constitute an overwhelming majority. Flutes are usually of the recorder type, with varying numbers of finger holes; the tunes they are used to perform are frequently those of songs that are also sung. True flutes, without the plug of the recorder, also appear. In some cases, ornamentation in the vocal line is faithfully reproduced on the flute; in others, the flute embellishes the tune. Flutes are most frequently used to play love songs, and they are played almost exclusively by men. Whistles of various sorts, made of bone, pottery, or wood, are used in conjunction

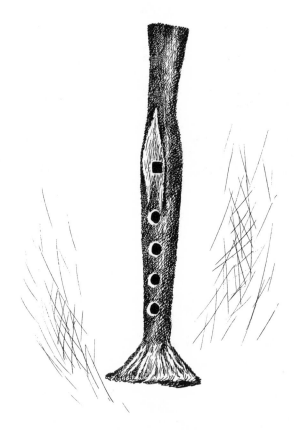

Ancient Mexican clay flute.

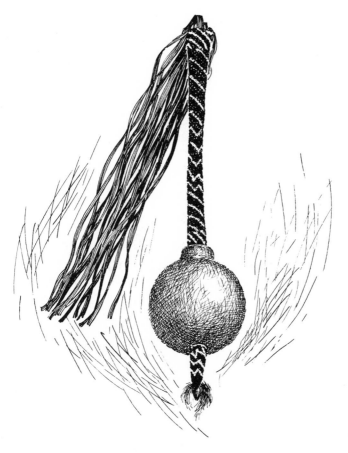

Plains Indian gourd rattle.

with songs and ceremonies. Drums and rattles are the main percussion instruments of North America. The drums are usually beaten with sticks rather than the hand, and they (as well as the rattles) are used only to accompany song. Most Indian drums have a single drumhead; some are so large that they can be played by several players simultaneously. Some are held in one hand, the player grasping the leather thongs that hold the skin against the rim. Kettledrums, sometimes filled with water, are also used. The Peyote ceremony requires such a drum, its drumhead moistened to attain appropriate pitch. Typically, each drum is associated with one or several specific ceremonies and is an object of importance beyond its musical service.

Rattles are also of various types and associated with specific ceremonies. Gourd rattles (with pebbles inside the gourd) are used for Peyote ceremonies. Also used in North America are rattles made of deer hooves strung together; rattles made on a base consisting of a turtle shell; notched sticks held against a basket resonator and rubbed with another stick; and wooden bells. The South American Indians also have a larger variety of rattles, but they are particularly distinguished from the North American tribes in their development of panpipes and of chordophones (string instruments). Panpipes made of fired clay and of wood seem to have been used in the highlands of Peru and Bolivia for centuries. Some have pipes up to five feet tall. The number and arrangement of pipes vary, but, interestingly enough, this type of instrument has been altered and its scale made to fit Western popular music, so that some of the present-day Indians of Peru, for example, use them to play tunes in the prevalent Hispanic style. While there is inconclusive evidence that some North American tribes used hunting bows to play simple tunes, the musical bow, played in much the same ways as in Africa, appears among several South American tribes, including the simple Araucanians of Patagonia. The high cultures of Peru, Colombia, and Mexico had rather elaborate instruments of various sorts, but we know little about the music produced on them.

STYLES BY AREA IN NORTH AMERICA

The distribution of musical styles among the North American Indians coincides more or less with that of the culture areas. There appears to be, however, a somewhat smaller degree of correspondence here than there is in Africa. South American Indian music is not yet sufficiently well known for us to construct musical areas. In North America (north of Mexico) there are six main areas; in some cases these cannot be distinguished on the basis of single pieces of music, and the distinctions among them are statistical, that is, they depend on the frequency of a given trait rather than its simple presence or absence.

1. The Northwest Coast-Eskimo area contains, besides the areas mentioned, the Salish Indians in the interior of British Columbia and in the state of Washington. While these groups have little in common culturally, they seem to be among the most recent immigrants from Asia. Their music is characterized by nonstrophic forms, by complex and sometimes nonmetrical rhythmic organization, by the prominence of small intervals such as minor seconds, and by a relatively small range in the melodies. The melodic contours in Eskimo music tend to be undulating, while they are more frequently of a pendulum type in Northwest Coast and Salish music. One important characteristic is the use of rhythmic motifs in the percussive accompaniment. Generally, in Indian music, drums and rattles follow a simple pulse. But in the Northwest Coast-Eskimo area, designs such as ♪♪♪♪ or ♪♩ ♪ are found. In spite of unity, however, the Eskimo music is generally simple while that of the Northwest is complex and, in its relative wealth of instruments, indicates some relationship to the culture of the Mexican civilizations.

2. The California-Yuman area, consisting of tribes in Central California and of the Yuman-speaking tribes of the extreme Southwestern United States, is characterized by singing in a relatively relaxed manner. Most Indian tribes use a tense, harsh vocal technique, but here the singing is more in the style of Western or Central European folk singing. The songs are not in strophic form; rather, they consist of two or more separate sections or phrases which are repeated, alternated, and interwoven without a predetermined pattern. The most characteristic feature of this area is the so-called rise, a form discovered and labeled by George Herzog.[3] The rise itself is a section of a song that is slightly higher in pitch than the rest of the song if not very obviously so. The Yuman Indians recognize this feature and use a word roughly translated as "rise" to indicate it. The rise is found in most songs of the Yuman-California area, and also elsewhere, mainly along the coasts of North America. Thus, it is found in some twenty or thirty percent of the songs of some Northwest Coast tribes, and in those of the Southeastern Choctaw; in ten to twenty percent of the songs of the Northeastern Penobscot and the Northwestern Nootka, and in less than ten percent of the repertory of the Southeastern Creek, Yuchi, and Tutelo.

3. A third area is centered in the Great Basin of Nevada, Utah,

---

[3] George Herzog, "The Yuman Musical Style," *Journal of American Folklore,* LXI (1928), 183–231.

and northern interior Canada, basically a desert area with simple hunting and gathering cultures. The style of the music here became the style of the Ghost Dance songs further to the East. Singing is in a relatively relaxed manner, melodic range is small, and the typical form is that of paired phrases, with each phrase repeated once. In the northwestern part of the area, some tribes with even a simpler style—the Modoc and Klamath, for example—have many songs consisting of a single repeated phrase. This kind of form is found, of course, in traditional musics throughout the world, and there are a few Indian tribes such as the previously mentioned Sirionó of Bolivia whose entire repertories don't go beyond this level of simplicity. But it seems possible that the simple repetitive forms of the Modoc and Klamath are historically related to the somewhat more complex but still essentially repetitive forms of the Great Basin proper. Because of long-standing contacts with the Plains Indians, the Great Basin tribes also have songs in the Plains style. And an interesting exception to the tendency of Indian songs to be short and to eschew narration is the existence, among the Ute, of some songs that serve as vehicles for reciting tales. These narrative songs do not have strophic forms (as do European ballads), but continue in unstructured fashion, liberally repeating and varying a few basic musical motifs. Example 8-3 illustrates the Great Basin style.

EXAMPLE 8-3. Paiute Indian song, transcribed by the author from the recording, *Great Basin. Paiute Washo, Ute, Bannock, Shoshone* (Library of Congress AAFS L38), recorded and edited by Willard Rhodes.

4. A fourth area, the Athabascan, seems to coincide with a language family by the same name. It consists of the Navaho and Apache tribes and, possibly, of another group of tribes, the Northern Athabascans in Western Canada. Though these northern tribes have for centuries been separated from the Navaho and Apache by a thousand miles, there is evidence that the musical styles of the two areas are related. The music of the Navaho is the most complex of this area, perhaps because it has been greatly influenced by the neighboring Pueblo tribes. Its melodies have a large range, a pendulum-like melodic movement, large intervals, and liberal use of falsetto. The Apache songs tend to have smaller range and tenser singing. What relates them is the form— usually nonstrophic and resembling that of the California-Yuman tribes

—and the rhythmic structure, in which meter is rather well established but changes frequently and suddenly. The note values in each song are few, usually just two, quarters and eights, and it seems likely that the style of Peyote music, as described for the Arapaho above, is in this respect based on the music of the Apache, from whom the use of Peyote for ceremonies had spread to the other tribes. Example 8-4 is a Navaho song.

EXAMPLE 8-4. Navaho Indian Enemy Way ceremony song, from David P. McAllester, *Enemy Way Music* (Cambridge, Mass.: Peabody Museum Papers 49, no. 3, 1954), song no. 35.

5. The Plains-Pueblo area takes in two of the most important cultural groups, the Plains Indians (Blackfoot, Crow, Dakota, Comanche, Kiowa, etc.) and the Pueblo Indians. The most recent aboriginal form of living of the Plains Indians was nomadic; their economy was based on the buffalo. Their loose political and ceremonial structure contrasts with the elaborate organization of life and religion among the Pueblo Indians (Hopi, Zuni, Taos, etc.), and in recent centuries there has been only slight contact among these two groups. Yet their music shares some im-

portant characteristics, particularly the great amount of tension in the singing and the two-part song form, which was described above for the Arapaho. The use of terrace-like melodic contour, gradually descending and leveling off on a long, low tone, is also typical (although the Pueblo songs often precede this form with a low-pitched introduction). The area directly east of the Plains, including such tribes as the Pawnee and the Eastern Woodland tribes such as the Menomini, Chippewa, and Winnebago, shares the main traits of the Plains but adds some characteristic ones of its own. Typically the Plains songs do not have strongly pronounced metric units, nor are repeated rhythmic patterns or motifs usually evident. Among the tribes to the east, however, repeated rhythmic motifs can be identified, and a good many songs have elements of isorhythmic form—a rhythmic pattern repeated several times, with different melodic content each time. Of course, this practice is also found here and there among the typical Plains tribes. Example 8-5 presents an Arapaho song.

EXAMPLE 8-5. Arapaho Sun Dance song, from Bruno Nettl, *Musical Culture of the Arapaho* (M. A. thesis, Indiana University, 1951), p. 100.

Song is repeated four times. Drum begins before the singers.
* Women enter here in repeat.
During last rendition, women finish alone, without drum.

6. The eastern portion of the United States and Southern Canada may be considered as one musical area, although it is only sporadically known. Perhaps the most distinctive feature is the development of responsorial singing—shouts thrown back and forth between leader and chorus, probably as a result of rudimentary rounds. Forms are frequently elaborate and composed of several phrases, some of which recur. Thus the Eagle Dance ceremony of the Iroquois has many songs with the form of AABAB, in which section A is always accompanied by quick shaking of a rattle, while B has slower percussive accompaniment. Similarly,

some of the southeastern tribes have social dances accompanied by groups of songs strung together in series that are repeated and interwoven in intricate sequences. Vocal technique is tense, and melodic contour usually descending, though not in the predictable terrace patterns of the Plains. The tribes living in the Gulf of Mexico area seem to have had, before the advent of the whites, a very complex culture related to that of the Aztecs, but it is possible that their music was similarly more complex. But little of this remains. Example 8-6 is an Iroquois song, an example of music from the eastern area.

EXAMPLE 8-6. Iroquois thanksgiving ritual song, from Wallace Chafe, *Seneca Thanksgiving Rituals* (Washington, D.C.: Bureau of American Ethnology, Bulletin 183, 1961), p. 66.

The level of musical complexity among these areas varies. Pueblo, eastern, and Northwest Coast are the most complex and developed, while the Great Basin is, on the whole, the simplest. Although the musical areas do not correspond precisely to the culture areas, they do coincide at various major points. Such easily defined culture areas as the Plains and the Northwest Coast have a unified musical style. The greatest cultural diversity as well as the greatest musical variety is found in the western part of the continent. On the other hand, the large number of language families found in North America do not coincide in their geographic distribution with either the musical or the culture areas.

INDIAN MUSIC OF LATIN AMERICA

It is interesting to find some of the North American stylistic traits paralleled in South America. This is true of the terrace-shaped melodic contours of the Plains tribes, which are found also among tribes in Northern Argentina. But in contrast to North America, the South American Indians seem to have developed some polyphony to the level of definite intention; thus the tribes of Tierra del Fuego occasionally sing in parallel fifths.

The Latin America area produced several Indian cultures whose technology and whose social and political organization were considerably higher than those of most nonliterate tribes, and which were comparable perhaps to some of the ancient civilizations of Europe and Asia. We are speaking, of course, of the Mayas of the Yucatan peninsula (who developed a kind of written communication), the Aztecs, and some of their predecessors, the Inca of Peru, and the Chibcha of Colombia. Little of their musical culture has remained, but there is archeological evidence to support the belief that they had rather elaborate musical practices and styles. Their instruments were larger in number,, though not much more complex, than those of other tribes. Pictorial representations of groups of instrumentalists indicate that playing in ensembles was a common practice. The Mexican cultures, though together they span hundreds of years, seem to have used essentially the same instruments: Prominent were the *teponatzli*, a log drum with a slit similar to some of the West African signal drums; the *tlapitzalli* (our names here are the Nahuatl forms—this is the language of the Aztecs), a true flute with four finger holes, made of clay, reed, or bone, with major seconds and minor thirds as the main intervals; the *huehuetl*, a kettle drum which was produced in several distinct sizes and pitches; a conch-shell trumpet; rattles; and rasps. The Incas added to these types a large number of ocarinas, flutes with varying numbers of finger holes (three to eight), and panpipes. The identity of tuning of some Peruvian panpipes with some of Oceania has been a factor in the debate about the possibility and nature of contact between native South America and Oceania.

According to early Spanish accounts[4] of the remnants of Aztec culture, the Aztecs recognized only religious music, and musical life was

---

[4] See Robert Stevenson, *Music in Mexico* (New York: Thomas Y. Crowell Company, 1952), pp. 14–19.

largely in the hands of a professional religious caste. Some instruments themselves had divine power. Music was normally performed by groups in concert, and responsorial singing was heard. Musicians were trained rigidly, and performances had to be completely accurate in order to please the deities; performers who made errors, such as missed drumbeats, were punished.

Before their discovery by the Spaniards, the Inca evidently had an even more elaborate musical culture than the Aztecs. The ruler had specially trained musicians for entertainment at his court. A school of music was instituted at Cuzco by the Inca Roca about 1350,[5] and in the fifteenth century the Inca Pachacuti ordered the collection of narrative songs about the deeds of the earlier Inca rulers; these were organized in song cycles.

THE WORDS OF INDIAN SONGS

The words of Indian songs are of considerable interest, for they frequently fit into the musical structure in unexpected and interesting ways. For example, the Plains Indians, with their two-part song structure, have developed a rather dramatic but simultaneously utilitarian way of setting words to music. Most of the song is taken up with meaningless syllables, such as "he-he" or "ho-ho," but meaningful text appears at the beginning of the second section, which starts again (as does the first) on a high note and works its way downward. The text's structure does not have the characteristics, such as rime or meter, of European poetry; it is rather like prose, although meaningless syllables sometimes appear between words and even between the syllables of one word, presumably in order to keep the stressed syllables on stressed musical beats. The text does not fill the whole second part of the song; when it is finished, meaningless syllables are again used to fill in the rest of the melody. This kind of structure gives considerable flexibility to the composer or poet, for it enables him to substitute new words for old in the same tune, or to make slight changes in the words in order to keep up with the times. Thus warriors of the Plains would report on their exploits in such songs, and the same tune could be used for various exploits. After World War I in which many Indians served as soldiers, old tunes with new words recounting stories of the war began to appear. Such words as "Germany" and an Arapaho word for submarine began to appear in the songs. Frequently these songs used texts from the tribal wars, but simply substi-

[5] Robert Stevenson, *The Music of Peru: Aboriginal and Viceroyal Epochs* (Washington: Pan American Union, 1959), p. 39.

tuted German soldiers for Indian tribes; for example, "The German officer ran and dragged his blanket along." The following are song texts of the Arapaho:[6]

Woman, don't worry about me; I'm coming back home to eat berries.
I am the crow; watch me.
The bird has come; it makes yellow the sky.
Young man, be brave; you're going to a dangerous place; your chieftainship will become famous.
Really it is good to be young, for old age is not far off.
The Ute Indian, while he was still looking around for me, I scalped him alive.
Young man, it is good that you are going to war.

Elsewhere among the North American Indians, however, meaningless syllables are not so prevalent, and entire tunes are accompanied by words; the subjects range from serious thoughts about the gods to lyrical complaints about the weather, to frivolous love songs. But the meaningless syllable songs occupy an important role, analogous perhaps to instrumental music. Thus there are entire bodies of song that use meaningless syllables. The famous night chant of the Navaho, the "yeibetchai," includes a group of songs sung by masked dancers in falsetto with only syllables. Many of the Peyote songs use only meaningless words, but, interestingly enough, they use special patterns such as "yowitsini," "heyowitsi," and "heyowitsinayo," which can easily be identified as belonging to the Peyote. Some of the Indian texts are long and elaborate; the Navaho songs may enumerate holy people, places, or things in great numbers. More commonly, however, a short sentence or phrase is repeated several times.

INDIAN MUSIC IN MODERN AMERICA

Considering the small number of Indians and the tremendous impact of Western culture on their lives, it would be surprising if their music had remained uninfluenced by that of the West, and particularly by Western thought and ideas about music. The effect of Westernization can be seen in many, sometimes contradictory, ways. It is important, first, to note that there is an important difference between North and Latin American Indian cultures. The Indians of Latin America, who in several countries now make up the bulk of the Spanish-speaking popula-

[6] Collected by Bruno Nettl.

tion, have learned the folk music styles of Spain and have also developed styles that are to a considerable extent mixtures of European and Indian materials. For example, in the Andes of Peru, tunes in an essentially Hispanic style are played on the aboriginal Indian panpipes; many similar illustrations could be cited. On the other hand, in North America —probably because the Indians have largely been segregated—such a mixture of styles did not take place. But there is a great deal of evidence that principles of musical thought, aesthetics, and social organization from the white Americans have made their mark in contemporary North American musical culture. To be sure, many American Indians now participate in purely Western musical practices; but they do not have, as a major part of their repertory, music that sounds both Indian and Western, although their way of singing the strictly Indian music may be influenced subtly by Western ideas of making music.

The fact that North American Indian and European musical styles have not merged is probably in part due to the great difference between them, a difference verging on incompatibility (in contrast, for instance, to the greater compatibility between European and African musics). But despite the points made in the previous paragraph, there are some changes in style that have come about through Western music. More recent Indian songs appear to have an interval and intonation structure more like that of Western music than do older songs. Accompaniment of piano or guitar is occasionally found.

Even so, the influence of Western civilization on Indian music is most commonly felt in less direct ways, and this is true of both the historical and the contemporary Indian cultures. In Mexico and Peru, the relatively high developments of music were reduced to simpler levels and styles through the annihilation of the aboriginal ruling classes, and through the introduction of Christianity. In Central America, the presence of simple xylophone-like instruments facilitated the introduction of the African *marimba*. In North America, tribes with radically different cultures became neighbors and learned from each other. One example is the Shawnee tribe, which at the time of first white contact was located in the southeastern United States, but had probably come from the Northeast a few centuries before. The Shawnee tribe participated in the music of the eastern musical area but was forced to migrate repeatedly and was finally located largely in Oklahoma, near the Plains Indians. Its repertory today contains songs in both the Eastern and Plains styles, simple songs of an older layer which the Shawnee may have brought with them from the Northeast, and songs in the Peyote style.

The spreading of the Peyote and Ghost Dance styles to tribes with other kinds of music, such as the Plains Indians, was also a result, though somewhat indirect, of the impact of Western culture, which caused the rapid spreading of new religions that were needed to cope with the drastically changed condition of the Indians, and which brought about the equally rapid distribution of musical styles. These kinds of indirect influences of Western civilization that we can trace in the period of American history before 1950 continue into the present.

Among the Indians of the United States, and of the Northern Plains in particular, music is developing and flourishing. Its role now is primarily that of a symbol of Indian identity, because it is one of the few aspects of Indian life into which the white man has not penetrated, and which he is usually unwilling to take the trouble to imitate. While Indians can hardly avoid trying to enter the Western economic and political systems, and while they have been converted religiously as a result of centuries of missionizing, there is little reason why they should not continue to sing in distinctively Indian musical styles. But many of the activities to which music was essential in the past are now gone—religion, war, the buffalo. On the other hand, the fact that Indians of various tribes have been thrown together on some of the reservations, and also their relatively greater mobility (along with other Americans), has added to a desire on their part to retain single, Indian identity, rather than separate tribal identity, and has facilitated musical contact and exchange of materials among Indian tribes. All of this has led to a pan-Indian culture and musical style, based essentially on the culture of the Plains, as far as music is concerned, but distributed throughout a large part of the United States and Canada. In this culture, the older, largely ceremonial musics live on only as relics, to be occasionally dusted off and brought out for the sake of tradition, and living vividly only in the memory of older persons who remember earlier times. (But there is evidence that each generation, as it grows older, begins to take an interest in this older material, so that it does not completely die out.)

Flourishing, however, is the music accompanying social dances. Here we find many songs being composed each year, and we see the development of a class of singers and drummers who are semi-professional, admired not for the power which their knowledge of songs brings them but for their knowledge of a repertory, and for the excellence with which they perform it—a way of thinking about music typical of Western culture. We see Indians recognizing musical composition as a human rather than a supernatural act. We find older practices, such as the Sun Dance, translated into the modern powwow, which has the social functions of the old Sun Dance—bringing the tribe together and permitting social interchange, gambling, and athletic contests—but which no longer has the religious function. We find a higher degree of standardization of musical forms, due perhaps to the greater standardization in the forms of Western music known to the Indians, hymns and country and Western music, but also perhaps due to the need for learning songs from other tribes as quickly as possible. Large intertribal festivals in such places as Anadarko, Oklahoma, and Gallup, New Mexico, accelerate the inter-tribal contacts and provide a Western-style forum for star Indian musicians and dancers. Because Indian languages are no longer spoken by all Indians, and because speakers of various languages will sing a song together, there is an acceleration of the old Plains practice of singing songs without words, with meaningless syllables only, or, occasionally, of singing Indian songs with English words. And Indian music has become, like Western music, something which expert musicians perform for an audience (both Indian and white), rather than as an integral part of many everyday activities. Record companies now issue disks primarily for an Indian market. All of this shows that Indian musical culture in North America is still very much alive, but that its functions and uses have changed as the life-style of the Indians has changed, in the direction of Western culture. Thus the role of music in Indian life is today very much like the role of folk music in the life of other minorities in North American culture.

BIBLIOGRAPHY AND DISCOGRAPHY

Since this chapter introduces the music of the Americas generally, besides covering American Indian music, some publications on the entire subject may be cited here. Charles Haywood, *A Bibliography of North American Folklore and Folksong*, rev. ed. (New York: Dover, 1961, 2 vols.) and Gilbert Chase, *A Guide to the Music of Latin America*, 2nd ed. (Washington: Pan American Union, 1962) are indispensable bibliographies. Bruno Nettl, *An Introduction to Folk Music in the United States* (Detroit: Wayne State University Press, 1960) is a brief survey.

Two attempts to show the various styles in North American Indian music are Helen H. Roberts, *Musical Areas in Aboriginal North America* (New Haven: Yale University Press, 1936) and Bruno Nettl, *North American Indian Musical Styles* (Philadelphia: American Folklore Society, 1954). The most prolific author on North American Indian music was Frances Densmore, and all of her publications, many of them published by the Bureau of American Ethnology, Smithsonian Institution, Washington, D.C., are worth examination. Recent developments in this field are discussed by Willard Rhodes, "Acculturation in North American Indian Music," in *Acculturation in the Americas*, ed. Sol Tax (Chicago: University of Chicago Press, 1952).

The best overall study of the music and musical culture of an American Indian tribe is Alan P. Merriam, *Ethnomusicology of the Flathead In-*

dians (Chicago: Aldine Press, 1967). Special problems and styles are discussed in David P. McAllester, *Peyote Music* (New York: Viking Fund Publications in Anthropology, 13, 1949) and *Enemy Way Music* (Cambridge, Mass.: Peabody Museum of Harvard University, 1954), and Bruno Nettl, "Studies in Blackfoot Indian Musical Culture," *Ethnomusicology*, 11–12, 1967–68.

Among the important publications on Indian music in Latin America are Robert Stevenson, *Music in Aztec and Inca Territory* (Berkeley: University of California Press, 1968), Marguerite and Raoul d'Harcourt, "La musique des Aymara sur les hauts plateaux boliviens," *Journal de la Societé des Américanistes*, 48, (1959), 5–133, and Karl G. Izikowitz, *Musical and Other Sound Instruments of the South American Indians* (Goteborg: Elanders, 1935).

The Library of Congress has issued a number of recordings made from Frances Densmore's and Willard Rhodes's collections in its series, *Folk Music of the United States*. North American Soundchief Enterprises has issued a number of records, primarily of Plains Indian music, and mainly illustrative of recent developments, in a series, *Songs of the Red Man*. This series, and the records issued by Indian House, Taos, N.M., are for use by scholars as well as American Indians interested in hearing songs of their own heritage. Other recordings of North American Indian music of interest are *Indian Music of the Canadian Plains*, Folkways P 464; *American Indians of the Southwest*, Folkways FW8850, and *Music of the Sioux and Navaho*, Folkways P 401. Indian music of Latin America is presented on *Indian Music of Mexico*, Folkways P 413; *Music from the Mato Grosso*, Folkways P 446; *Indian Music of the Upper Amazon*, Folkways P 458; *Instruments and Music of Bolivia*, Folkways FM4012; and *Mountain Music of Peru*, Folkways FE4539.

NINE

LATIN AMERICAN FOLK MUSIC

by Gérard Béhague

The Latin American continent presents, on the whole, cultural traits obviously inherited from the Iberian Peninsula, but its folk music traditions have generally preserved less of that old heritage than North American folk music has kept of British lore. Many parts of what (for the sake of convenience) is called "Latin America" are virtually devoid of any Latin cultural elements. Many tropical-forest Amerindian cultures, for example, and some Indian groups of the Bolivian *altiplano* are still relatively untouched by European traditions. Moreover, in many cases the prevailing cultural influences are Afro-American and not Latin American. The study of folk music in individual countries or territories is bound to be somewhat artificial, although common cultural traits do exist in very large geographical areas, such as the areas, formerly occupied by the Inca Empire, that extend from Western Argentina to the highlands of Northern Ecuador, or in the areas of Afro-American populations, found in Brazil, Trinidad, Cuba, and Western Colombia, Ecuador, and Venezuela with their analogous developments. In such areas a geographical approach to the study of folk music could be justified.

The degree to which a single culture predominates—Hispanic, Amerindian, or African—varies greatly among the nations; and, within nations, among regions. For example, Bolivia, whose people of Indian descent represent about seventy percent of the total population, has essentially traditional music (Aymara, Quechua) in the *altiplano* area but, in the valleys and the eastern provinces, has typical mestizo (a term indicating culturally and racially mixed groups in Latin America) folk music, characterized by Spanish tunes and words but using Indian instruments and accompanying dances of Indian origin. Conversely, it is not uncommon to find rather isolated highland Indian groups using string instruments clearly of Spanish descent, such as the ubiquitous *charango* (an instrument with five double strings, made in its most rustic form out of an armadillo shell) and the harp. As opposed to Indian music of tropical forest cultures (Mato Grosso, Upper Amazon), Indian music of the Andean countries represents, as a whole, a dominant ingredient of the folk music traditions of the area. In the transfer of Hispanic or African material to the Americas, syncretism accounts for the creation of certain forms and the preservation or rejection of others. It is, therefore, accurate to assume that genuine Latin American folk music traditions are the result of mestizo cultures.

In addition, the actual history and ethnohistory of a given country or area should be considered in accounting for specific stylistic traits. A case in point would be a comparative historical study of such Caribbean islands as Haiti, Jamaica, and Trinidad. While all three countries have a large majority of population of African descent, they were at various periods of their history under the political and cultural domination of Spain, France, and Great Britain. In the case of Trinidad, although France actually never dominated her, French influences (e.g., Trinidadian *créole*) have been considerable. In addition, the Western African cultures transferred to those areas have quite diverse origins: Ewe (Dahomey) in the case of Haiti, mostly Yoruba (Nigeria) and Ashanti (Ghana) in Jamaica and Trinidad. The problem becomes exceedingly intricate when one considers the immigration of East Indians to Trinidad, Guiana, and Surinam, or more recently, that of Germans and Italians to Brazil, Uruguay, and Argentina.

The Latin American folk music arena is, then, a very complex one, and a macroscopic exposition alone will be presented here, resorting to a few illustrations of what is found rather than a survey of the entire wealth of song, dance, and instrument types. For the sake of clarity, though somewhat arbitrarily, we should distinguish between the Hispanic related folk music genres, on the one hand, and Mestizo folk genres, subdivided into Indian-Hispanic and Afro-Hispanic, on the other. Afro-American music in Latin America is discussed in Chapter Ten.

SOUTH AMERICA

Folk Songs

Examples of autonomous folk song genres are relatively few in South American folk music, since, in a very high proportion of the repertory, song functions as an accompaniment to dancing. Throughout the continent we find a multitude of song types derived from the old Spanish *romance*, a narrative song form dating back to the early Renaissance, typically based on eight-syllable lines and four-line stanzas. Under different local names, *romances* have been preserved sometimes in their original form (e.g., in Colombia) and sometimes with significant variations which reveal the characteristic thought and feeling of the creole of a given region. The *copla*, a ballad type derived from the *romance*, is common throughout Colombia, the Andean countries, and Argentina. Typically, *romances* and *coplas* describe, in an epic lyrical manner, famous historical events of a region or episodes of everyday life. Apart from their poetic and musical value, they often provide significant sociological data. Other folk songs, such as the Argentine and Chilean *tonadas* and *tonos*, have maintained old Spanish literary forms besides that of the *romance*. The *glosa* and the *décima* are forms consisting of two parts, the first a quatrain which sets the basic subject, the second a development of it in a stanza of ten octosyllabic lines. This structure is found in Chilean, Peruvian, Ecuadorian, and Colombian *décimas*, Argentine *estilos* and *cifras*, and in many other genres, such as the *guabina* of Colombia or the *romances* and *xácaras* of Brazil. The classical rhyme scheme of the Spanish *décima*, ABBAACCDDC, prevails in most of the folk song types mentioned. Example 9-1 shows two versions of a traditional *romance* known in Lima, Peru. Entitled *La esposa difunta o la Aparición*, its origin has been traced to sixteenth century Spain. The regular two- and four-bar phrases and their isometric structure are characteristic of Spanish folk song. Literary versions of the same *romance* have been collected in New Mexico, California, Mexico, Nicaragua, Cuba, the Dominican Republic, Puerto Rico, Venezuela, Ecuador, and several provinces of Argentina, which attests to the wide diffusion of the *romance* tradition in Latin America.

But actual Iberian folk melodies still extant in Spain and Portugal today are very rare in Latin America. Children's songs seem to be the

EXAMPLE 9-1. Two versions of the romance *La esposa difunta o la Aparición*. From Emilia Romero, *El Romance Tradicional en el Perú* (Mexico: El Colegio de México, 1952), p. 89.

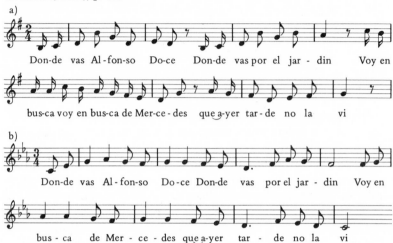

notable exceptions, for many of them remain basically the same in both areas. The problem of the origin of Hispanic tunes in Latin American folk music is generally unsolved. But we can say with some certainty that the tunes sung in Latin America are for the most part not simply imports from Spain and Portugal (the texts more frequently are). They are more usually songs either composed in Latin America in the styles brought from Europe, or they are indeed songs brought from Europe centuries ago but so changed by the process of oral tradition that the tunes in Europe that are related to them can no longer be recognized as relatives; or perhaps it is the European tunes that have undergone change. This situation is not completely paralleled by the traditions of minority groups living in South America—Germans, East Europeans, Italians—for these have preserved many of the songs that they brought from Europe, but they have not to a large extent created new material in the traditional styles.

A recent study of the Chilean *verso*,[1] a traditional type of sung poetry, has conclusively shown stylistic similarities with Spanish Medieval and Renaissance genres (*cantigas, villancicos*), especially as to modality and cadential practices. Such archaic elements are also found in

[1] María Ester Grebe, *The Chilean Verso: A Study in Musical Archaism* (Los Angeles: Latin American Center, University of California, 1967).

Brazil in some folk melody types associated with the *desafio* (literally "challenge"), with texts consisting of questions and answers, that are performed by two singers, often presenting antiphonal musical structure with instrumental interludes (guitar) between the vocal sections. The most common literary form of *desafio* in Brazil is the six-line heptasyllabic stanza, common in Portuguese popular poetry. One of the most popular song types, closely related to the *desafio*, is the *embolada*, found throughout Brazil's hinterland. Mostly improvised, it presents a characteristic refrain in addition to the six-line stanza. As in many Brazilian songs, the refrain makes use of alliteration, assonance, and onomatopoeia in a syncopated melodic line and an unusually fast tempo. The text of the *embolada*, based on stereotyped models, comments on local customs and criticizes figures and events of the community in a very provocative manner. The *embolada* has actually penetrated the urban areas in the last few decades; there it is used mostly as a chronicle of current events. But, as a whole, *desafios* and *emboladas*, together with songs of praises (*louvações*) constitute the main bulk of the folk song repertory of Northeastern Brazil. This particular folk music tradition is referred to in Brazil as the "caboclo" tradition, i.e., showing traits inherited from the Portuguese and some local Amerindian cultures. In this tradition, we generally find modal melodies, with frequent occurrences of the Lydian and Mixolydian modes. In addition, an artificial mode consisting of a major diatonic scale with the fourth degree sharpened and the seventh flattened often appears in the *caboclo* repertory.

Song genres similar to the *desafio* are widely used elsewhere in South America, variously called *contrapunto* and *cifra* in Argentina, *payas* in Chile, or *porfias* in Venezuela.

Folk songs of lyrical character whose subject matter is associated with love abound in South American folk music. Generically known as *tonadas* in the Spanish-speaking countries, and *toadas* in Brazil, they appear, typically, in four-, five-, or ten-line stanzas, sometimes incorporating a refrain. The Argentine *estilo* will serve as an example. According to Isabel Aretz, the *estilo* is a well defined lyrical song genre; made up of two melodic ideas, the "theme," properly speaking, and a somewhat faster strain known as *alegre*.[2] The overall formal aspect of the song is ternary, ABA. The text of the *estilo* is generally set in quatrains or *décimas*. In the Cuyo province of Argentina as well as in Chile, the *estilo* is known as *tonada*, and in the northern provinces it is called *verso* or *décima*. The *estilo* is also common in Uruguay. Example 9-2 illustrates

---

[2] Isabel Aretz, *El folklore musical argentino* (Buenos Aires: Ricordi Americana, 1952), p. 144.

the characteristics of this folk song species: guitar accompaniment (both picked and strummed styles), vocal duet, and the "theme" and "alegre" sections.

EXAMPLE 9-2. *Estilo.* From Isabel Aretz, *El Folklore Musical Argentino* (Buenos Aires: Ricordi Americana, 1952), p. 147.

An interesting example of folk song in South America is the Brazilian *modinha*, for its origin has been traced to cultivated musical circles in Portugal and Brazil of the eighteenth century. It is a love song type whose actual printed examples from the nineteenth century reveal a strongly melodramatic character, fairly similar to salon music of the period. *Moda* is a generic term applied vaguely to a song, or any melody. The *Moda-de-viola*, however, is a lyrical folk song type known especially in the rural areas of the central and southern states. Its Portuguese antecedents are most obviously seen in the singing in parallel thirds and the ·guitar accompaniment. The text assumes very often a narrative, satirical, or sentimental character, with strong reminiscences of the Iberian *romance*. *Modinha*, the diminutive of *moda*, actually became part of Brazilian folk music only in the latter part of the nineteenth century, when it lost gradually its original Italian operatic flavor and became a simple sentimental song. In the course of its popularization it acquired simpler structures, such as ABACA, or a refrain and a stanza. With its cultivated origin, the *modinha* clearly illustrates the transplanting of European musical culture into the popular music of Brazil.

A fairly important body of folk songs in South America comes from popular religious customs accompanying the liturgical calendar of the Catholic church. Here again, the repertory exhibits close relationship with the Iberian Peninsula. Brought to the New World by Spanish missionaries, hymns and songs of praise are still found today and are known as *alabados* and *alabanzas*. Most of them are prevailingly modal and follow the traditional pattern of folk-hymn singing, i.e., alternation of refrain (*estribillo*—chorus) and stanza (*copla*—solo). In the Chocó province of Colombia, the *alabado* is also used at wakes to pay tribute to the dead person; the text represents the autobiography of that person and is improvised. Most religious folk songs are associated with the Christmas season. Thus the traditional Spanish *villancico* has developed into numerous folk song genres, known as *aguinaldo, adoración, coplas de Navidad, esquinazo*, and others in the various countries of Latin America. While most of this body of songs obviously relates to its Spanish counterpart, it also displays many mestizo or *criollo* characteristics. For example, the Venezuelan *villancicos* and *aguinaldos* present a regular meter in 2/4, 6/8, or 3/4, regular phrases of two- and four-bar lengths, major and minor mode or bimodality, melodies in parallel thirds with a range not exceeding a sixth, almost total absence of modulation and chromaticism, and syllabic setting of the text.[3] All of these features are part of the Hispanic Christmas *cancionero*. But most *aguinaldos* differ from the

[3] Isabel Aretz, *Cantos navideños en el folklore venezolano* (Caracas: Casa de la Cultura Popular, 1962), pp. 40–42.

Spanish *villancico* in rhythmic structure. In addition to the indispensable *cuatro* (a small four-string guitar), they are accompanied by various percussion instruments, such as a double-headed drum (*tambora criolla*), a friction drum (*furruco*), a shaker-rattle (*chineco*), a *güiro*-type rattle (*charrasca*), and maracas. This accompaniment typically is based on the alternation of binary and ternary rhythmic figures, so common in mestizo dances such as the *merengue* and the *guasa*.[4] The melodies of the Venezuelan *aguinaldos* tend also to be more syncopated than the Spanish *villancico*. Example 9-3 shows some of the features of the Venezuelan *aguinaldo*.

EXAMPLE 9-3. Venezuelan Aguinaldo. From Isabel Aretz, *Cantos navideños en el folklore Venezolano* (Caracas: Casa de la cultura popular, 1962), p. 111.

[4] *Ibid.*, p. 92.

Autos and Dramatic Dances

Many of the Latin American Christmas songs are associated with popular dramatizations of the Nativity and the journey of the Three Kings, as well as with processions of various kinds. Such festivities are known throughout the continent and are variously called *posadas, auto sacramental, pastoris,* etc. Dance forms an integral part of such revelries.

True rituals associated with the Roman Catholic feasts of the Lord and the commemoration of saints' days, offering examples of cycles of syncretic feasts, are quite common in Latin America. Among these, the carnival is the most popular one. Many folk dances and songs function within the summer and winter cycles of feasts, such as St. John's day or feasts to the Virgin, in which syncretism with African deities is often present. In Brazil, for example, there exist many dramatic dances whose central subject is always religious. Conversion is the main theme of such dramatic dances as *congada, marujada,* and *moçambique,* while *quilombo caiapó, cabocolinhos,* and *lambe-sujo,* among others, are concerned with resurrection. Most of these dances appeared during the colonial period as a result of the Hispanic catechization. In Brazil, specifically, the Jesuits were responsible for diffusing many of them and for giving them unity and uniformity. Indeed, the *congada,* for example, is known all over Brazil. It combines elements of the popular religious theatre of the Peninsula and Afro-Brazilian traditions and customs, such as the coronation of Black Kings during the slave period. But in spite of its name and the fact that Blacks participate in it in large numbers, the history of the dance suggests that it is not of African origin but simply "a remembrance of the *Chanson de Roland* (the medieval French *chanson de geste*) wisely turned to the advantage of the catechist."[5] A consideration of the musical components of this dramatic play points to the absence of any particularly evident African element, although call and response pattern is often found, and drums frequently accompany the chorus. The songs accompanying the cortege, which is led by the main characters, show typical traits of Portuguese folk songs. The text of the play always appears in verse rather than prose, resulting in the adoption and transformation of the main incidents of the medieval epic poem.

[5] Alceu Maynard Araújo, *Folclore Nacional,* Vol. I (São Paulo: Edições Melhoramentos, 1964), p. 216.

Folk Dances

In the category of "secular" folk and popular dances the Latin American continent enjoys a well-known distinction. Many such dances originated in the Iberian peninsula, and while they have undergone considerable changes in the New World, choreographic traits specific to much Spanish folk dancing, such as shoe-tapping or finger snapping, remain significant in many dances. This is the case of the Argentine *chacarera* whose actual origins remain to be uncovered. The name of the dance is apparently derived from *chacra* meaning "farm" (from the Quechua *chagra*—"corn field"); thus it is believed that the *chacarera* was probably created by the farmers of the plains in the province of Buenos Aires, although it is used in almost all Argentine provinces. The choreography includes stamping of the feet and snapping of the fingers. Musically, Spanish ancestry appears, among other elements, in the hemiola rhythm (alternation of 6/8 and 3/4 meters) of the instrumental introduction, generally six or eight measures long. The rhythmic pattern of that introduction is ♪ , and that of the vocal part which follows is ♪ ; both are very common in Spanish folk music.[6] The vocal part is generally sung by one soloist, although trios have gained much popularity in the last few decades. The text, of good-humored, satirical, or comic character, consists of four quatrains of octosyllabic lines, coinciding with the six figures of the dance. The *chacarera* also appears in exclusively instrumental versions; the instruments used are harp, guitar (*punteada*), violin, or accordion, with a drum accompaniment.

One of the most important *criolla* dances (i.e., native, indigenous) of the Argentine countryside is the *gato*. Not only is it widespread, but other dances derive from it. Here also the Spanish heritage comes to light. Dance figures include shoe-tapping steps performed by women. Much like *flamenco* female dancers, the women lift their long skirts to show the agility of the foot movements. Another familiar choreographic figure is the so-called *escobillado* (or *escobilleo*), a very fast foot movement performed by men, consisting of swinging one foot after the other with scraping of the ground. Rhythmically and formally, the *gato* presents singular features. The text of the sung *gato* follows the form of the *seguidilla*, a four-line verse pattern in which the second line is assonant with the fourth. But the lines of the *gato* are of seven and

[6] Cf. Isabel Aretz, *El folklore musical*, pp. 202–205.

five syllables, in alternation. This textual irregularity creates, in a strict syllabic setting, a rather uneven melodic phrasing. In actual performance, however, the difficulty is surmounted by anticipating the last accent of the seven-syllable line and by augmenting the note values in the melodic phrase corresponding to the five-syllable line. The *gato* is accompanied by a guitarist who also sings. The specific Spanish guitar technique known as *guitarra rasgueada* (strumming) is used here consistently, in a 6/8 meter. Picked guitar is used only in the prelude and interludes. Characteristically, the rhythmic formula of the *gato* alternates between 6/8 and 3/4 meters (the hemiola rhythm again). Generally, the sung *gato* is made up of four melodic phrases, repeated with some minor variants in the following order: prelude, AABB, interlude, AB, interlude, CD, in which prelude and interludes are strictly instrumental. Whenever it is sung in duet, parallel thirds prevail, a characteristic of Iberian folk polyphony.

Among the many Argentine folk dances for couples, the *zamba* should be mentioned. Together with such dances as the *aires* and the *lorencita*, it is a "scarf dance" (*danza de pañuelo*). According to Carlos Vega and Isabel Aretz, there exists in Argentina (and in Chile, Peru, and Ecuador for that matter) a true code involving the use and function of the scarf. The *zamba* has a rather obscure history. An old colonial Peruvian dance known as *Zamacueca* or *Zambacueca* (today *marinera*) was introduced into Argentina during the first half of the nineteenth century. Out of this dance emerged the *zamba* on the one hand, and the *cueca* on the other. The latter became one of the most familiar dances of Chile and Bolivia. In the Western provinces of Argentina the name *chilena* was used to designate the Chilean *cueca*. Thus the three names *zamba*, *cueca*, and *chilena* have survived and have, nowadays, specific meanings. Choreographically, *zamba* and *cueca* differ considerably. While the basic figures are similar, the overall development of the dances depart from each other. The *cueca* allows extemporized shoe-tapping, whereas the *zamba* adheres more strictly to less vivid and traditional figures. Musically, both dances are indistinguishable as to general form but present different melodic types. Both show preference for four musical phrases, the last two of which are repeated. They both start with an eight-measure introduction and end with a coda in which new melodic material is presented. The prevailing meter is 6/8, with subdivisions of ternary and binary figures. For the *zamba* the basic rhythmic formula for both accompaniment and melody is $\frac{6}{8}$ ♩♩♩ ♪♩ , although a $\frac{3}{4}$ ♩ ♩ ♩ accompaniment figure occurs rather frequently. The *zamba* is essentially instrumental, although vocal versions also exist.

Traditionally, the performing ensemble includes the violin for the melody, the guitar for harmonic support, and the drum (*bombo*) for accompaniment. In recent times, the accordion tends to substitute for the violin. Older *zamba* melodies tend to exhibit a modal ambiguity, due to the alternation of major and minor thirds, or that of B natural and B flat in the dorian mode; the melodic minor scale also appears. More recent melodies adhere strictly to the major mode; so do *cueca* melodies, which tend, however, to end on the fifth degree of the scale. But it is in their rhythmic cast that *cuecas* differ intrinsically from the *zamba*. *Cuecas* are essentially vocal and their texts follow the *seguidilla* form, resulting in the same metric irregularity observed previously with the *gato*. Only the guitar accompanies the *cueca*, with the occasional addition in the Western provinces of the *charango*, under the influence of the Chilean and Bolivian *cueca*. The accompaniment consists typically of a regular strumming in 6/8 (♩ ♫ ♫ ♩ ♩ ♩), creating cross-rhythmic effects with the vocal line.

Many Brazilian folk songs and dances also exhibit considerable European retentions. For example, many of the round dance types used in the *fandangos* in southern Brazil are of Portuguese derivation. These *fandangos* are popular rural revelries in which regional dances, such as the *tirana, tatu, balaio, recortado,* and many others, are performed. One of the most frequent components of these dances is shoe-tapping; another, in the state of Rio Grande do Sul, is the use of castanets. Thus *fandango* was transformed in Brazil into a generic term, which suggests that the Spanish dance of the same name was once popular there, as it was in Portugal. The numerous designations of these dances derive from the song texts. Typically, the singing, which alternates stanza and refrain and is always in fauxbourdon style, is the responsibility of the guitar players.

The Andean Area

Bolivia, Peru, and Ecuador are good examples of nations in which the Spanish culture was greatly influenced by that of the Indians. The combination of stylistic elements from the Indian and Spanish populations in the whole area formerly occupied by the Inca Empire—a combination which did not occur with the English and Indian styles in North America—was probably due to the greater musical sophistication of the Andean populations as compared to the relatively simpler musical cultures of the North American Indians. In his study of instruments used by the Incas and their predecessors, Robert Stevenson (see bibliography for this chapter) has conclusively shown that the Andean peoples had, at the time of the conquest, the most refined musical culture of the whole American continent. Not only did they know five- and six-hole flutes with unequal finger-holes, fourteen- and fifteen-tube *antaras* (panpipes made of clay), double-row panpipes with unequal pipe-growth, and cross flutes, but their instrument making proves their intent to use predetermined pitches. Today, in the Andean area there is hardly any village or town (even in the Spanish-speaking villages) that does not have a kind of traditional music with elements of Indian musical culture. The widespread use of pre-Colombian instruments, such as the panpipe (called *sicu* by the Aymaras and *antara* by the Quechuas) and vertical flute (*pincollo, pincullo*), attests to that influence. The ubiquitous end-blown flute known as *quena* is used along with European types of drums in processions for Catholic saints, and in social dances, along with post-Colombian indigenous instruments such as the *charango*. It is very difficult in Bolivia, Peru, and Ecuador to separate the musical elements of Indian origin from those of the European tradition. Acculturation began in the sixteenth century; it was consciously fostered by the Catholic missionaries, who realized that the survival of Christianity depended in part on its absorption of native elements. The elements of the two cultures combined to form inseparable units. Essentially, the tunes are European in style, but a very large number show a great deal of repetition and make use of tetratonic and pentatonic scales. The introduction of diatonic scales in modern times has required adjustments in instrument making. Thus, today, six- and seven-hole *quenas* are more common than the three- or four-hole models. In addition, European string instruments (violin, guitar, lute, harp) have, to a great extent, modified the essential character of highland Indian music. For example, European harmonic patterns have been added to a music that was probably essentially monodic. These patterns form today the basic support for melodies of clearly non-European character. In their study (see bibliography), the d'Harcourts have analyzed the various modes used in Quechua music. Out of some two hundred melodies collected in the highlands, the majority show a descending progression and are built on the pentatonic scale without semitone, G-E-D-C-A, where the highest tone tends to act as a dominant. Literally hundreds of songs in the highland Andean area present this melody type. Obviously mestizo melodies abound, many of them based in part on the European diatonic scale. But all tunes maintain a modal flavor, a prevailingly descending tendency, large intervals, and few modulations. Rhythmically, Indian traits also prevail. Duple meters, with binary and ternary divisions, are the most frequent, especially a dactylic formula for percussion accompaniment. Syncopated melodic lines are also very common in pure song genres, such as the *yaravi,* and in dance types, such as the *huayno*. Particularly important is the syncopation of ♪♪ ♩ together with ♩. ♩.While the same syncopation occurs in most Afro-American music in Latin America, the resulting effect (here) is quite different, partly because the first note of each beat tends to be strongly accented. Another rhythmic peculiarity of much Andean melodic material is an emphasis of shorter note values when they occur at the beginning of a beat. Example 9-4, taken from the d'Harcourts' study, illustrates these peculiarities. 6/8 meters are also very common

EXAMPLE 9-4. Rhythmic formulas of Andean music. From Raoul and Marguerite d'Harcourt, *La Musique des Incas et ses survivances* (Paris: P. Geuthner, 1925), p. 156.

and frequently used in alternation with 3/4 (again the hemiola we noted in Argentine dances). Triple meters are found in mestizo music in which Spanish elements appear more clearly, but tunes of song types of Indian descent, such as the *yaravi*, are also often cast in triple meter. Finally, many Indian and mestizo song melodies are of a non-mensural nature. Typical accompanimental rhythmic figures of the Andean area represent the unmistakably Indian percussion style. This style consists, for the most part, in a straightforward, systematic repetition of the simplest figures. In addition to the dactylic rhythm in 2/4 already mentioned, the percussion presents the following figures: ¾ ♩ ♪♪ ♩ and ⁶⁄₈ ♩ ♪♪♩. . In some instances, such as the *cachua* (or *kashua*) dance of the Aymaras of Bolivia, the percussion accompaniment consists of a simple continuous rolling of the drum. String accompaniment, whether with harp, *charango*, or guitar, also presents distinct features. Among these, one particularly favored pattern which can be considered as a true trademark of the Andes is a series of arpeggios based on two fifths, with roots a minor third apart, presented in a rhythmic figure of an eighth followed by two sixteenths (Example 9-5). This pattern represents the basic accompaniment of many dances, such as the *wayno* (*huayno*), *carnaval*, *pandilla, and pampeña*, to name a few.

Formally, strophic form dominates much of Quechua and Aymara music. The simplest types of variation are fairly common as well. Improvisation does exist but does not have a major role. Mestizo songs or tunes tend to be in binary or ternary structures, with parallelism

EXAMPLE 9-5. Accompanimental patterns of Andean dance music. From Raoùl and Marguerite d'Harcourt, *La Musique des Incas et ses survivances* (Paris: P. Geuthner, 1925), p. 162.

in thirds. Aymara instrumental ensembles, on the other hand, very often present the melody doubled at the fourth and the octave, especially in the *sicus* ensembles.

Many indigenous dances of the Aymara and Quechua Indians, including pantomime dances, have become traditional for celebrating Catholic religious feasts as well as their own rituals. For example, the dance of *Kena-Kena* (or *Uturunku*) is used for the feast of the Holy Cross; that of the *Wipfala* is associated with the agrarian rituals (to the deity of the earth, Pachamama) and is preferably performed during the harvest season and on August 15 (Assumption day). The Quechua and Aymara peoples also have dances like the numerous dramatic dances of Latin America involving Christians and Moors, but reminiscent of events from the conquest period, or of the glory of the past. For example, the *Chunchus and Collas* dance of Peru involves two sides representing Spanish soldiers and Indians, and the well-known *Baile del Inca* of the Quechuas and Aymaras reminds one of Atahualpa's cruel death.

Among the principal social dances of the Andes is the *huayno*, popular from Northern Argentina to Ecuador where it is known as *sanjuanito* (this term could be derived from "huainito" rather than San Juan). Although an Indian dance, it has been adopted by mestizos of the highlands as their own. The Aymara and Quechua *huaynos* still exhibit an aboriginal character, but with an increasing degree of Spanish flavor in both music and texts. Indian *huaynos* are generally sung in the native languages, although lyrics in both Spanish and Quechua, for example, are not uncommon. In lively tempo, the *huayno* appears most of the time in duple meter and in binary form, consisting of two phrases (AB) of equal length (generally four measures each) repeated *ad libitum*. Versions alternating triple and duple meter (or compound duple), or simply alternating binary and ternary divisions in a single meter, are fairly frequent. Most tunes associated with the dance take the pentatonic mode (G-E-D-C-A) as their basis. Example 9-6 shows one of the most typical versions of the *huayno*.

EXAMPLE 9-6. The typical *huayno kaypipas,* from Cuzco, Peru. From *Cancionero Andino Sur,* ed. by Consuelo Pagaza Galdo (Lima: Casa Mozart, 1967), p. 13. Collected by Consuelo Pagaza Galdo and transcribed by Rodolfo Holzmann.

Afro-Hispanic Folk Music

The last major South American folk musical tradition to which we shall turn our attention derives from the complete fusion of African and Hispanic styles. This Afro-American tradition is particularly important in Brazil, Venezuela, and Colombia, and to a lesser extent in Uruguay, Argentina, and the lower coastal regions of Peru and Ecuador.

The special character of Brazilian folk music is largely due to the importance of the Black population in much of the national culture as a whole. Not only do the Black communities have their own traditions, which often revolve around styles that are still very close to Africa, as we indicate in Chapter Ten; the folk music of the Brazilian mestizos and whites, in many instances, can hardly be distinguished from that of the Afro-Brazilians, since they both result from basically identical syntheses. The Afro-Brazilian components are especially recognized in the driving rhythms, the particular performance practices, and the explicit importance of percussion instruments. The emphasis on dancing can also be interpreted as a result of the same syntheses. The number of Brazilian distinct folk dance forms of Luso-African derivation is genuinely striking. Among these, the best known are *batuque, samba, jongo, côco, lundu, baiano,* and some purely urban types, such as the *samba de morro, maracatu, maxixe, chôro,* among others. All Afro-Brazilian folk dances include specific choreographic traits, such as tapping, marked movement of the hips and the shoulders, and *umbigada*. *Umbigada* (from the Portuguese *umbigo* meaning navel) is the most characteristic choreographic elements of these dances, a sort of "invitation to the dance" manifested by the touching of the couple's navels. When there is no *umbigada* in a given dance, the dance generally belongs to the *caboclo* folklore or has an Hispanic origin. The *umbigada* is therefore a diagnostic trait defining the different origins of these dances.

Samba is a generic term designating, along with *batuque,* the choreography of certain round dances imported from Angola and the Congo area. We should distinguish between the various rural versions of the folk *samba* and the popular urban dance which developed only after World War I. The rural versions have different musical characteristics from most urban dances, although the responsorial singing and the use of syncopations are elements of both. The vocal line of the rural expression (as studied by the Brazilian musicologist, Mário de Andrade) tends to be divided into irregular patterns: three to five units for the stanzas, four to seven for the refrain, with variants. The melodies rarely go beyond the range of a sixth. Syncopations do occur in the folk *samba* but not as frequently as, and without the numerous variants found in, the urban expression. The exclusively percussive accompaniment of both versions is based on the following rhythmic figures: $\frac{2}{4}$ ♩. ♪♩♪ , ♫♩♫♫ , and the superimposition of the dotted figure on four regular sixteenths. A peculiar variety of *samba* which developed mostly in the city of Rio de Janeiro and has become the carnival dance par excellence is the *samba de morro*. This type, cultivated among the poor people inhabiting the hillside slums of the city (*morro* means "hill" in Portuguese), preserves some aspects of the rural *samba:* responsorial pattern, with solo part often improvised; mostly two-part form; and accompaniment exclusively by percussion instruments. Example 9-7 is a typical *samba de morro,* transcribed from a field collection made in the late 1930s. It shows most of the rhythmic-melodic patterns of the rural *samba,* i.e., repeated notes, intervallic skips within a melodic progression up to the sixth, offbeat phrasing of accents (represented notationally by ties across beats), frequent descending melodic movement, and the contrasting regularity of the solo part. Many varieties of *samba* are found through-

EXAMPLE 9-7. Brazilian *samba de morro.* From Egydio de Castro e Silva, "O samba carioca," *Revista Brasileira de Música,* VI (1939), 49–50. (*Surdo* is a low-pitched drum, *cuíca* a friction drum, *pandeiro* a tambourine, and *tamborim* a tabor-like instrument.)

Solo (without accompaniment)

out the country. Some, such as the *samba de roda,* maintain the typical Afro-Brazilian accompanimental formulas, but the melodic material tends to show Hispanic influences (regular phrasing, parallelism).

Afro-American musical traits are quite prominent in some aspects of Venezuelan and Colombian folk music. Marked Black musical influence in these countries is to be found above all in the coastal regions which properly belong to the Caribbean area. The most authentically African drumming and dancing in Venezuela comes from the states of Zulia and Trujillo, along Lake Maracaibo. Among the various percussion instruments, three types of drum should be mentioned: the *mina* drum (or *tambor grande*), more than six feet tall, with a single head fastened by ropes and wedges; the *curbata* drum, of the same family but smaller; and the *tambor redondo* ("round drum"), double-headed and always played in a battery of three (these round drums are also called *culepuyas*). Stamping bamboo tubes, called *quitiplás*, are also part of the African heritage of Venezuela. Most of the percussion instruments have an almost exclusively accompanimental function. The fact that a significant body of Afro-Venezuelan folk music is used in connection with Catholic feasts (e.g., feasts of St. John, St. Benedict) is again indicative of the strong local cultural blending.

One of the most typical dances and songs of Venezuela today is the *joropo*. The term itself has a generic sense of music for dancing. According to the Venezuelan ethnomusicologist Ramón y Rivera,[7] there are four main categories representing the music used to sing and dance the *joropo;* the *corrido, galerón, pasaje,* and *golpe.* As a result, the melody of this dance presents greatly diversified aspects. But the urban *joropo,* which is generally composed and has significantly penetrated the rural regions as well, is a fast dance in triple time, with a strongly syncopated accompaniment and frequent hemiola effect. Its choreography (for solo couple) seems to be analogous to that of the Colombian *pasillo* and *bambuco.* The latter is one of the most representative dances of the Colombian mestizo. It also alternates 3/4 and 6/8 meters. Its text, Spanish-derived, consists of four octosyllabic lines with an occasional refrain, and its accompaniment calls for Spanish folk instruments, such as the *tiple* and the *bandola* (respectively, a small guitar and a mandolin). In the Pacific Lowlands the *bambuco* is related to the *currulao.* (See Chapter Ten).

CENTRAL AMERICA: MEXICO AND THE CARIBBEAN

Mexican folk music is largely in the Spanish tradition, and while the Mexican Indians retain to some extent their native musical styles, there seems to have been less influence of the Indian styles on the Spanish-derived folk music here than in the Andean countries. Therefore, the basic difference between the Inca and the Aztec areas seems to be that the former could be considered as "the product of Hispanic influence upon an indigenous foundation," while the latter appears to reveal "an indigenous influence upon a Hispanic foundation," as Rodney Gallop has characterized Mexican art. This Hispanic foundation is manifested in Mexico mainly in the melody types of mestizo folk songs, the Spanish-derived choreography in numerous mestizo folk dances, and the widespread adoption of Hispanic instruments, even among rather isolated Indian groups. But one important difference between Spanish and Central American folk music in general is the importance of instruments in the

---

[7] Cf. Luis Felipe Ramón y Rivera, *El joropo: baile nacional de Venezuela* (Caracas: Ministerio de Educación, Dirección de cultura y bellas artes, 1952).

latter. In Mexico, the Spaniards at the time of the conquest found highly sophisticated instruments (mainly percussion instruments, flutes, ocarinas, and the famous multiple flutes) and a refined melodic system, if we can accept as evidence the testimony of early Spanish missionaries and the conclusions that have been drawn from the study of archaeological instruments.

The early missionaries in Mexico evidently tried hard to suppress the native Indian musical culture. They did not succeed entirely, but as a result of their work much of the folk music of the Hispanic tradition has found its way into the culture of some Mexican Indian groups. Vicente Mendoza,[8] a well-known authority on Mexican music, presents songs of the Otomí Indians of Northern Mexico which show the characteristic triplets of Spanish folk song and have elements of major tonality emphasizing tonic and third. Other Otomí songs give even greater evidence of European influence in their parallel thirds and sixths, which are hardly to be found in aboriginal Indian music. This is not to say that these songs are simply Spanish songs sung by Indians; their style is simpler than the Spanish, for they typically have short melodies, few tones, and small range. More likely they are songs composed by Indians who were still steeped in the Indian tradition but who had had contact with Hispanic folk music in Mexico. Likewise, the most typical mestizo musical forms are a result of the local adoption and gradual adaptation of both Spanish and Indian material throughout post-conquest Mexican history. Almost never has a Spanish folk song form or dance been adopted *in toto*. For example, the Spanish *romance* was transformed in Mexico and some Caribbean countries into the *corrido*, although its general character remained closely identifiable with that of its generator. The *corrido* continued to be essentially a narrative song type, with a four-line stanza or a *décima* form but with repetitive melodic structure, with many regional sub-types. *Corridos* often dealt with current events, crimes, and love stories, much as the English broadside ballads tell of sensational happenings; new ones are still coming into existence. Art songs are also sometimes reshaped into the form of the *corrido* by the folk tradition.

Among the numerous kinds of mestizo songs and dances, the *jarabe, jarana, huapango, son, canción,* and *valona* should be mentioned. The *jarabe* is one of the oldest and most popular folk dances of Mexico. Indians, rural and urban mestizos, and white people dance to it. It shows preference for triple meter, occasionally alternating with 6/8, and follows a binary form. The name *jarabe tapatío* is given to that form of

---

[8] Vicente Mendoza, "Música indígena Otomí," *Revista de Estudios Musicales* II, No. 5–6 (1950–1951), 527.

the dance which developed in Jalisco. The name "hat dance" by which the *jarabe* is called in the United States, is derived from a choreographic section in which the man puts his sombrero on the ground and his partner dances around in the wide brim. The urban *jarabe* has become a conventionalized and abbreviated version of the old dance still performed in many villages. Each section has its own melody, called a *son*, of sixteen or twenty-four measures. In the sixteen-measure *son*, the first half is instrumental and the last half vocal with accompaniment. The twenty-four-measure *son* has an eight-measure addition of an instrumental ending.

Similar to the *jarabe* is the *jarana*, the most popular dance in Yucatan. The music has the same lively character as that of the *jarabe*, but the dance proper is generally not accompanied by singing. The word *jarana* is said to be derived from the small stringed instrument of the same name, belonging to the *vihuela* family. The dance is accompanied by an ensemble composed of *jaranas*, drums, cornets, and sometimes *güiro*-type rattles.

The *huapango* is a well-known folk dance from the Gulf coast province of Veracruz and the central region of Huasteca. According to Paul Bowles, the Huasteco and Veracruzano types have in common "an extremely successful exploitation of contretemps: voices go along seemingly unaware of each other or of the rhythmical variations in the accompanying bass. The Huasteco is the simpler of the two, the disparity in rhythm between the melody and accompaniment is less, and the melodies themselves are less involved and less soaring."[9] Other musical characteristics, noted by Stevenson, are (1) the rapid shift from 3/4 to 6/8; (2) the rapid gait of the beats and alternation of accents; (3) a frequent sharp accent on the last eighth note in a measure; and (4) the frequent harmonic use of interior tonic pedals. In modern *huapangos*, such as the well-known *La Bamba*, the typical instrumental accompaniment includes a violin, two *guitarrones* (large five-string bass instrument, with a convex-shaped body), and a *jarana*, although the *huapango* ensembles also use harps and *jabalinas* (similar to the *guitarrón*).

Considerable confusion accompanies the use of the word *son* in Mexican music. As has been mentioned previously, the word sometimes refers to individual sections of *jarabes* and *huapangos*, sometimes to any song or portion of a song. It is also used to designate a separate choreographic genre. But the precise meaning of *son* also depends on association with a particular region or state: *son huasteco*, *son veracruzano*, *son jaliciense*, etc.

Vicente Mendoza depicts the *son* as one of the most genuinely

[9] Paul Bowles, "On Mexico's Popular Music," *Modern Music*, XVIII, 4 (May–June, 1941), 225–226.

Mexican of all folk genres. It is associated with an instrumental group comprising violins, guitars, *jaranas*, and *guitarrón*, and sometimes harp. To this combination the *mariachi* bands add trumpets, trombone, or clarinets. The development of the *mariachi* orchestras—groups of three to a dozen players of string instruments—is an interesting manifestation of the instrument culture in Mexico. In recent decades, brass instruments have been added to the traditional ensemble. The *son* constitutes an integral part of the *mariachi* band repertory. Rhythmic vigor characterizes the *son*, and alternating or simultaneous use of 3/4 and 6/8 meter are again standard. Often a unit of three notes and one of two notes is combined with a resultant 5/8. Example 9-8 shows six characteristic rhythmic patterns for *sones* from the Jalisco region.

EXAMPLE 9-8. Characteristic rhythmic patterns of Mexican *sones*. From Paul Bowles, "On Mexico's Popular Music," *Modern Music*, XVIII, 4 (May–June, 1941), 227.

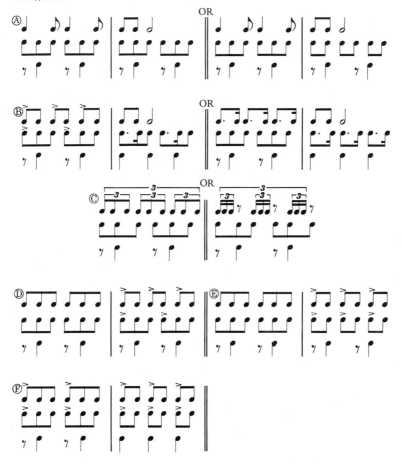

The song associated with the *son* intersperses short vocal verses with ritornello-like instrumental sections. Sequences abound, and parallel thirds, sixths, and triads accompany the melodic line.

The *canción* is a Mexican song of lyric expression which has assimilated many characteristics of nineteenth century Italian opera. It is not confined within any given meter or rhythm, but its form generally is a binary structure consisting of the song itself and an instrumental ritornello. The variety within the boundaries of the genre is abundant. Mendoza classifies the *canción* according to the following criteria: the meter of the versification, the musical structure, geographical features which it describes, area of the country in which it is sung, the time of day or the circumstances in which it is sung, the character of the tune, age or occupation of the users, and the rhythm of the accompaniment expressed in terms of European dance forms.

The *valona* (or *balona*) is a declamatory genre whose poetic form follows the *décima* model. The themes of this genre run the gamut of human sentiment, from dramatic to humorous and satirical. The vocal part is in parlando-rubato style, while the instrumental part (known as *sinfonía*) is strictly metrical. The instrumental ensemble in Jalisco includes usually two guitars, two violins, harp, and possibly *jaranas*.

The most typical performance characteristics of Mexican folk music comprise a high tension of the voice, producing an extremely vigorous incisive effect; a slight continuous nasalizing of the voice and a preference for high pitch, frequently passing into falsetto; instrumental pieces often beginning in a slower tempo than is used in the main body of the piece, with a gradual acceleration to the desired tempo, which is then maintained rigorously until the final cadence. Improvisation is not emphasized in Mexican music, and melismatic ornamentation, of the Andalusian *cante hondo* type, is largely absent, as it is in all of Latin America.

The states of Central America, from Guatemala to Panama, have greatly varied musical traditions. In addition to the same Hispanic foundation of Mexican folk music, the area has a number of aboriginal Indians with traditional music and a marked Black influence. For example, in spite of the fact that the most popular dance of Guatemala, the *son chapín*, exhibits clear European traits, the national instrument of the country is the marimba. Likewise, the *sique*, the most characteristic folk dance of Honduras, is closely related to the Spanish *jota*. But it is also in Honduras and Nicaragua that Black Carib settlements are to be found. The Black Caribs are descendants of Arawak and Carib Indian tribes and former African slaves. But in spite of their Afro-Indian past, their culture and their music are derivative of West Africa, combined with ceremonial dancing of tropical forest Indian cultural derivation.

Panama is a good example of a country whose musical traditions clearly reflect its ethnohistory. Traditional music is found among Indian groups, such as the *Cunas* and the *Guaymíes;* Hispanic music is represented by various folk song genres and dances, above all the *mejorana* or *socavón;* and African-derived music is represented mostly by dances of the *tamborito* type.

The *mejorana* is a ballad type, although purely instrumental pieces accompany a dance of the same name. The sung version, exclusively for male voice, is commonly referred to as *socavón* and shows the following traits: a descending tendency of the melodic phrase, progressing by disjunct rather than conjunct motion, and a text based on the *décima* preceded by a quatrain with the typical rhyme scheme ABBA. Although many *mejorana* melodies are cast in the major and minor modes, the mixolydian mode also occurs frequently. Typically the accompanying instrument is a modern guitar or the native *mejoranera* whose tunings are either e, b, a, a, d, or e, c sharp, a, a, d. Hemiola rhythm between the voice and the accompaniment is quite common. The singing style involves a penetrating harsh voice (without tremolo), with frequent alternation of falsetto and normal voice, extending the range to more than two octaves. As a dance, the *mejorana* presents traditional Spanish choreography divided into two parts: the *zapateo* (foot figures) and the *paseo* (promenade as in the square dance).

The most typical example of Afro-Panamanian singing and dancing is to be found in the *tamborito,* danced by mixed couples but sung exclusively by women (both solo and chorus). Generally a short phrase is sung alternately by soloist and chorus, although other forms may occur, such as two different phrases of equal or varying length; in the latter case, the longer phrase is that of the soloist. Typically the dance is in duple meter and is accompanied by hand clapping and drums. The drums are played in a battery of three, in complex rhythmic combinations.[10]

In general terms, two folk traditions form the basis of the music in such "Latin" Caribbean islands as Cuba, Puerto Rico, and the Dominican Republic: the Hispanic tradition and the African tradition. Among the Cuban peasants (the *guajiros*) of the Eastern province and the interior of the country there survive two song types, the *punto* and the *guajira,* showing the same stylistic peculiarities as most Spanish-related folk music of Latin America. The *punto* is spread throughout the Caribbean; it is found in Puerto Rico, the Dominican Republic, Colombia, Venezuela, and Panama.

[10] Fourteen notated examples of *tamborito* are given in *Boletín del Instituto de Investigaciones Folklóricas*, Vol. I, no. 1 (Panamá: Universidad Inter-Americana, 1944).

Afro-Cuban music, in addition to the cult-related music examined in Chapter Ten, is represented by such important dance forms as the *conga*, the *rumba*, and other well-known hybrid forms, such as the *son*, the *danzón*, the *guaracha*, the *habanera*, and the *bolero*. Together with the various drum types associated with cult music, the typical Afro-Cuban instrumental ensembles include *maracas*, *güiros*, *claves*, and bongo drums. The *tres* and *cuatro* (small three- and four-string guitars) are commonly added to the percussion. Example 9-9 illustrates the fundamental rhythmic figures of Afro-Cuban music. The first figure, called *tresillo* in Cuba, is often notated as a simple triplet (A), but in actual performance appears as in (B) or (C). In other words, by taking the sixteenth note as the unit, the duple meter is actually subdivided as 3-3-2. The second figure, notated as (D) but performed as (E), is further complicated in the basic *conga* rhythm by tying together the first two notes of that rhythmic cell (F). The third figure (G) is perhaps the most characteristic formula of Cuban folk and popular music. It is known as *cinquillo* and results possibly from a contraction of the rhythm (H), quite African in its symmetry. It also forms the basis of much ritual drumming of the Haitian *vodoun*, as well as the Caribbean dance known as *merengue* (Haiti, Dominican Republic). It sometimes appears as (I), and it generates the basic rhythm of the Cuban *danzón* (J). The last two models show the typical figures, in duple and triple meters, associated with the *claves* in almost all Afro-Caribbean dances. The first measure of the duple meter

EXAMPLE 9-9. Rhythmic figures of Afro-Cuban music. From Gaspar Agüero y Barreras, "El Aporte Africano a la Música Popular Cubana," *Estudios Afrocubanos*, (1946), p. 77.

example is the *habanera* rhythmic formula, the epitome of Latin American dance music.

BIBLIOGRAPHY AND DISCOGRAPHY

The best and most comprehensive bibliographical discussion of Latin American folk and primitive music is found in Gilbert Chase, *A Guide to the Music of Latin America* (Washington, D.C.: Pan American Union, 1962). An updated account of the literature appears in the music section of the *Handbook of Latin American Studies,* published annually by the Hispanic Foundation of the Library of Congress.

A very useful study of Aztec and Inca musics and their development is Robert Stevenson, *Music in Aztec & Inca Territory* (Berkeley and Los Angeles: University of California Press, 1968). Mexican folk music is also studied, with many musical examples, in Stevenson, *Music in Mexico: A Historical Survey* (New York: Thomas Y. Crowell Co., 1952); in Vicente T. Mendoza, *Panorama de la Música Tradicional de México* (México: Imprenta Universitaria, 1956); and in Mendoza, *La Canción Mexicana* (México: Universidad Nacional, 1961). Gertrude P. Kurath and Samuel Martí, *Dances of Anahuac* (Chicago: Aldine Publishing Company, 1964), discusses the Maya and Aztec traditional dances and music and the extent of their preservation in present-day Middle America.

Studies of Latin American folk and popular musical instruments abound. For Central America, Vida Chenoweth, *The Marimbas of Guatemala* (Lexington: The University of Kentucky Press, 1964), Samuel Martí, *Instrumentos musicales precortesianos,* 2nd ed. rev. (Mexico City: Instituto Nacional de Antropología e Historia, 1968), and Charles L. Boilès, "The Pipe and Tabor in Mesoamerica," *Yearbook* of the Inter-American Institute for Musical Research, Tulane University, Vol. II (1966), should be consulted. For South America, the most useful single-volume items are: Isabel Aretz, *Instrumentos musicales de Venezuela* (Cumaná, Venezuela: Universidad de Oriente, 1967), and Carlos Vega, *Los instrumentos musicales aborígenes y criollos de Argentina* (Buenos Aires: Ediciones Centurión, 1946). Works mentioned below also contain sections on instruments.

Most studies of South American folk, primitive, and popular music are in Spanish or Portuguese. Items in English appear in specialized journals, such as the Latin American issue of *Ethnomusicology,* Vol. X, no. 1 (January, 1966). For the Andean area, Raoul and Marguerite d'Harcourt, *La Musique des Incas et ses survivances* (Paris: P. Geuthner, 1925) is still valuable. A more recent study is Marguerite and Raoul d'Harcourt, *La Musique des Aymara sur les Hauts Plateaux Boliviens* (Paris: Société des

Américanistes, 1959). Important collections of folk music for the same Andean area are: *Cancionero Andino Sur* (Lima: Casa Mozart, 1967) and *Panorama de la Música Tradicional del Perú* (Lima: Casa Mozart, 1966). A good survey of Argentine folk music is the study of Isabel Aretz mentioned in the text, p. 185. Oneyda Alvarenga, *Música Popular Brasileira* (Rio de Janeiro: Editôra Globo, 1950) is the best introduction to its subject. Rossini Tavares de Lima, *Melodia e rítmo no folclore de São Paulo* (São Paulo: Ricordi, 1954) presents numerous musical notations and excellent photographs of musical instruments. Aspects of Colombian folk music are discussed in José Ignacio Perdomo Escobar, *Historia de la Música en Colombia*, 3rd ed. (Bogotá: Academia Colombiana de Historia, 1963).

Among the many recordings of Latin American folk music available commercially, the following items are recommended. Folkways Records catalogs contain some of the most useful recordings. Mexican and Central American material appears on *Songs of Mexico*, Folkways FP 15; *Mexican Folk Songs*, Vol. 2, Folkways FP 815/2; *Folk Music of Honduras*, Folkways FP 834; *Black Caribs of Honduras*, Folkways P 435; and *Mexican Corridos*, Folkways FW 6913. Caribbean collections include *Caribbean Dances*, Folkways FP 840; *Calypso, Meringues*, Folkways FP 8; *Songs & Dances of Puerto Rico*, Folkways FP 80/2; *Música del Pueblo Puertorriqueño*, Troutman Press, UB-137; and the recent *The Music of Trinidad*, National Geographic Society, 3297.

South American materials are found in *Folk Music of Colombia*, Folkways FW 6804; *Folk Music of Venezuela*, Library of Congress, Archive of Folk Song, AFS L15; *Venezuelan Folk and Aboriginal Music*, The Columbia World Library of Folk and Primitive Music, Columbia KL-212; *Music of Peru*, Folkways P 415; *Traditional Music of Peru*, Folkways FE 4456; and *Kingdom of the Sun*, Nonesuch H-72029. The music of Bolivia is well represented in *Instruments and Music of Bolivia*, Folkways FM 4012; and *Songs and Dances of Bolivia*, Folkways FW 6871. An excellent collection of Argentine music is *Argentine Dances*, Folkways FW 8841 and 8842. The album *Argentine Folk Songs*, Folkways FW 6810, presents selections of songs accompanying such dances as the *gato* and the *chacarera*. The music of Brazil is not well represented on the United States record market; however, the album *Songs and Dances of Brazil*, Folkways FW 6953, includes good examples of *emboladas*.

TEN

AFRO-AMERICAN FOLK MUSIC
IN NORTH AND LATIN AMERICA

by Bruno Nettl and Gérard Béhague

One of the truly important developments in the recent history of world music was initiated by the forced migration of great numbers of Africans, as slaves, to various parts of the Americas. Coming mostly from West Africa but also from other regions, such as Angola, they brought with them their music and other elements of their cultures, which served to provide a common context for the continuation, at least in part, of the African traditions. The Africans in the New World came into contact with a large variety of European musics, and the nature of the contact was different in North and South America, in the Caribbean, on plantations, and in towns. Their reactions to these European—and sometimes American Indian—musics called into being a whole group of musical sub-cultures that have had an impact on all strata of twentieth-century music in the West and elsewhere.

Not only are the folk musics of the various Black populations and communities in the New World intrinsically interesting and alive, they have also influenced the folk music of the whites to the extent of having played a major role in the development of some typical North and Latin American forms. They are responsible for the development of a great deal of Western popular music; their role in the development of ragtime and jazz cannot be overestimated; their urban outgrowths, such as gospel, rock, and soul music, are major forces in everyday musical life; and their effect on composers of art music in the United States and Latin America as well as on such Europeans as Antonin Dvořák and Igor Stravinsky has been considerable.

The origin of the styles of Black music in the New World has been the subject of much debate. Extreme and opposing views have been advanced: the music is actually African, unchanged by migration; the music is simply a copy of Western form and style; the Black American is a superlatively creative individual; he is capable of creating nothing but the simplest spontaneous musical utterances. The definition of "Black" music has been argued as well: is all music composed or performed by Afro-Americans Black music? Or is it only that part of the repertory of Afro-American musicians that shows a distinctly African-derived character? Much as the latter view seems more reasonable, the former one corresponds to a great deal of ethnomusicological practice, since scholars, in assessing the musical style of a culture, tend to base their findings on a sample of that culture's complete repertory, whatever its origins.

A more moderate view of the origins of Afro-American styles is now widely accepted. There is no doubt, of course, that the slaves from Africa did bring with them their music. In areas in which they greatly outnumbered their white neighbors and masters, and where they were isolated from the whites, they retained this African heritage with relatively little change. It is even conceivable that they now retain some practices that have changed more rapidly in Africa than in the New World. Some of their songs and rhythms can still be found in Africa, but their repertory appears to be largely material actually composed in the Americas, although using styles and patterns very largely derived from Africa. In areas in which Afro-Americans associated more closely with whites, and lived in less self-contained communities, they appear to have taken over a great deal of folk, church, and popular music from the whites (while probably also holding on to aspects of the African tradition), gradually absorbing it. Everywhere, in any event, they were influenced by the music of the whites (and in some cases by that of the Indians), and accordingly they modified their own way of singing to some extent. Thus their musical acculturation could take three forms: they may have learned the songs of the whites together with white performance practices; they may have learned the performance practices of the whites and superimposed these on their own songs; or they may have learned the songs of the whites and superimposed on them African performance practices.

All of these things happened to some degree. The Blacks of the United States learned songs from their white masters, from missionaries, and from neighbors in the towns. Some songs they sang in styles indistinguishable from those of the whites, but on most of them the Blacks imposed some stylistic traits derived from Africa. They presumably also continued to sing African songs and to compose new songs in the African styles; this appears to have been true more in Brazil and the Caribbean than in the United States to which slaves were not brought directly from Africa but rather from the Caribbean, where linguistic and tribal ties were broken down. The African elements that were retained were among those also found, at least to some extent, in European folk and popular music, a fact that stimulated anthropologists to develop a theory of culture change symbolized by the word "syncretism." According to Waterman,[1] when one culture is, as it were, absorbed by another, those traits of the two cultures which have similarity or compatibility tend to syncretize, or grow into a new combined form. Thus, for example, since both Africa and Europe have harmony, Afro-American music also has it, and its character is derived from both African and European models. In contrast, since North American Indian and European music have little in common, a form of music having features of both did not arise.

What actually are the African features that were carried into the New World? One that comes to mind immediately is the emphasis on rhythm; it appears in many different forms, including the importance of drums and other percussion instruments in the Black cultures of the Americas, the use of syncopation and complicated rhythmic figures in North America (and of complex rhythmic ensemble music in Latin America), and an emphasis on the beat, and a tendency to adhere very strictly to meter and tempo (the "metronome sense" of West Africa). Another feature is the tendency to use call-and-response patterns, so important in Africa, that is manifested not only in ordinary antiphonal or responsory techniques but also in more complex alternating devices, such as the rotation of the solo part in jazz. The love of instruments and instrumental music is also one of these African features, although only some Afro-American instruments are derived from Africa, others being ordinary Western instruments, such as guitar and harmonica, or adaptations of them, such as the gutbucket. Extremely important among African features is the use of improvisation and a tendency to vary a short theme. Polyphony, although not really typical of West African music or, for that

[1] Richard A. Waterman, "African Influence on American Negro Music," in *Acculturation in the Americas*, ed. Sol Tax (Chicago: University of Chicago Press, 1952), p. 212.

matter, of much Black music in the Americas, may perhaps, where it is found, be traceable to African roots. Most important, the manner of singing, the way in which the voice is used and the typical vocal tone color in the Black musics, appears to be closely related to Africa.

These are the features of music that appear to have been brought from Africa. They are techniques of making music, and the actual musical sounds that Afro-Americans produce when using such techniques may actually not seem very much like African music. It is frequently difficult to decide whether something that we notice about a piece of Black music results from the African heritage or not. As has been pointed out, African musical techniques have maintained themselves in a hostile cultural environment largely because their counterparts in Western folk and popular music are somewhat similar. But it is interesting to find that, on the whole, those features of music that were most strongly developed in Africa have to some extent also been retained in Afro-American music; and, conversely, those which were not developed to any great degree of complexity or distinctiveness (such as scale) seem to have given way to traits bearing the European trademark.

Students of the relationship between African and Afro-American cultures have often remarked on the extent to which African characteristics have remained in the Afro-American musical repertories, in contrast to the lower degree of retention in most other aspects of culture. At times this fact has been ascribed to the presumably special native musical talent of Blacks, and it has even been supposed that certain elements of music (rhythm, call-and-response, etc.) are part of the Black's biological heredity. The question of musical talent is unsolved, but until concrete evidence to the contrary is presented, it must be presumed that no racial group differs from others in the inheritance of such a complex group of behavioral patterns. And it has never been possible to prove the biological inheritance of specific aspects of musical behavior. The explanation is probably much closer at hand. Music plays an important role in African life, especially in ritual; as such, it is of major cultural value. It is not surprising that Africans cherished their musical heritage when they were brought to the New World. (Similarly, we find that European immigrant groups also tended to lay greater stress on their musical traditions in the strange environment of America than they did in the old country.) Furthermore, music was in various ways more complex and more highly developed in Africa than in the Western folk cultures with which the Blacks came into contact in the Americas.

It is possible to rank the various Afro-American communities by the degree to which their musical styles adhere to African models. Among the musics that are reasonably well known, those of Haiti, the Guianas, and Northeastern Brazil (particularly the state of Bahia) are closest to the African. Jamaica, Trinidad, and Cuba are next, followed by the Southern United States and, finally, the United States North. Generally speaking, religious music tends to be closer to African styles than does secular. In general, also, Africanisms are more readily found in rural than in urban situations, for the culture of the cities lends itself more to Westernization and acculturation, and a resulting modernization. This is particularly true of the United States, but there appear to be exceptions, as in the city of Salvador, Brazil, West African religious cults remain an important force, and are accompanied by extremely African-sounding music.

The kind of ranking produced here is complicated by the fact that each Afro-American community has a variety of styles. For example, the island of Jamaica provides a characteristic microcosm of this variety. Inhabited almost entirely by Blacks, it contains a number of distinct musics related in various ways to Africa. In the rural areas there are remnants of cult music with African-sounding melodies and drum patterns; there are also the songs of revival cults, based on Protestant fundamentalism, with songs that are European in character but sung with African modes of performance. In the port of Kingston, dock workers sing work songs in a style closely related to the music of Haiti and Cuba. The popular music of Kingston, however, is distinctively Jamaican, having developed, in the last two decades, three types of style, the Ska, the Rock-steady, and Reggae, all based essentially on North American models but with prominent African and Latin American elements. Jamaica participated, of course, along with Trinidad, in the development of a distinctive song type, the calypso. Thus, while we may rank Jamaica at a particular point in the scale denoting degrees of Africanism or African retention in music, we must realize that this ranking is not based on a homogeneous musical culture. The same sort of statement could be made about each of the communities mentioned here.

AFRO-AMERICAN INSTRUMENTS

A great many instruments that are at least partly of African origin are used by the Afro-American communities of Latin America. For example, in Haiti certain drums are made of hollow logs. Normally they have single heads and are cylindrical in shape. Their height varies from six feet to eighteen inches. Among the idiophones, the *ogan*, a kind of iron bell struck with an external clapper, is prominent, as are gourd rattles. Double-headed drums are also used, and so are shallow, single-headed, open drums similar to a tambourine. Various kinds of sticks are used to beat the drums, each cult having its own type of drum sticks and combination of drums. The mosquito drum, a type of musical bow, of which one end is attached to the ground while from the other extends a string attached to a piece of skin covering a hole in the ground, is used as an accompaniment to singing. In this instrument, the hole in the ground functions as a resonance chamber, much as the calabash or the player's mouth adds resonance to the sound of musical bows in Southern and Central Africa.

Stamping tubes, hollow tubes struck on the ground or on a board, provide another kind of rhythmic accompaniment. A rather large and deep-sounding version of the African *sansa* or *mbira* (called *marimba* in Haiti and *marimbula* in Puerto Rico) is also found in the Caribbean. Horns and trumpets made of bamboo, each capable of playing only one pitch, are used, as are cows' horns, conch-shell trumpets, and horns improvised from various objects, such as phonograph loudspeaker horns. The *claves,* short sticks made of hardwood that are struck together by hand, are important in the Caribbean. The xylophone, common in Africa, is not as widespread in the Afro-American cultures but does seem to have become one of the important instruments of Central America. In Guatemala, the marimba (xylophone with gourd resonators) has become a national instrument. A form of musical bow with gourd resonator, called *berimbau,* is used in Brazil and played in an essentially Central and South African manner. Throughout the area under discussion, the Negro community has brought instruments directly from Africa, has adapted Western materials and technology to the needs of African instruments, and has exerted an African cultural influence by its interest in instruments and instrumental music and its creation of many musical types, also by the prestige and ritual significance that it has placed on the instruments themselves and on the instrumentalists.

The steel drum, an instrument invented in Trinidad during or after World War II, is a fascinating example of the results of the acculturation of African practices in modern Western civilization. Steel oil containers, abandoned and available, their tops hammered into shapes producing the desired scales, were combined into groups of three or four different sizes and accompanied rhythmically by idiophones—rattles, *claves,* or bells. The bottom sections of the containers were cut off later, and the steel drums were placed on special stands. Each "drum" is capable of playing simple melodic material. The result is music of a strongly rhythmic character, with polyphony of an ostinato nature, and with each "drum" (or "pan," as they are called by the players) having a particular musical function, as in a jazz band.

Aside from African-derived and invented instruments, Western instruments such as the guitar and the banjo (which may itself have been

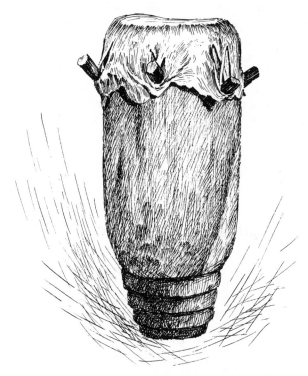

Drum type common in West Africa and the Caribbean.

developed under African influences) are widely used in the Negro communities of Latin America and the Caribbean.

In the Black folk music of the United States, instruments play a
larger role than in the Anglo-American tradition, although the Blacks'
interest in instruments appears to have infected the white communities
to a certain extent in the course of the twentieth century. Many of the
Afro-American instruments in the United States are European-derived
(mouth organ, banjo, fiddle, brass instruments), while others are actually
derived from African models or fashioned so as to produce sounds
similar to those produced by African instruments. In the former category
are several that are hardly found today but are reported to have been
present in the United States in the nineteenth century and earlier: the
sansa or *mbira*, hollowed log drums, and gourd rattles. In the latter category we find the gutbucket or washtub, related to the musical bow and to
the Haitian mosquito drum; washboards used as scrapers and placed on
baskets for resonance; and frying pans, cowbells, bottles, wood or bone
clappers to replace the bells and rattles of the West African percussion
ensembles. These instruments are not themselves descendants of African
forms, but they seem to have been invented or improvised to fulfill the
functions once performed by African instruments.

AFRO-AMERICAN MUSIC IN LATIN AMERICA

In the Latin American context, the definition of "Black" music, as
discussed above, becomes extremely complex. First of all, the general
acceptance of what constitutes, culturally and ethnically, an Afro-
American is not as unequivocal as in North America. There are several
examples in Central and South America of Black groups whose African
cultural identity is virtually non-existent, such as the Caribs of Honduras
and Nicaragua who are Black representatives of an Indian culture. Conversely, important non-Black segments of certain communities have perfectly definable African-related cultural traits, such as, for example, some
East Indian groups of Trinidad, or the Cayapa Indians of Western Ecuador. In many areas of Latin America, Negro acculturation has been considerable and has affected other ethnic groups or the wide range of mixed
groups. In such cases we are confronted with ethnically diverse groups
with a remarkably homogeneous "Black" culture. Race alone cannot, then,
be considered a valid criterion in discussing Afro-American musical styles
in Latin America. Although we are stressing Africanisms in our discussion
here, it should always be borne in mind that Afro-American music cuts
across ethnic lines.

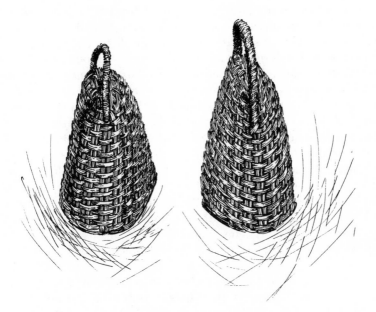

Basket rattles, as found in Haiti or West Africa.

Black music in Latin America functions in both sacred and secular contexts, but generally it is in the sacred context that African musical elements are most strongly preserved. Various cults involving deities (called *orishás, vodouns,* saints, etc.) that have been transferred from the West African homeland but whose character has often changed in the process are found conspicuously in Cuba, Haiti, Jamaica, Trinidad, and Brazil. Among the Afro-American communities of Latin America a cult implies the recognition of African deities and a belief system essentially African. Syncretism, however, has taken place almost everywhere, in varying degrees. Most cults show features of Christian belief systems, although not necessarily a recognition of a Christian God or saint. Often, as a result of socio-historical accommodation, a Catholic saint has been assimilated into the personality of an African deity, but the equivalence of saints and deities is by no means uniform throughout the continent. West African religions as developed in the Americas are monotheistic, animistic in nature, and involve a pantheon of major and lesser deities, each of which is worshipped with characteristic ceremonies, songs, and drum rhythms. The most obvious African features prevailing in such ceremonies include the ritual use of blood (animal sacrifices), initiatory rites, ritual dancing with a highly symbolic choreography, personification of the *orishás* through spirit possession, and offering of food to the gods. The most outstanding Christian or reinterpreted Christian elements include the use of the Bible, Catholic prayers, cross and crucifixes, candle burning, and lithographs of saints. Misconceptions about Afro-American belief systems, epitomized by the term "Black magic," arise from the fact that most cult leaders practice some aspect of folk medicine.

The most important Afro-Cuban cults include the *Lucumi* (derived from the Yoruba of Nigeria), the *Kimbisa* or *Mayombé* (from the Congo area), and the *Abakuá* (combining beliefs and practices of the other cults; its members are referred to as *ñáñigos*). In Brazil, the cult groups are called the *candomblé* in Bahia, *xangô* (shango) in Pernambuco, and *macumba* in the central and southern states. The Bahian groups include the *Ketu* (or *Nago*) and *Jesha* (Yoruba), the *Gêgê* (Dahomey), the *Congo-Angola,* and the *Caboclos* (derived from some Amerindian beliefs combined with those from the other cults). Most important among the Haitian cult groups are the *Vodoun* or *Rada* cult (*Arada-Nago* family) and the *Pétro* group (*Congo-Guinée* family). According to Courlander (see bibliography) other lesser family groups include the *Ibo-Kanga,* the *Congo,* and the *Juba-Martinique,* each with a distinct set of dances and accompanying songs. In Jamaica and Trinidad the groups include respectively the *Kumina* and the *Shango* cults, in addition to Afro-Christian groups under Protestant denominations' influence, such as the Pukkumina, Revival and

Revival Zion of Jamaica, and the Spiritual Baptists (or Shouters) of Trinidad. Revivalist cult music in these areas is quite similar to much Black Protestant music of the Southern United States. It is basically a mixture of various types of traditional Protestant hymnody, with an important body of Gospel hymns of the type composed by Ira Sankey and disseminated throughout the area by various evangelical crusaders during the nineteenth century. In both Jamaica and Trinidad the word "Sankey" has actually become a generic term for "hymn." A basic difference of Revival cult music from that of the other cults is the constant presence of harmonized choruses, much like congregational hymn singing in southern United States Black churches, and the nature of the accompanying rhythmic patterns, substantially less African than in the Cuban, Haitian, or Brazilian cults. The type of call and response practice in Jamaican revivalist music could be considered a retention of an African feature, although it is not unlike that of the commercial gospel music that one can hear in all large American cities.

Protestant-related cults excepted, the most obvious stylistic trait common to the musics of cult-groups in Latin America is the predominant use of call and response patterns. The leader or solo singer may be either a woman or a man, but the chorus is usually composed of women. The chorus sings in monophonic fashion, but occasionally individual singers deviate from the main melodic line. Among the most acculturated groups (*Abakuá* in Cuba, *Caboclo* and *Umbanda* in Brazil), heterophony is not uncommon. Sometimes soloist and chorus overlap. The scales are most commonly pentatonic without semitones, although diatonic scales are found in many songs. Tempo varies considerably from one cult group to another and, within the same cult, in accordance with a particular song cycle. Gradual acceleration in many songs or in drum music is fairly frequent, depending on their particular ritual function. The ranges of the melodies are not uniform; for example, the *Gêgê* cult of Bahia has songs with wide range (most with more than an octave), while those of the *Jesha* cult in the same area average less than an octave. The melodic contours are generally descending, but frequent pendulum-like movements are also characteristic, as in the series of songs to the deity *Exú* in the Bahian *Ketu* cult. Melodic intervals are frequently quite large. Whenever there is leader-chorus alternation, the melodic phrases tend to be short, but with solo songs or duets the melodic line becomes longer and more complex. The form, within the framework of the solo-chorus alternation, is frequently based on the repetition of a single phrase, with some variations through ornamentation. The soloist is likely to present a theme with variations as the basis of his tune. Leader and chorus often use the same tune, sometimes related tunes, and sometimes completely unrelated materials. Occasionally the chorus uses material from the last portion of the soloist's line. The large majority of songs follow the strophic form. Examples 10-1 and 10-2 illustrate some of these characteristics of the Afro-Bahian cult songs. In Example 10-2, the *rumpi* and *lê* figures, taken together, form the following pattern:

EXAMPLE 10-1. Brazilian Gêgê cult song (text omitted), from Alan P. Merriam, "Songs of the Gêgê and Jesha Cults," *Jahrbuch für musikalische Volksund Völkerkunde* I, ed. Fritz Bose (Berlin: Walter de Gruyter & Co., 1963), 122.

EXAMPLE 10-2. Brazilian Ketu cult song (Field collection of G. Béhague). Transcribed by Robert E. Witmer and G. Béhague. Text omitted.

Leader 1)

Cho.us 2)

Agogó
Rumpi & Lê }3)
Rum

The singing styles of most Afro-American cults are essentially like the relaxed, open manner of singing common in Africa. Female voices present a characteristically hard, metallic quality, with a preference for the upper range of the voice. Falsetto is often used by both soloist and chorus.

The song repertories of Afro-American religions have never been fully codified, but we know that a multitude of songs attributed to a given deity form the bulk of the repertories. Cycles of songs are performed in a ritual order, according to a well established tradition. Song texts appear in various languages, from Yoruba (Nago), Fon, various Congo dialects, to Spanish and Portuguese, Haitian *créole*, or a combination of all of these. Typically, song texts are simple praise or imprecation directed to the gods; sometimes they refer to specific events in the lives of the deities or to their remarkable feats, following West African mythology as reinterpreted in the New World through the influence of popular Christianism.

Although the large majority of song repertories are traditional, evidence has been gathered recently pointing to stylistic changes and to the elaboration of a more recent repertoire. According to the testimony of cult leaders in Salvador, Bahia, many songs attributed to specific deities have disappeared from the repertory, and new songs are being incorporated. These are not, in general, songs composed by the priest or priestess of a cult house; they are spontaneously created when an initiating member, in a state of possession, sings his or her song to his or her *orixá*. Such songs are apparently remembered afterwards. Especially among the Congo-Angola and the Caboclo cults, these "new" songs frequently include elements from folk music or urban musical culture (such as carnival street music) foreign to the tradition but familiar to the songmakers.

The single most important ritual and musical element in Afro-American cults is the drumming. Drums are considered sacred instruments. They undergo ritual baptism by means of animal sacrifices and food offering. In the case of the Cuban *Abakuá,* some have an exclusively symbolic function and are never played. Such complex ritual involving drums is essential since they alone are thought to have the power to communicate with the deities. In most cult groups, drums are played in a battery of three, in conjunction with an iron gong or a rattle. They vary in size and shape among the various cults, but the trio always comes in three different sizes. The largest drum (called *rum* in the *Ketu* of Bahia, *iyá* among the *Lucumis* of Cuba, *maman* in the *Vodoun* cult, *mama* or *bemba* in the *Shango* of Trinidad) is played by the master drummer. The medium size drum (known as *rumpí, itótele, seconde,* and *congo,* in the same order) and the smallest one (respectively *lê, okónkolo, bébé, oumalay*) usually repeat a single steady rhythm. In contrast, the largest and lowest drum varies its beats, producing some of the complex and intensely exciting rhythms typical of the Afro-American styles. The gong (variously called *agogó, gan, ogan,* or *ekon* in Brazil and Cuba) or the rattle generally sets the fundamental beat; the drums join in a few seconds later. As Herskovits has pointed out, the melody of the song is but the accompaniment to the rhythm of the drums. This emphasis on rhythm is an obvious African heritage. Each cult, dance, ceremony, or deity has its characteristic rhythms, on the basis of which the master drummer improvises. Drum music per se, that is, separate from an accompanimental function, also exists in large quantity. Its major function is to "call" the gods and to bring on "possessions," also to provide materials for the many ritual dances. Cross rhythms and polyrhythms form the major substance of the music. Examples 10-3 and 10-4 show several rhythmic patterns, with their respective names, of the Bahian *Ketu* cult, and the Afro-Cuban *Lucumi.* The *rum* part of the *avaninha* pattern often presents a subtle duple-triple ambivalence. For example, it sometimes sounds like ♪ ⁷ ⁷ ♪ ⁷ ⁷ ♪ ⁷ ⁷ ♪ ♪ ⁷ ⁷. Likewise, in the *toque de Iansa,* the 4/4 gong pattern often approaches a triple feeling, as for example ♪ ⁷ ♪ ⁷ ♪ ⁷ ⁷ ♪ ⁷ ♪ ⁷ ⁷. In the same pattern, the *rum* also expresses a duple feeling, like the gong: 4/4 ♪ ♪♪ ♪ ⁷ ♪ ♪ ⁷.

In general, the meters of this cult music are most commonly duple but often also triple, and the hemiola rhythm—African par excellence—finds its way into much of the drum music repertory. While there is no definite evidence of the retention in Latin America today of the African talking drum techniques, it is believed that the various ritual drum patterns (attributed to each deity) were, originally, rhythmic renditions of the melodic shape of certain phrases of the Yoruba language which is a tone language. Such renditions would have been learned, memorized, and transmitted by use of onomatopoeias.

EXAMPLE 10-3. Abstract of some basic patterns in Afro-Bahian drumming.

"Avaninha"

(1) The duple triple ambivalence is subtle,

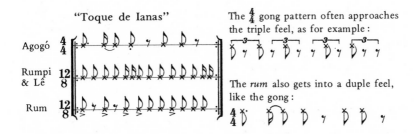

sometimes sounds like:

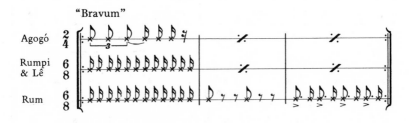

"Toque de Ianas"

The $\frac{4}{4}$ gong pattern often approaches the triple feel, as for example:

The *rum* also gets into a duple feel, like the gong:

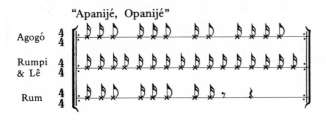

"Bravum"

"Apanijé, Opanijé"

224   *Afro-American Folk Music in North and Latin America*

EXAMPLE 10-4. Lucumi Bata drum pattern to the deity Obba. From Fernando Ortiz, *La Africanía de la Música Folklórica de Cuba* (Habana: Ediciones Cardenas y Cia., 1950), pp. 417–18.

Allegretto

Within the social structure of the Afro-American cults, women have a particularly important position. In the Afro-Bahian cults, while many leaders are men, the great majority are women; so are most of the initiates. The leaders, referred to in Bahia as "Pai" or "Mãe-do-santo," in Cuba as "Padrino" or "Madrina," represent the maximum spiritual and temporal authority of the cult house, and determine the degree of orthodoxy in it. They are, for the most part, leading singers themselves, responsible for transmitting the knowledge of their vast repertory and for the supervision of instruction in music and dancing in the house. Drummers have a very exalted position. They are musicians par excellence. According to Herskovits, the master drummer "moves about the scene, confident, respected. . . . Relaxed, the drum between his legs, he allows the complex rhythm to flow from his sure, agile fingers. It is he who brings on possession through his manipulation of these rhythmic intricacies, yet he himself never becomes possessed."[2] Drummers go through a series of tests before they are allowed to perform in ritual ceremonies. Their acceptance into the cult is publicly signified by means of a "confirmation" ceremony. A drummer may become a master drummer only after many years of experience, and only under certain circumstances, for it is considered as a very special privilege.

There also exist, in Latin American Black culture, instances of what might be termed "secular rituals" in which, once more, music appears as a cultural focus. The *currulao*, or marimba dance, of Southwestern Colombia and Northwestern Ecuador is such a ritual, i.e., a socializing occasion at which a highly symbolic behavior takes place. According to Whitten, the *currulao* gives us an excellent example of the function of music not only in social integration but also in the "development of personal networks." One of the important conclusions of Whitten's study is that "the currulao provides an expressive context which permits household and marital structure to be realigned when necessity demands it. . . ."[3] The music itself of this marimba dance preserves many African patterns. It requires an ensemble of six to seven male musicians, two of whom play the marimba and the others drums. The marimba may have from twenty to twenty-eight hardwood keys (each with bamboo resonators), and it functions both melodically and harmonically. The player called *bordonero* is in charge of the melody on the lower half of the instru-

[2] Merville J. Herskovits, "Drums and Drummers in Afro-Brazilian Cult Life," *Musical Quarterly*, XXX (1944), 477–80.
[3] Norman E. Whitten, Jr., "Personal Networks and Musical Contexts in the Pacific Lowlands of Colombia and Ecuador," in *Afro-American Anthropology, Contemporary Perspectives*, ed. Norman E. Whitten, Jr., and John Szwed (New York: The Free Press, 1970), p. 214. See also by the same author the essay "Ritual Enactment of Sex Roles in the Pacific Lowlands of Ecuador-Colombia," in *Afro-Hispanic Culture* (Cambridge, Mass.: Shankmann Press, 1972).

ment; the *tiplero,* on the upper half, of the counterpoint and harmony. The tuning of the marimba is by no means uniform. Solo-chorus alternation predominates in the *currulao.* Many female singers, called *respondedoras,* participate in the chorus. The leading male musician is the *glosador;* his function is to lead the singing, to give the shouts, and to indicate to the women what part of the repertory should be sung at a given time. Accompanimental drumming is produced by two *bombos* (large double-headed drums), two *cununos* (single-headed cone-shaped drums played with the hands), and rattles (maracas and *guasás,* the latter being bamboo tubes filled with seeds and into which hardwood nails are driven).

The relationship of the religious material to social dance and song is, in Latin American Black culture, always a close one, and one for which explanations vary from area to area. Some of the Haitian and Afro-Bahian ceremonial material has lost its religious significance and has become part of the social side of musical life. This is also true of the *Candombe,*[4] an Afro-Uruguayan ritual dance performed at the time of the Mardi Gras carnival in Montevideo. Here are found certain stock characters—the *gramillero* (an agile young dancer representing a tottering old man), an old Negro woman, a broom-maker, a drummer, and a trophy-bearer. These characters dance in the parade, but it is likely that they represent figures from the earlier time of slavery and the period after emancipation, when African cults and tribal rivalries dominated the life of the urban Negro community.

Among the Afro-Bahians, a particular secular form of singing and dancing, although not entirely dissociated from the sacred context, is the sort of athletic game known as *Capoeira Angola.* In spite of its name, this game seems to have been invented in Brazil by former slaves, and must have been, in its original form, a simple offensive and defensive type of fight.[5] Today it is reduced to a simulated fight, with the preservation of stylized steps (strokes). Only the legs and feet are involved in this dance-like game. The *capoeira* makes use of a small instrumental ensemble, including the *berimbau* (musical bow, also called *urucungo*), the tambourine (called *pandeiro*), a cone-shaped drum (*atabaque*), and a little basket rattle (*caxixi*) of the type illustrated in this chapter. Sometimes, though infrequently nowadays, a *ganzá* or *reco-reco* (*güiro*-type of rattle) and an *agogó* (iron gong) may participate in the ensemble. Specific rhythmic patterns (each with a special name, such as *São Bento Grande,*

---

[4] Paulo de Carvalho Neto, "The Candombe," *Ethnomusicology* VIII (1963), 164–74. See also Nestor Ortiz Oderigo, *Calunga, Croquis del Candombe* (Buenos Aires: Editorial Universitaria de Buenos Aires, 1969), pp. 29–41.

[5] Cf. Waldeloir Rego, *Capoeira Angola, Ensaio Sócio-Etnográfico* (Salvador, Bahia: Editora Itapuã, 1969), pp. 30–46.

Benguela, and *Angola*) accompany the dancing and the singing. *Capoeira* songs are among the oldest in Brazil; very often they originate in repertories of the music of other folk dances and from songs such as the children's round songs or *samba de roda* described in the previous chapter. One of the most significant characteristics of the *capoeira* song is its dialogue form, between the *capoeira* singer himself and some abstract, imagined character. Fernando Ortiz[6] has observed the same characteristic, under its multiple aspects, not only in Cuba but in various other Afro-American areas of Latin America. Strikingly similar genres still exist in distant areas of the continent. For example, the well-known stick-fight game of Trinidad associated with the *kalinda* and accompanied by drum music has its equivalent in Bahia: the *maculelê*.

While the ceremonial music (sacred and secular) of the Black communities of Latin America and the Caribbean is its most prominent—and stylistically most African—musical expression, we must not forget that other kinds of music are also produced. There are work songs, social dance songs, narrative songs of various sorts, love songs. The calypso, which presumably originated in Trinidad and spread rapidly throughout the Caribbean (but there are satirical songs in Africa), is a unique kind of satirical song that grew out of the racial tensions present in the island; musically, it is a combination of African, North American Negro, and Spanish popular styles. Jamaican Negroes sing spirituals and sea shanties whose words are of English and North American origin but also preserve the call-and-response pattern of the African tradition (which may have been reinforced by the existence of similar forms in the English sea shanties). Likewise, Afro-Cuban, Afro-Brazilian, Afro-Colombian, and Afro-Venezuelan urban popular musical species exhibit various patterns that can be related to several stylistic origins. Some of these are mentioned in Chapter Nine.

BLACK FOLK MUSIC IN THE UNITED STATES

The musical development of North American Black communities has proceeded rather differently from that of other Afro-American groups. Rather than living in relatively closed communities in which African tribal groups could still function, the Blacks were brought to the

---

[6] Fernando Ortiz, *Los Bailes y el Teatro de los Negros en el Folklore de Cuba* (Havana: Ediciones Cárdenas, 1951), pp. 6–36.

United States from the West Indies, where elements of African culture had already begun to change and to disappear; and, once on the continent, they tended to live in close contact with their white masters. While the survival of the West African religious cults was to some extent assured in Latin America because of their similarity to some aspects of Roman Catholicism, the impact of the Protestant denominations in the United States was of such a nature as to annihilate many, if not most, of the West African religious practices. Nevertheless, much of the value structure of the African heritage was retained, and while most of the Black folk music in the United States does not sound like African music in the way that the cult music of Haiti and Bahia does, it contains some African stylistic features. More important, the independent developments that took place in Afro-American music were frequently the result of African musical values. For example, call-and-response patterns, in pure form, are not found too frequently in Black folk song of the United States. But the original importance of this kind of practice—essentially alternation, dividing up of a tune between leader and chorus, and the encouragement of improvisatory variations—seems to have led to other practices involving alternation and improvisation, for instance, the sophisticated dividing up of a performance among different soloists in jazz and the principle of improvisatory variation that is the essence of jazz. Similarly, the importance of rhythm in West African music became part of the American Black tradition, even though the rhythmic structure of North American Black folk songs is very distant from that of Africa. When it comes to singing style, of course, Black Americans share the qualities of other Afro-American groups and exhibit a really close tie to West Africa.

There are reports of the southern scene by nineteenth-century American observers which mention the existence of musical practices, such as African-derived cults and cult music, similar to those that can be observed in twentieth-century Brazil and the Caribbean. The songs of the southern slaves were numerous and were associated with a large number of uses. There were work songs, many of them rhythmic to accompany the hard labor performed by groups but some, such as the field blues, slow and languid. The work songs with driving rhythms were related to similar songs used in Africa to accompany rowing and other group activities, but they also derived in part from British work songs, such as the sea shanties. Dance and play songs, related to the playparty songs of the whites, were used when time for recreation was available. A few narrative songs, similar to the Anglo-American broadside ballads, or derived from the African practice of singing while telling stories about animals (like the stories of Uncle Remus, with heroes like Br'er Rabbit or Anansi, the spider), are still used and were probably once much more numerous. Short field and street cries or hollers, consisting of a single, repeated, and varied musical line, are also an important ingredient of the Black folk music repertory. Most important, perhaps, is the spiritual, the religious musical expression of the slaves, which exists in many different forms and styles, from the slow, lyrical, and devotional spirituals sung at services, to the quick, driving, and ecstatic "shout spirituals" of the revival meetings.

The spiritual, in its basic content, is closely associated with the "white spirituals" sung in the South, particularly in the Appalachians. Many of the Negro spirituals use words and tunes also found in the "white spirituals" sung in the South, particularly in the Appalachians. more percussion accompaniment, the use of antiphonal techniques, and improvised variation. (Parenthetically, we should point out that the question of the origin and development of the Negro spiritual's style has not been answered in a satisfactory way, for the white spirituals are also frequently sung in a very vigorous and rhythmically un-hymn-like way, whether through Black influence or not, we don't know.

George Pullen Jackson (1874–1953)[7] found, in tunes he took largely from nineteenth-century published collections, a great number of parallels between Negro and white spirituals. However, although he presents the tunes of the songs, the early notation gives us no information about the style(s) of singing used. Nevertheless, obviously some tunes were used as both white and Negro spirituals, like the one shown in Example 10-5: it is the famous "Swing Low, Sweet Chariot," which is similar in melodic content to a white American hymn tune entitled "Gaines."

Many songs of the Black Americans have simply been taken over from the heritage of the whites, and others, although composed by Blacks, are patterned after the music of the Anglo-American community. The Black tradition has always been influenced by the whites, and much of the basic material in it is essentially of European origin; it is in the style of performance that we can detect definitely African roots.

But there are exceptions to the tendency of Blacks to take over the forms of white songs. One such exception is the blues, a term actually referring to a number of different types of forms. The so-called "field blues" are simply short calls and wails, frequently with indefinite pitch, repeated several times, which perhaps originated as communication by field hands in the cotton fields; sometimes they are sung alternately by two persons. This type of song gradually developed into the "rural blues,"

---

[7] George Pullen Jackson, *White and Negro Spirituals* (New York: J. J. Augustin, 1943); also his *White Spirituals in the Southern Uplands* (New York: J. J. Augustin, 1933).

EXAMPLE 10-5. Negro spiritual, "Swing Low, Sweet Chariot," and analogous white spiritual, from George Pullen Jackson, *White and Negro Spirituals* (New York: J. J. Augustin, 1943), pp. 182–83.

Swing low, sweet char - i - ot, Com-ing for to car-ry me home, Swing low, sweet char - i - ot, Com-ing for to car-ry me home. I look'd o-ver Jor-dan and what did I see— Com-ing for to car-ry me home, A band— of an-gels com-ing af-ter me,— Com-ing for to car-ry me home.

O— for a thous-and tongues to sing My— great Re-deem-er's praise, The glo-ries of my God and King,— The— tri umphs of— his grace, The tri umphs of— his— grace.

accompanied most frequently by guitar, and, eventually, to the "urban blues" style, which is based on a specific harmonic pattern and has a definite though flexible musical and textual form.

The Afro-American community in the United States has produced a great number of prominent musicians who have become widely known outside the folk culture and, indeed, have gone on to become nationally famous. A typical example is Leadbelly, whose real name was Huddie Ledbetter, a Texas convict who was discovered by the pioneer folk song collector, John Lomax. Leadbelly sang many songs, but perhaps his main contribution was a number of blues songs. Typically the form of these was also adopted by the early jazz bands that played blues. It consists of three parts, the first two similar in content (both musically and textually), while the third contrasts. This form can be observed in such well-known pieces as "St. Louis Blues" and also in some of Leadbelly's songs, such as "Shorty George" and "Fort Worth and Dallas Blues." Many songs in the rural blues category have different forms, some of them based essentially on one musical phrase. Thus "Now your man done gone" (Example 10-6), collected in Alabama, is essentially a descending set of variations on the first phrase. Typically, Afro-American folk songs tend to be based on a smaller number of different melodic phrases than are most of the songs of the American whites—another possible survival of African music.

A frequently mentioned characteristic of Afro-American music is the so-called "blue note," the flatted or sometimes just slightly lowered third and seventh degrees in a major scale. The origin of this phenomenon is not known, but it cannot with certainty be traced to Africa. If indeed it is African in origin, it must have been selected from a considerable number of deviations from Western scales (or, rather, differences between African and Western scales) that African musics exhibit. Its survival must have a special reason, such as compatibility with Western

EXAMPLE 10-6. U.S. Negro folk song, "Now your man done gone," collected in Alabama, from Harold Courlander, *Negro Folk Music, U.S.A.* (New York: Columbia University Press, 1963), p. 108.

musical patterns. Possibly it originated among urban Afro-American musicians and moved from them into the folk music repertory.

Another group of Black songs in North America that is rather distinct from its counterpart in white culture consists of counting-out rimes and other children's game songs and rimes. These, again, are performed in a style perhaps derived from Africa, with strict adherence to metric patterns, some rhythmic complexity such as syncopation, and the undeviating tempo typical also of much West African music and perhaps resulting from the "metronome sense" described in Chapter Seven. These rimes, among the most popular of which are "I asked my mother for fifty cents" and "Head-shoulder baby," are sometimes sung, sometimes spoken. Call-and-response techniques are very common. The melodic materials are part of a world-wide pattern of children's songs with few tones, intervals of the minor third and major second, and repetitive structure. These children's songs are found not only in the South, but also in the Black ghettoes of the Northern cities, and they are frequently disseminated from Black to white children.

In the work songs of Afro-Americans, African patterns also appear. Work songs that are actually sung to accompany rhythmic labor are not common in the white American tradition, with the exception of sea shanties. But they are widespread in West and Central Africa, and their existence may have contributed to their prominence in the Afro-American folk tradition, as may the fact that rhythmic labor was very much a part of the slaves' way of life. The style of these songs is a mixture of Anglo-American and African elements. Some of the songs, such as "Pick a bale of cotton," actually deal with the work. Others, such as Leadbelly's "Elnora," are simply a group of words, euphonious but hardly related to the job, which supply a pleasant rhythmic accompaniment to work.

The use of the voice by Afro-American folk singers is often traceable to African singing styles. The much more relaxed, open way of singing, sometimes varied by the use of purposely raucous and harsh tones, is rather similar to African singing and certainly quite different from the rather tense and restrained manner of singing common among southern whites. It is important to repeat that there is no evidence to support the idea that the difference is due to heredity; much more likely, it is due to the persistence of African musical ideals in the Afro-American community, and possibly it is related to the difference between the culture patterns of the Anglo-Americans and the Afro-Americans, a difference due both to the African heritage of the latter and to the life-style developed from slavery and gradual, though partial, emancipation.

BIBLIOGRAPHY AND DISCOGRAPHY

Among the numerous publications on Black folk music in the United States, the following older ones are most useful: Harold Courlander, *Negro Folk Music U.S.A.* (New York: Columbia University Press, 1963); John and Alan Lomax, *Negro Folk Songs as Sung by Lead Belly* (New York: Macmillan, 1936); and, for its study of the relationship between Black and white spirituals, George Pullen Jackson, *White and Negro Spirituals* (New York: J. J. Augustin, 1943). A more modern view is presented in Charles Keil, *Urban Blues* (University of Chicago Press, 1966) and the very important survey by Eileen Southern, *The Music of Black Americans* (New York: Norton, 1971). Among the many publications in jazz, we mention only Marshall Stearns, *The Story of Jazz* (New York: Oxford University Press, 1958; also Mentor Books); Andre Hodeir, *Jazz, its Evolution and Essence* (New York: Grove Press, 1956); and Neil Leonard, *Jazz and the White Americans* (University of Chicago Press, 1962).

Two publications by Richard A. Waterman provide theoretical background for the study of New World Negro music: " 'Hot' Rhythm in Negro Music," *Journal of the American Musicological Society*, I (1948), 24–37, and "African Influence on American Negro Music," in *Acculturation in the Americas*, ed. Sol Tax (Chicago: University of Chicago Press, 1952). Several studies of South American Black music are important reading: Alan P. Merriam, "Songs of the Ketu Cult of Bahia, Brazil," *African Music*, I (1956), 53–82; Melville J. Herskovits, "Drums and Drummers in Afro-Brazilian Cult Life," *Musical Quarterly*, XXX (1944), 447–92; Luis Felipe Ramon y Rivera, "Rhythmic and Melodic Elements in Negro Music of Venezuela," *J-IFMC*, XIV (1962), 56–60; and Mieczyslaw Kolinski, "Part III, Music" in *Suriname Folklore* by M. J. and Frances Herskovits (New York: J. J. Augustin, 1936). Black music in the Caribbean is discussed, with musical transcriptions, in Harold Courlander, *The Drum and the Hoe* (Berkeley: University of California Press, 1960), a study of Haitian voodoo culture. Peter Seeger, "The Steel Drum: A New Folk Instrument," *Journal of American Folklore*, LXXI (1958), 52–57, presents a recent development.

The most important studies on Afro-Cuban music are those of Fernando Ortiz. In addition to the two references in the text, see his *Los instrumentos de la música afro-cubana* (Havana: Ministério de Educación . . . , 1952–55), 5 vols. For Jamaican music, see the introductory study by Olive Lewin, "Jamaican Folk Music," *Caribbean Quarterly*, XIV

(1969), 49–59. A systematic study of cults in Jamaica is George E. Simpson, "Jamaican Revivalist Cults," *Social and Economic Studies* V, i–ix (1956), 321–42.

Important recordings of Black music in Latin America are: *Music of Haiti* collected by Harold Courlander, Folkways P 403, 407, 432 (3 disks); *Cult Music of Trinidad*, Folkways 4478; *Afro-Bahian Religious Songs of Brazil*, Library of Congress AAFS 61–65; *Cult Music of Cuba*, Folkways 4410; *Afro-Hispanic Music from Western Colombia and Ecuador*, Folkways 4376; *Jamaican Cult Music*, Folkways FE 4461; and *From the Grass Roots of Jamaica*, Dynamic (Kingston, Jamaica) 3305.

Among the numerous recordings of North American Black music, we recommend two large sets of records, *Music from the South*, recorded by Frederic Ramsey, Folkways FP 650–58 (9 disks), and *Southern Folk Heritage Series*, edited by Alan Lomax, Atlantic 1346–52 (7 disks, including white and Negro music). Also worth mentioning are *Leadbelly's Last Sessions*, Folkways FP 241–42 (4 disks) and *The Rural Blues*, edited by Samuel B. Charters, RFB Records RF 202 (2 disks).

ELEVEN

FOLK MUSIC IN
MODERN NORTH AMERICA

The culture of modern North America is essentially a European one; its most prominent ingredients have come from Great Britain and, to a somewhat smaller extent, other Western European countries. But there have been other major influences, such as Hispanic culture, although this is largely confined to certain areas of the continent, principally the Southwestern United States. Eastern and Southern European elements are also important. And among the most important distinguishing features is the influence of two originally non-Western cultures: the African, which has had an enormous impact, and the American Indian, whose thrust has been less noticeable but is nevertheless pervasive. At certain levels of activity and thought, North American culture is a rather homogeneous blend of all these ingredients. At other levels, however, it is a conglomeration of enclaves—Scotch-Irish in the Appalachians, Mexican-American in Arizona, French-Canadian in the province of Quebec and in northern New England, Polish-American in Chicago and Detroit, Afro-American in the ghettos of large cities and in parts of the rural South, with small pockets of separation, such as the Indian tribes on reservations and various communities of religious groups (the Amish in the Midwest or the Doukhobors in the western United States and Canada). Each of these enclaves has kept a distinctive way of life; thus, in certain respects, there is enormous variety in the panorama of North American culture. In some ways, then, this continent is in the vanguard of what appears to be a gradually developing universal culture; in other respects, it functions as a museum, preserving in isolated and archaic forms the otherwise rapidly changing cultures of other lands.

The profile of folk music in modern North American is similar. The songs of peoples from everywhere have been brought here, sometimes sung for generations, sometimes rapidly forgotten; sometimes developed into new, more distinctly American phenomena, sometimes preserved in old forms; sometimes combined with the music of other groups from elsewhere, and with strange styles, but sometimes held in isolation. We find that the enclaves of European, African, and American Indian cultures have retained their old songs and styles; but we also find that new styles, resulting from combinations, have come about. We are forced to conclude that the homogeneity of modern American life, and particularly the prominence of radio, television, and the record industry has also homogenized musical life to the extent that the old tri-partite view of music (art, popular, and folk) has lost much of its meaning, and that all elements of the population share in a musical culture dominated by what we have for some time called popular music, based on rock, with elements of jazz, blues, country and western, folk, and even to some extent art music—a musical culture with a certain amount of stylistic unity based on aesthetic as well as technological criteria.

Our task here is to describe the role of the surviving traditional folk music in this complex situation; to a smaller extent, it is to point out those elements in the homogeneous culture that come from folk music.

ETHNIC MINORITIES IN RURAL AMERICA

We have mentioned the existence of isolated groups which retain their traditional culture essentially outside the framework of modern American civilization. Among them are the English-descended New England farmers and the Scotch-Irish of the Appalachians, we have already (in Chapter Four) examined their retention of older British songs and singing styles. Although their place in American history and the character of their culture is different, the American Indians occupy something of a similar role. In both cases, distinctiveness of musical culture helps to provide a feeling of cultural and, to some extent, racial identity. The most dramatic examples of such conservatism in both life-style and music is found in some of the religiously-based enclaves.

In many cultures, religious and ceremonial life tends to reveal the most conservative elements, and the most archaic aspects of a tradition are usually to be found in its religious manifestations. Thus, perhaps the oldest European folk music preserved in the Americas is that which is associated with religion. The Spanish liturgical dramas are one example; another is the tradition of German spiritual folk song which is found especially in Pennsylvania and also among the Amish of the midwestern United States.

The Amish are a religious community related to the Mennonites. Of Swiss and German origin, they began leaving Germany in the seventeenth century, some migrating first to Russia and then, in the early nineteenth century, to the United States, others coming directly to America. Their austere manner of living and their conservative traditions have kept them essentially out of contact with other German-Americans. Devoting themselves exclusively to farming, they use music only for worship. Their hymns are of two types, an older one that is possibly a survival of a medieval hymn-singing tradition, and a newer one evidently part of the German-American spiritual tradition of Pennsylvania.

To most listeners, the older hymns of the Amish scarcely sound like a product of Western musical culture. They are monophonic and sung without accompaniment, without perceptible meter, with syllables drawn out over many tones, and with slowly executed ornaments. Only when one becomes acquainted with the style does one see in it any resemblance to the hymn tunes of the German reformed churches. This can be done by connecting the first notes of the textual syllables to each other, even when they are short and seemingly insignificant. Since this style of singing is not found in Europe today, how did it come about? Possibly the Amish, after arriving in Russia or the United States, began to slow down the hymns they had sung in Germany, to add ornaments, and to draw out the metric structure until it was not to be recognized. On the other hand, possibly their way of singing was once widely used in the German-speaking rural areas of Europe, and has simply been retained by the Amish in America although undergoing complete change in Europe under the impact of the all-pervading musical influence of the cities and courts. At any rate, the Amish hymns are an example of the marginal survival that characterizes some of the musical culture of the Americas to the extent that it is derived from Europe.[1]

The newer hymns of the Amish correspond to the spiritual tradi-

[1] Bruno Nettl, "The Hymns of the Amish, An Example of Marginal Survival," *Journal of American Folklore*, LXX (1957), 327–28.

tion of the Pennsylvania German culture. This culture represents an interesting mixture of German—particularly South German—and British elements, including a special dialect of German that includes certain elements of American English phonology. The songs of the Pennsylvania Germans are in part simply those of the German tradition, in part based on tunes from the Anglo-American heritage. Thus the so-called Pennsylvania spirituals, folk hymns with German words, are really products of the spiritual revival of the early 1800s, which involved Methodists and Baptists in the English-speaking community, and the influence of Negro music and of Negro spirituals, all converging on the Pennsylvania German community. As a result, the tunes are of various origins. Some are those of secular German folk songs; a few are derived from early German hymns; some come from the white spiritual tradition ("The Battle Hymn of the Republic" appears with several sets of words). The Pennsylvania German spiritual is not, of course, a purely folkloric type of music. Hymn books were printed and professional hymn writers contributed to them. But much of the musical material was and is identical to that which lives in the authentic folk culture; and most of the tunes, in contrast to the words, were actually passed on by oral tradition, performed at camp meetings without the use of books, and lived by means of variation and communal re-creation.

Just as the German folk culture lives on in the small towns of Eastern Pennsylvania, other Western European traditions can be found thriving in other rural areas of North America. Northern Michigan and Minnesota are repositories of Scandinavian and Finnish folklore. The southern Midwest and Louisiana are the homes of people who still sing, or at any rate can occasionally remember for a collector, the folk songs of France. Of course the eastern part of Canada, especially the province of Quebec, is rich in the folklore of French-Canadians. Much as the United States yields a repertory of English songs at least as large as that of England herself, the French-Canadians sing essentially all of the older French folk songs; and Marius Barbeau, veteran collector of songs in this tradition, records that for song upon song more variants have been found in America than in France. One group of individuals who particularly carried the French tradition was the *voyageurs*, French Canadians who paddled canoes through the Great Lakes in the fur trade, and who sang for amusement and in order to provide rhythmic accompaniment to paddling. On the whole, the French-Canadian folk song heritage does not seem to differ appreciably from that of France, and in its wealth it parallels the Anglo-American folk song tradition. The penetration of French melodies to other repertories can be seen in some of the tunes of the Haitian voodoo cults, whose musical style is generally Caribbean and closely related to African music but among whose songs are tunes and fragments of melodies highly reminiscent of French music. A similar situation obtains among the Cajuns of Southern Louisiana, descendants of the Acadians whose deportation from Canada to Bayou Teche, Louisiana, in 1755 was chronicled by Henry Wadsworth Longfellow in "Evangeline." The Cajuns continue to speak French and to sing French songs, but their music has also absorbed elements of Anglo-American and Afro-American styles, paticularly in the repertories of their string bands.

THE ROLE OF FOLK MUSIC
IN URBAN AMERICAN CULTURE

The early settlers in America who came from the British Isles, Scandinavia, France, and Spain developed a largely rural culture, and their folk music is preserved mainly in small towns, in villages, and on farms. On the whole, the peoples who came to North America from Italy, the Balkan peninsula, and Eastern Europe arrived later, when cities had already developed into centers of industry; they emigrated at the end of the nineteenth century and the beginning of the twentieth, to work in these cities. Thus their folk music, to the extent that it is preserved, is found in an urban milieu. These same cities also draw upon the rural population, and thus many of the Western European immigrants also found their way into them as did members of non-European minorities— the Blacks, Mexican-Americans, Chinese, Japanese, and even some American Indians. The rapidly expanding North American city—different from the typical European city, which took centuries to grow to its present size—tended to become a complex of sections, neighborhoods, villages almost, that served as focal points for various ethnic groups. These tended to try to maintain in some respects the culture and tradition of their countries and places of origin, as a way of preserving identity and of easing the dislocations of Americanization, Westernization, and modernization. They could obviously not retain their rural work habits, economic systems, transportation, and so on, but they could attempt to retain their folklore, art, and music.

At the same time, the North American cities, in the twentieth century, have been wellsprings of technical innovation and social change. It is difficult to imagine that music could have escaped the impact of the kinds of development that resulted from the turmoil caused by the throwing together of many disparate cultural groups, and of the constant pressure to change the approach to all of life's problems. Thus the folk music of the American city also reflects the most important social attitudes that developed, and we find song associated with various movements of social and political forces, particularly with movements whose function was to protest.

Preservation and response to the pressures of modernization are both evident in the music of Eastern European groups in those cities, particularly in the Midwest, which grew primarily as industrial centers. By no means have the folk song repertories of all groups been collected and studied, but a generous sampling is already available. Thus large collections of Hungarian and Slovak songs have been made in Cleveland;[2] Yiddish and Puerto Rican folk music has been studied in New York, and the songs of Poles, Syrians, and many other groups have been recorded in Detroit. In some cases, old songs can be found relatively undisturbed, and the American city acts as the agent of marginal survival. At other times, the European traditions are changed because of the pressures of urban American culture. Thus there seems to be a tendency to favor dance and instrumental music over other types; perhaps this is due to the fact that young Americans of foreign descent have less interest in the words of the songs, which they may not even understand, than in the tunes. Organized teaching of folk songs, even from song books, by members of the ethnic group who are noted for their knowledge may be one way of preserving the material. Group singing is more prominent than in the European parent traditions. Singing clubs and dance groups are formed in order to keep the tradition alive, for music and dance play an important part in keeping an ethnic group in a city from losing its identity.

Furthermore, the musical style of Eastern European folk songs sung in the American cities may change, for those songs which come closest to being acceptable in terms of the American popular tune tradition are those which are preserved by the ethnic groups. The younger individuals in these communities, who by the middle of the twentieth century were no longer able to speak the languages of their grandparents, have been stimulated by the appearance in concerts of professional dance and instrumental groups from Europe. The original functions of the folk songs on the whole have disappeared in the American city, and the music must serve mainly as entertainment, as an expression of sentimental feeling, and as accompaniment to dancing. Occasionally, new songs in Polish, Hungarian, Slovak, and other languages are created, though in such cases it is usually only the words, dealing with American life, that are new and that serve as a setting for an old tune. On the whole, the ethnic groups in the United States perform the music of the old country,

---

[2] Stephen Erdely, "Folksinging of the American Hungarians in Cleveland," *Ethnomusicology,* VIII (1964), 14–27.

sometimes preserving tunes already forgotten in Europe, but more frequently singing the old tunes in less ornamented, shorter, and frequently impoverished style, and often tending to change modal tunes to major or minor, heterometric structure to isometric, and unaccompanied tunes to songs with chordal accompaniment or singing in parallel thirds. Example 11-1 illustrates a Polish folk song (possibly unchanged in transit) collected in Detroit.

EXAMPLE 11-1. Polish folk song, "Czterty Mile za Warszawa" ("It was four miles out of Warsaw"), collected in Detroit. Reprinted from *Merrily We Sing, 105 Polish Folksongs* by Harriet M. Pawlowska by permission of the Wayne State University Press. Copyright 1961.

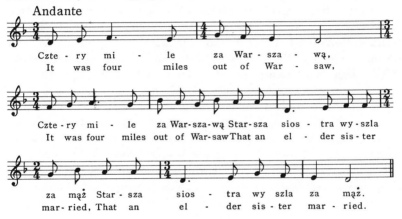

To a smaller extent than the non-English-speaking groups, the Anglo-American and Black communities in the cities also have a folk music tradition, largely because many members of these two groups are recent immigrants from the countryside. The older, traditional sort of Anglo-American folk song, when known to urban individuals or families, tends to live essentially in the memories of singers rather than functioning in social situations. In the music of urban Afro-Americans, on the other hand, folk music has functioned as an inspiration for the creation of various popular styles and musical forms, like jazz, blues, and gospel song.

Throughout Western history, music has been used as a symbol of political actions and positions. Songs of political and social protest are known even from the late Middle Ages; nations and political parties developed solemn anthems for inspiration and rousing songs to stimulate rallying to a cause. It is not surprising that folk music, the music most closely associated with the poor, the minorities, and the disestablished, has provided the natural stylistic symbol, even in the mainstream of society, for social criticism and for protesting intolerable conditions, while music associated with the established order was more likely to hew closely to a stylistic line derived from art music. Folk songs voicing protest have been composed in many corners of the world; it appears that thoughts that would not be acceptable in speech are frequently permitted in song.

Of great interest in this connection is the body of songs revolving about, and in some cases integrally a part of, the labor movement. These are songs of relatively recent origin, their poets and composers are normally known, and they are usually learned first from song books and taught by trained organizers. Stylistically they are part of the broadside ballad tradition, and they use original tunes composed in the broadside idiom, or tunes from other folk songs, hymns, and popular music. One of the best known is the ballad of "Joe Hill," a martyred leader of the IWW, whose ghost returns to exhort laborers to organize. Some of these songs have passed into oral tradition and are also sung outside the labor movement. Many of them have words protesting the bad treatment of factory workers, miners, migrant farmers, and minority groups. Others sing the praises of labor organizations. Usually, tunes of older folk songs, hymns, music hall ditties, and minstrel songs are used. Often the words parody songs already in the folk tradition. For example, a song sung during a New York State milk strike in 1939 is a parody of "Pretty Polly," a version of the British ballad of the "Cruel Ship's Carpenter":

Mister farmer, mister farmer, come go along with me (twice)
Come hitch up with the milk trust and we'll keep the system free.
So they followed the milk trust stooges and what did they find? (twice)
Nothing in their pockets and a knife from behind.[3]

The use of folk songs as protest has deep roots in Afro-American culture and is an essential ingredient of the texts of entire genres such as blues and spirituals. It was not adopted as rapidly by the white mainstream of American society. But beginning in the 1930s, the idea of protesting through folk song began to spread to segments of the white population. One of the characteristics of this movement was the development, especially in the 1950s and '60s, of star folk singers who performed songs with important elements of Anglo-American folk song styles (e.g., characteristic melodic devices and contours, text patterns with the basic structure of folk poems, accompaniment by folk instruments, such as the guitar, dulcimer, banjo, etc.). But although traditional folk songs

[3] John Greenway, *American Folksongs of Protest* (Philadelphia: University of Pennsylvania Press, 1953), p. 215.

are occasionally used, it is more typical of these singers to perform original songs only reminiscent of the rural tradition. Many of these songs —and indeed, the most famous—are songs of protest. The Vietnam War in particular produced a large number of such protest songs; many of the performances of singers, Bob Dylan, Joan Baez, and others fall in this category. While some of these performers, including Dylan and Baez are very close to the traditional folk styles, others, such as Simon and Garfunkel, have adopted styles intermediate between folk music and the mainstream of urban popular music; still others (such as the Byrds) exhibit a style essentially in the realm of popular music but influenced by folk song. Precursors of this movement, Pete Seeger, Burl Ives, and others, tended to adhere more closely to the folk tradition; thus the urban folk singing movement in the middle of the twentieth century follows a course of gradual assimilation into popular music, and simultaneously an increasing popularity and acceptance among many segments of the population.

Those who believe in authenticity as a major criterion may decide that the phenomenon described above is not really folk music. But the role of folk music in contemporary popular culture is a musical and cultural phenomenon worthy of detailed study. This kind of folk music differs from the authentic folk tradition mainly because the songs are learned not from friends and family but from books, records (field recordings and professional performances), and trained musicians; because many of the songs are composed especially for city consumption (but this may also have been true of many "real" folk songs when they were first composed); because the performer consciously tries to develop certain idiosyncracies and to repeat them in an identical way each time; and because the style of singing—polyphonic, sometimes with virtuoso accompaniment on banjo, guitar, piano, etc.—may be completely different from the style in which the same songs are sung in the countryside. And an urban folk singer may use several traditions and many languages.

As was pointed out in Chapter One, it may be possible for a song to be a folk song and not a folk song at the same time. And thus we may insist that folk songs sung by musicians in the popular music tradition, by professionals who make use primarily of the mass media, in styles which may have little to do with any rural folk tradition, are no longer really folk songs. It may be simply a semantic problem. But perhaps a good solution to this definitional dilemma is to regard the music that consists of actual folk songs, and of songs composed in a style derived from folk music by urban song writers and performed by professional entertainers, as the true folk music of urban culture.

The relationship of this kind of music to the broadside ballad traditions of the eighteenth and nineteenth centuries cannot be overlooked.

Both kinds of music made use of a variety of musical sources; both depended on the current interest of their subject matter for rapid dissemination; both dealt with content close to the interests of many segments and classes of society; and both depended upon rural and perhaps ancient singing traditions for important elements of their performance practice. Thus there is at least some justice in calling this urban material folk music, and in considering it the logical result, in a rapidly urbanizing and modernizing society, of the rural folk music tradition.

The use of folk music by urban musicians in the twentieth century is, of course, not unique to the United States. Folk songs have been used as a way of representing political and social views, and also as a method of music education, in Europe and elsewhere as well. In the Soviet Union, songs praising the communist way of life and Joseph Stalin were introduced and passed into oral tradition in city and countryside long before the 1950s. In Nazi Germany, the singing of German folk songs was obligatory in patriotic organizations. In Hungary, authentic folk music has become the mainstay of elementary music education. Even in Vietnam, a folk singing movement using traditional tunes with new words treating matters of war and liberation, and with American-style guitar accompaniment, has become widespread, largely due to the efforts of the famous singer, Pham Dui. Thus the kind of urban folk singing that is now so prominent in the United States has precedents and analogues in many parts of the world.

THE RURAL ANGLO-AMERICAN TRADITION

In the United States, the development of urban folk song culture is partly a result of the maintenance of a strong folk music tradition in the rural Anglo-American community. We have pointed out the importance of this tradition to the survival of British folk music, and we have noted that British material is often better preserved in the New World than in the Old. Of course, the British folk song tradition has undergone changes in America, influenced by the peculiar course of American history and the development of American culture.

The music of Anglo-American folk songs is partly composed of British and Irish tunes that are not easily distinguished, individually, from their forms as they are found in the British Isles. Some come from popular song and from broadside ballad tunes. The differences between American and British song are greater in the words than in the music, for the words are much more frequently of American origin (often they are parodies of British songs), embodying specific events of American history or reflecting particular features of American culture—the frontier, the religious revival of the 1880s, the love of humor and exaggeration, the presence of various ethnic minorities, and the particular occupations (cowboys, miners, Indian fighters, etc.) in which Americans engaged while building a new country.

Taken as a whole, the style of American folk music in English has more melodies in major, fewer pentatonic tunes, more songs in duple meter, less use of accompaniment (but more use of the drone principle in instrumental accompaniment) than the style of Britain. Like the British tradition, but unlike the Afro-American and some of the ethnic group styles, it is essentially one of solo singing. Melodies that are obviously of nineteenth-century origin, with a definite implied harmony, are common. The words of the English songs in America have also been changed, and Americans have made a special selection of material from the British repertory. Thus there are more humorous folk songs in the American repertory than in the British. Tall tales and other humorous exaggerations are typical. Folk heroes, such as the Black superman John Henry, the bad-man Jesse James, and the Slavic steel worker Joe Magarac, abound. Broadside ballads telling of the murders and railroad wrecks of a locality are particularly popular, and songs telling of shipwrecks are a specialty of the populations of Newfoundland, Labrador, and New England. Besides preserving British broadsides, Americans have composed a body of broadsides of their own, especially during the nineteenth and early twentieth centuries. These are more apt to deal with violence and romantic love and less with the supernatural and with battles than are their British counterparts.

Regional differences do, of course, appear in folk singing of the United States. According to Alan Lomax,[4] northern folk singers produce a rather relaxed, open-voiced tone, while southern ones are tenser and "pinched-voiced," and those of the West are a blend of the two. Lomax attributes these differences to deep-seated cultural differences involving the relationship between the sexes, the hardships of frontier life, and the presence of the Negro minority in the South.

The fact that dancing was prohibited or at least frowned upon by many religious leaders of early America tended to drive dance music from the British Isles into the background, but it produced a distinctly American type of song, the "play-party song," which accompanies marching and dance-like movements similar to those of some children's group games. Dancing has, however, played a part in the British-American folk culture, as may be seen from the prominence of the square dance, which

[4] Alan Lomax, *The Folksongs of North America in the English Language* (New York: Doubleday & Company, Inc., 1960), p. 1.

is derived from the eighteenth- and nineteenth-century quadrilles of European high society. A distinctive American feature is the presence of a "caller," who speaks or sings verses instructing the dancers in the routine required in the execution of the dance.

There is also in the American tradition a large body of instrumental music that is used for dancing, some of which was at one time also used for marching. As a matter of fact, the earliest jazz bands in New Orleans were brass bands that played marching music for funerals and other processions. At the same time, in the white North, fiddle and fife players played ornamented versions of song tunes as well as tunes of popular and art music origin. The main instruments of the American folk tradition are the guitar, the banjo, the mandolin, the dulcimer, the violin, and the mouth organ. The dulcimer appears in various forms, some of them similar to those of the Swedish dulcimer described in Chapter Four. As in Europe, the American string instruments are frequently used for music in which the drone principle somehow appears.

Just as many of the instrumental tunes came from the vocal repertory, many tunes originally played were eventually sung. Again, this is a tendency found also in some European cultures. Example 11-2 is a fiddle tune with words; its large range suggests that it may have originated as an instrumental piece which only later began to be used vocally.

Finally, the Afro-American impact on the white American folk song tradition has been enormous. It can be felt in the occasional "hot

EXAMPLE 11-2. Fiddle tune and song, "Prettiest Little Gal in the County, O," collected in Florida, from Alton C. Morris, *Folksongs of Florida* (Gainesville: University of Florida Press, 1950), p. 226.

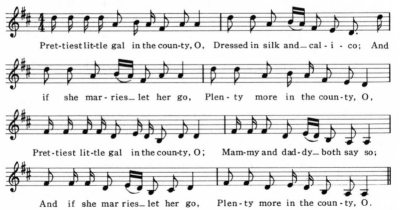

rhythm" of singing and accompaniment, in the development of the so-called hillbilly style, in the tendency to stick to one meter (although many white singers do not do this but sing in the parlando-rubato style), in the use of rhythmic handclapping by white folk audiences, and, of course, in the many Negro songs that have become part of the white repertory.

If the singing of Joan Baez, Pete Seeger, Bob Dylan, and Simon and Garfunkel is the consequence of the impact of urbanization on folk music, then the result of modernization and the use of the mass media on rural America must be the large body of country and Western music. Beginning with music growing directly out of the traditional folk songs of the Appalachians, taking with it musical elements of the broadside ballad and a large repertory of folk hymnody that goes back to colonial times, and constantly interacting with the developments in urban culture, this highly distinctive musical style remains exceedingly prominent in contemporary American culture despite the shrinking of rural America and the all-pervading influence of television, to which it has readily adapted. And while country and Western music has traveled far from traditional folk song in its style, its origins nevertheless remain obvious. The relationship to the old Appalachian folk music is most evident in the structure of the melodies and the physical stance of the singers and particularly in the singing style, that least changeable aspect of musical performance.

CONCLUSION

The American folk music scene is a fitting one for closing a survey of folk and traditional music in the Western continents, for it shows us many of the things that are typical and interesting in folk music everywhere—the preservation of archaic forms, the creation of new styles under the impact of acculturation, special developments due to particular trends in cultural values, and the growth of a special kind of folk music culture in the modern city.

One of the things that our consideration of folk music in the Americas and, indeed, of folk and traditional music everywhere, has shown in the condition of flux in which the material is constantly found. Change, brought about through intercultural contact and through the creative elements within each society, has evidently been present in even the simplest cultures, and it has increased in rapidity as the world's traditions are thrown into contact and conflict with each other as a result of the accelerating Westernization of the entire planet. Will it be possible for traditional musics to survive and to retain some measure of the distinctiveness that has characterized them in the past? Prognostication is not our task here. But if we consider folk music as merely the product of the rural, unlettered classes, and if we consider "primitive" music as nothing but the product of backward peoples, we are bound to find that the traditions in which we are interested are receding and will eventually disappear. On the other hand, if we can retain an interest in the musical cultures of nations and peoples rather than only that of a musically professional elite, and if we are willing to bend our definitions of folk and traditional music to include such things as popular music, jazz, and urban folk song, we may be in a position to investigate the kind of music which is rapidly replacing, in its social function, the folk and traditional music of the past and present.

While we must perhaps concede the eventual disappearance of traditional musics in the present sense of the concept, we should not assume that this demise is imminent. For many decades, some collectors have pursued their material with the attitude of a last-minute rescue operation, proclaiming the doom of authentic folklore. And indeed, since traditional music is always changing, something of it must always be disappearing. Nevertheless, each year brings new discoveries of unknown styles, unexplored musical cultures, unexpected instruments, and new distributions of musical types, always requiring changes in theory and reorientation of scholarly thought. As long as this is the state of traditional music, one can hardly claim that it is a dying art.

BIBLIOGRAPHY AND DISCOGRAPHY

The developments in collecting and studying American folk song are discussed in D. K. Wilgus, *Anglo-American Folksong Scholarship Since 1898* (New Brunswick, N.J.: Rutgers University Press, 1959). A bibliographic survey of ballads originating in America is Malcolm G. Laws, *Native American Balladry* (Philadelphia: American Folklore Society, 1950). The classic collection of British song in the United States is Cecil J. Sharp, *English Folk Songs from the Southern Appalachians* (London: Oxford University Press, 1952, 2 vols.). A modern collection covering all types of song is Alan Lomax, *The Folk Songs of North America in the English Language* (New York: Doubleday & Company, Inc., 1961). Samuel P. Bayard, *Hill Country Tunes* (Philadelphia: American Folklore Society, 1944), is a collection of instrumental folk music. Charles Seeger, "The Appalachian Dulcimer," *Journal of American Folklore*, LXXI (1958), 40–52, discusses one important American folk instrument.

The role of folk music in entertainment and education is discussed in Sven Eric Molin, "Lead Belly, Burl Ives, and Sam Hinton," *Journal of American Folklore*, LXXI (1958), 58–78; and Charles Seeger, "Folk Music in the Schools of a Highly Industrialized Society," *J-IFMC*, V (1953), 40–44.

The music of other ethnic groups in America is presented in Marius Barbeau, *Jongleur Songs of Old Quebec* (New Brunswick, N.J.: Rutgers University Press, 1962); Harriet Pawlowska, *Merrily We Sing, 105 Polish Folk Songs* (Detroit: Wayne State University Press, 1961); Bruno Nettl, "The Hymns of the Amish: An Example of Marginal Survival," *Journal of American Folklore*, LXX (1957), 323–28; Stephen Erdely, "Folk-singing of the American Hungarians in Cleveland," *Ethnomusicology*, VIII (1964), 14–27; and Jacob A. Evanson, "Folk Songs of an Industrial City" in *Pennsylvania Songs and Legends*, ed. George Korson (Philadelphia: University of Pennsylvania Press, 1949), which deals with Slovak songs in Pittsburgh.

It is difficult to select a group of recommended records from the multitude available for the European-American folk traditions. For the United States, the series *Folk Music of the United States* issued by the Library of Congress is excellent. Especially to be mentioned among these recordings are *Folk Music from Wisconsin*, AAFS L55; *Songs of the Michigan Lumberjacks*, AAFS L56; *Anglo-American Songs and Ballads*, AAFS L12, 14; *Songs and Ballads of the Anthracite Miners*, AAFS L16; and *Sacred Harp Singing*, AAFS L11. Lectures on collecting by John Lomax appear on *The Ballad Hunter*, AAFS L49–53 (5 disks). Fine Canadian collections are *Maritime Folk Songs from the Collection of Helen Creighton*, Folkways FE 4307; *Folk Music from Nova Scotia*, Folkways P 1006 (also edited by Helen Creighton); and *Songs of French Canada*, Folkways FE 4482. An excellent collection of non-English language songs from the United States, with detailed notes, is *Lithuanian Folk Songs in the United States*, Folkways P 1009.

INDEX

DATE DUE

GAYLORD   PRINTED IN U.S.A.